T0367385

THE LAST

UNICORN

The Last Unicorn
The Life and Times of Fifi McFadden

iUniverse books may be ordered through booksellers or by contacting:

iUniverse
1663 Liberty Drive
Bloomington, IN 47403
www.iuniverse.com
1-800-Authors (1-800-288-4677)

ISBN: 978-1-4620-4874-8 (sc)
ISBN: 978-1-4620-4876-2 (e)
ISBN: 978-1-4620-4875-5 (dj)

Library of Congress Control Number: 2011915092

Printed in the United States of America

iUniverse rev. date: 10/5/2011

THE LAST

UNICORN

THE LIFE AND TIMES OF
FIFI MCFADDEN

Philip J. McFadden

For Kim

For the first time…

For Mom

For all the times…

ACKNOWLEDGEMENTS

I would like to gratefully acknowledge all the help and support that I have received over the course of time that Fifi and I have been working on this project.

First and foremost, my beautiful wife Kim, who has been so patient and understanding of my need to get this book written and the measures that I have taken to do it. She has been supportive of this endeavor from the very beginning, and has never wavered. She sacrifices so much of herself to my interests, and for that I will never be able to thank her enough, and will be eternally grateful. Her greatest gift to me, however, is allowing me to close my eyes at night with the peace of mind that comes with the unshakeable knowledge that I am loved, unconditionally.

My cousins; Eileen Budny Paul, MaryAnn Budny Suddarth, Mary Ellen Dick Westerfield and Marie Nelson Stowe, who all contributed there time and images from their own personal family archives.

My friends; Trish Broderick, Susan Storm and Gayle Langdraf, for their reinforcing that I was on the right track, and for their constructive criticism.

My sister in law, Joanne Higbie McFadden, who lent her expertise and talent to helping me edit the final manuscript.

Montgomery Delaney, former U.S. Marine and New York City cop who now toils as a successful trial lawyer during the day but who's true spirit is that of a proud son of Ireland and a gifted singer / songwriter, for lending his talents as a wordsmith, and laying bare his sensibilities to the subject matter on which we seem to share some common ground.

Jimmy Webb, the great American singer / songwriter, for graciously allowing me the use of his beautiful poem, "The Last Unicorn". Since the first time I heard it many years ago, I felt that it captured her spirit, and although I tried to consider other titles it was the first one I chose when I started to contemplate writing this book, and the only one that really captures the essence of what I want this tribute to my mother to convey.

~~~

THE LAST UNICORN

TABLE OF CONTENTS

Introduction – The look on their faces   i

1 – Irish Roots   1

2 – Helen and Mary   29

3 – Growing up in Tarrytown   45

4 – Fifi - A Willing Heart   73

5 – Brinie Marlin   94

6 – The War   126

7 – The American Dream   174

8 – That Godforsaken Island   246

9 – Bethpage   299

10 – Crooked Disciples   349

11 – Heart's Delight   380

12 – World Without End   430

13 – Lessons learned Along the Way   449

Epilogue   I

The Last Unicorn   VII

INTRODUCTION

The look on their faces

"I should write a book."

That is a phrase I have heard my mother say countless times over the course of my life.

That proclamation had invariably been preceded by some vivid account of one of the many facets of her life. Whether it was about growing up in Tarrytown, New York before World War II or her childhood friends and the exploits they had in school, or tales of her parents, uncles, siblings, and cousins, and their deep Irish roots. Her fierce Irish pride always coming through when she spoke of her family and their history.

There were stories of how she met my father and of their courtship. There were epic sagas about the war, some of which recalled her first hand experiences during those years, while others were second hand depositions of my father's experience as a Marine in combat in the South Pacific. She would relate those narratives of human suffering or acts of heroism to my brothers and me because my father rarely, if ever, spoke of them.

Then, of course, there were the exploits of my four brothers and me. Her "crooked disciples," that provided an endless fountain of drama, adventure, and comedy which she would proudly broadcast, play by play, to anyone who would listen.

There were parables of her twenty-nine years as a high school English teacher, and all that her coworkers and students had meant to her, and how rewarding she had found her teaching career to be.

Now I know that anyone who has lived on this earth has their stories to tell. We all do. Some people like to talk about their life's experience more than others, while some are very private and keep things to themselves. Still others just don't think their memoirs are worth telling or that anyone else would find any interest in them, so their stories go untold.

But not my mother.

Her descriptions of personal and public affairs were (and still are) told in the most vivid terms. She has the innate ability to turn her subject into near tangible reality. Always portrayed in the most descriptive prose, in the tradition of the great Irish story tellers, helped along by her unmatched knowledge of the English language and vocabulary, with more than a dash of drama thrown in for effect. When you sat and listened to one of her verbal renderings, it would be easy to make the mistake of thinking that she was reading from one of the great authors. Perhaps Hemingway, Hermann Melville or Mark Twain, rather than recounting an event from her own personal experience. And typically, she was always at her story telling best when she had an audience. Especially a new audience. But most especially when it was a young audience.

There were many times during our youth when one of my brothers or I were late to a party or a movie because we had brought home a new date and my mother would catch her ear with some entertaining yarn about our childhood or some other aspect of life, and the girl would be drawn in and want to hear it to the end. Most times there was no end, because her original monologue would go off into multiple tangents and morph into completely different topics which invariably had yet another nostalgic disclosure to go along with it.

Her best audience for the past forty years has been her grandchildren and now great grandchildren. And in return, my children, nieces and nephews are providing her with not only a great new audience, but have also added their own sub-plots to the voluminous archives of my mother's memory. Pages and chapters to be added to the great book that she would someday write.

But the thing that struck me most about her story telling was the way that she could capture the imagination of her listeners. Especially the young ones. And the look on their faces as they sat and listened. You could see the look of wide eyed wonder as they were drawn into the exploits of my grandfather and his brothers, my father, or my brothers and I. Always hanging on every dramatic word in what would lead to some climactic conclusion that would usually segue into another fantastic tale that the young listener was always eager to sit through.

Many of her narratives ended with a moral to be learned, others a punch line. But most were told just for the sheer joy of the telling. Her reward coming in the form of the look on our faces, and the knowledge that she was passing along bits of our family history, and by doing so, keeping the memory of those that had passed away alive. She may also have taken some small amount of comfort just by reliving certain times in her life through her own recounting of those times. Wrapping herself in those stories like a warm blanket. Bringing herself back to her own youth, her family, and to simpler times.

In some ways I think that my mother may have felt a responsibility to pass down her experience (and knowledge) to the generations that followed. To keep our Irish heritage from fading away and being lost. To convey the hardships of living through the experience of World War II. Or maybe her storytelling was a way of keeping the world in perspective. The sorrows and the joys of life all came through, although the joyous stories vastly outweighed and outnumbered the tales of bad times. Through it all my mother was, and continues to be, a woman of great optimism and determination. There were times when life dealt her crushing blows but she never let them defeat her. And although there are times when her storytelling will touch on those aspects of her life, her stories always embrace the positive aspects and the joys in her life. Not the bad times and the things that life took from her, but the many gifts that life has bestowed on her.

But for all of her great penchant for storytelling, and in spite of her constantly saying that she "...*should write a book*," her book never got written.

Too bad!

But maybe not too late.

And better late than never.

And that is why I sit here on this wet October morning. Trying to come up with the means of getting my mother's stories and thereby HER story told in the form of something that will convey the essence of her spirit. The same spirit that infused all of her stories for so many listeners for so many years.

It is a task for which I am ill prepared except for the desire to help her bring those proclamations of, "*I should write a book*," to fruition, and to memorialize her story for all those who know and love her. And in doing so, assist her to bestow a family gift; an heirloom for her grandchildren to pass along to their children, so that her testimony will be recorded into our family's history, and in fact be perhaps one of the few, if not only, historical accounts of our family covering five or six generations, beginning with her grandfather, parents and uncles.

I sit trying to create an outline for the form her book should take. I will put pencil to paper to record her words, but the book will be hers, not mine. If only I can somehow capture some of her spirit on the pages.

What it will be for me is a way to fulfill a very strong need to help her get her story written, and, in doing so, be close to her in the latter years of her life. To make sure that she knows that all of her stories were meaningful on many levels to me and so many others in her audience.

But not just her stories were meaningful. She was meaningful. She played an important, inspirational role in so many lives. She taught so many of us the importance of family and tradition. She gave us an appreciation of music, literature and humor. She provided us with a moral compass with which to navigate life's turbulent times, and then lead by example, teaching us lessons about courage, hard work and integrity, and about how to overcome our shortcomings and our fears. I don't mean to portray my mother as a saint. She wasn't. But she was and continues to be a woman of great substance and character.

I would like to be able to think that, personally, I have managed to carry myself through life in the mode of substance over style. Whether or not I have been successful in that regard is a matter for others to decide. However, my mother lacked neither, as she developed a style that was all her own and complimented her inner substance. Flamboyant and outgoing. Self-confident and ready to lead every charge. Always willing to pick up the gauntlet, yet always nurturing and loving. She embraced and took the role of teacher and mentor to great heights. She was the embodiment of tough love, and the consummate loving mother to her five sons.

I feel as if I am about to embark on a long journey that will take me back through history as we revisit some of her stories. I expect that many of them may sound somewhat mundane to my ears as I have heard them many times throughout my life. To that end, I will enlist my own grandchildren and my brother's grandchildren to accompany me during my writing sessions with my mother. So that she will have a fresh set of ears to hear her revelations. And some fresh young minds to enrich. And a new youthful audience that she can observe and see the look on their faces as she spins her tales.

The challenge for me will be to try to capture the zeal with which she tells her stories. The emotion that she injects into them. The tone of her voice, the cadence of her words, the altering of the mood, conveying the moment either through thunderous volume or by a whispered phrase. Through her body language, a furrowed brow, a frown or a smile. But mostly by the sparkle in her eye.

Recent circumstances in my own life have presented me with an unforeseen opportunity to help her get her book written. I carry no false illusions that it could be some great literary success. I do it for her. And in many ways, I do it for myself.

It is something I need to do. I expect that it will compel me to look deeper into myself and my relationships with my mother, my father, my brothers and my own children, and help me to understand how it is that my family and I have arrived at where we are today. It is something that if I didn't at least try, I know I would regret for the rest of my life.

So I will spend the coming weeks and months with my mother, and hopefully some of my grandchildren, in an effort to get her spoken words down in black and white. I expect the experience has the potential to be cathartic, and readily await whatever may lie in store. And I will relish the opportunity to sit in her room at the assisted living facility that has been her home for the past six years, and witness the magic in the air as she casts her spell over her young listeners.

And I will look forward to seeing the look on their faces as she speaks.

The children's faces.

And hers.

~~~

In the distance,

hear her laughter

Jimmy Webb
"The Last Unicorn"

The following chapters are the product of the story telling/writing sessions (Mom speaking, me writing) that I had with my mother between early October 2009, and mid December 2010, in my mother's room at the ARBORS, an assisted living facility in Islandia, NY.

We celebrated her eighty-ninth birthday in August of this year, and what I found is that she still has a remarkable ability for remembering names and dates and events that happened long ago, from the time she was a child, some eighty years ago, right through to today.

However, I still worried that some of the details of her stories may have been obscured or perhaps made grander by the passage of time. To that end I have invested quite a bit of time and effort to investigate the facts behind as many of these tales as possible, especially the older ones that were before my time, or those that seemed to stretch the limits of credulity. And in doing so, I found that there wasn't a single case where the available information, mostly family records and internet searches, refuted any of her recollections. Furthermore, the veracity of her stories is supported by the many photos and images that fill these pages.

People familiar with some of the events on these pages may find certain minor inaccuracies. Please indulge them. Good, bad or indifferent, these are her memories, her stories and her truth.

What follows, are Fifi's stories, in her own words. She, like her father Nick Egan, was a first generation American of Irish descent, but her mother emigrated from the old country, and that is where her thoughts took her that first morning as she started to speak.

So, as you begin to read the first chapter, try to imagine this indelibly Irish sage of a woman, this wonderful, white haired matriarch, sitting, hunched over in an armchair, in the room with me. She is speaking softly as she starts to reminisce. Now imagine that you are there with us and can almost hear her voice, and let her take you back to her family origins, to another time and place, when she was but a twinkle in the eye of her own beloved mother.

~~~

The Horgan family homestead in Abbeyfeale, Limerick.

Chapter One

IRISH ROOTS

My mother was born in Abbeyfeale, Limerick, in Ireland, on February 12th, 1885, and she was the ninth of twelve children. She lived in a little thatched roof, two room cottage.

No plumbing.

No electricity.

Dirt floors.

Her family were farmers back in Ireland, and very poor. Like so many others, they immigrated to America to escape the hardships in Ireland caused by the potato famine. She would tell me stories of how she

Ellen "Nellie" Horgan.

and her brothers and sisters would take off their shoes, stand in the Feale River, and catch fish for their dinner.

Her name was Ellen Horgan, but she was always called Nell or Nellie. She was only nineteen years old when she left Ireland and she knew that when she said goodbye to her parents, she would never see them again. My sister Helen found a copy of the "Ships Manifest" from the "Umbria", the ship that brought my mother to America in 1904, and it noted that she had just two and a half dollars in her possession when she sailed from Ireland. Her brother Danny was her sponsor here in America, and he and some of her other brothers were all guards in the New York City prison system.

Ellen Horgan's brother Danny.

Ellen Horgan - in graduation ball gown from nursing school.

Aunt Katie Horgan (front row on the right) - Nursing school graduation.

Margaret Horgan (Smith) - Mother's youngest sister.
August, 1912.

My mother and at least two of her sisters became nurses following their individual arrivals in America. She went to Tarrytown, New York to be a companion to a doctor's daughter who had had some kind of an emotional breakdown. She told us of how she taught herself to sew on an old pedal-driven sewing machine as she was sitting in the room watching over the young girl. She was a full-time, live-in companion to the girl and so lived in the doctor's house and shared a room with the afflicted child. One night she awoke in the middle of the night with the feeling that someone was watching her. When she opened her eyes, the girl was standing over her, staring directly into Mother's eyes, then she swept her arm toward the door and, pointing at it, ordered, "Satan, be gone." So Mother slowly reached under her pillow, got the key, left the room and locked the door behind her. She slept the rest of the night on a couch in another room. The next morning she told the doctor that if his daughter was going to be walking around and carrying on so in the night, that she could no longer care for her.

~~~

I don't know where she lived when she first landed in America, or when she started nursing school, but during her stay in Tarrytown my mother was noticed by a young policeman by the name of Nick Egan, and a mutual friend arranged a meeting between Nick and Ellen. I don't know how long they dated, but they were married on January 7th, 1911, at the Church of Ascension on Broadway and Amsterdam Avenue in New York City.

Nicholas Egan - Tarrytown Police Department.

Nick and Nellie Egan - Coney Island, - year unknown.

Nick Egan was the son of Bartholomew Egan, who had five sons and one daughter. Their names were Jack, Nick, the twins Philip and Joe, and Billy. His daughter's name was Rose.

Fifi's grandfather, Bart Egan - year unknown.

Bart Egan and his sons were teamsters. They would dig foundations and haul out the dirt and rock with teams of horses. My grandfather dug the foundations for the Catholic Church in Pocantico Hills, the Church of the Magdalene (The original marble Baptismal font for that church was donated by Michael and Honora Foley, my husband John's grandparents), and for the original Transfiguration Church in Tarrytown.

My grandfather, Bartholomew Egan, owned a large piece of property at the bottom of Sunnyside Avenue in Tarrytown, in the area known as Tarrytown Heights. Back in 1894 the village of Tarrytown bought the property from him in order to increase the water supply for the village,

Fifi's grandmother - Mary Goodman Egan (Bart's wife) - year unknown.

and created what is now Tarrytown Lakes. He had owned five houses on the property, and, after the village bought it from him, Bart and his sons moved the five houses using teams of horses to haul them up Sunnyside Avenue, a steep hill, to where they are today on Union Avenue. The task of moving the houses up from Sunnyside Avenue to Union Avenue took two to three weeks each, during which the families continued to live in the houses as they made their way up the hill.

They started with number 169 which was the house that I was raised in. The second house belonged to my father's cousin, Mike Moore. The third house was that of my uncle Billy Egan, his wife

Catherine and his daughter Alice. The next house was the one that Bart lived in with his daughter Rose, her husband Bill Rogers (who turned out to be a Son of a "B") and their daughter Florence Rogers. The fifth was that of my Uncle Jack Egan, his wife Betty, and their daughters Rosemarie, Dorothy, and Barbara May who married Jimmy Burns from Irvington. Dorothy married my husband John's cousin, Bobby Nelson, and they eventually built a house next to Uncle Jack's.

There was a time that the Tarrytown Village Board considered naming the area in the heights around Union Avenue "EGANVILLE" because everyone there was an Egan either by blood or through marriage.

~~~

I remember my father, Nick Egan, telling me and my sisters about the area near our house that was known as

Do You Know That—

A section of Tarrytown was once known as Eganville. It came to light recently when a letter arrived at the Tarrytown Post Office with an Eganville address. It was delivered because some old-timers recall that the far easterly section of Union Avenue was once unofficially known as Eganville. It was named after the late Bart Egan, contractor, who built a home to raise his six sons and one daughter. There were no improved roads, lights, water, sewer or gas when they settled there. Soon other houses were erected for members of the family. Today, that area of Tarrytown faces Tarry Crest, a fine development, and scores of home have been built. William Egan of Tarrytown, Joseph Egan of White Plains and Rose-Mary Egan Rodgers of Pittsburgh are the only surviving members of that family.

Newspaper article about Eganville.

Hackley Woods, and the time that my grandfather, Bartholomew Egan, had bought a team of horses from some gypsies that were camped out in tents there. During the negotiations the gypsies seemed to be in a big hurry to complete the transaction and get their money. The next day my grandfather, my father and uncles were working the horses, then, after a while, took them down to the little pond at the end of Union Avenue, known as Egan's pond, for some water. But, as they started to drink, the horses foundered. So Bartholomew and the boys went and got the Chief of Police and went out to the gypsy's camp. When they arrived there, there was a camp fire burning and a dog barking but none of the gypsies were to be found. The Police Chief called out for the gypsies, who were hiding in the woods, and finally, after threatening harsher punishment if they didn't show themselves, they came out into the open. The Police Chief made them return the money they had taken from my grandfather, and take back the sick horses. Then he ordered the gypsies to get out of town and not to come back. They knew that he meant business, so they moved on.

~~~

In those days there was a railroad track that ran along the bottom of Sunnyside Avenue adjacent to the Tarrytown Lakes, and there was a rail siding that came off the main track at the lakes. My father knew that one of his friends, Frank Gibson, had taken his horse and buggy over to Pleasantville to visit his girlfriend one evening, and he knew the approximate time that Frank would be returning. So my father and his friends, who were all in their twenties at the time, hid near the railroad siding with their faces covered with gunny sacks. When Frank came by they stopped him, pulled him out of the wagon and gave his horse a slap on the rump which sent him running home to his barn. They took his pants and threw them into the woods, and took his wallet, and then they loosely bound his hands and tied him to the tracks of the rarely used siding, where they left him to think that he would soon be run over by a train. Then they ran down into

Nicholas Joseph Egan.
Year unknown.

10

town to one of their local haunts on Neperan Road.

They were all casually standing on the corner of Main Street when a disheveled Frank Gibson found his way into town and told them of how he had been set upon in the woods by robbers, stripped and tied to the tracks and left to die, and of his fortunate escape. They never let on that it had been them, instead suggesting that it was probably some of the gypsies that were known to prowl the woods. They never told him the truth till years later. He was fit to be tied when he finally found out.

~~~

I can remember my father telling us a story about when he was a cop in Tarrytown. They didn't have prowl cars so they walked their beats on foot. His beat covered an area towards the north end of Tarrytown, and there was an apartment complex up there known as the "Peek a Boo's", where a lot of poor Blacks and Hispanics lived. One night while walking his beat, a guy came running up to him, all excited, and yelled, "Hey Nick. Get up to the Peek a Boo's right away. There's a razor fight goin on."

So he ran up to the Peek a Boo's, and, when he got there, some of the residents were standing outside and told him that the fight was going on up on the second floor. He sprinted up the stairs with his gun drawn, and, when he opened the door and went in, there were the two men, both already bloodied, fighting with straight razors. One of them had his hand holding the razor raised high above his head in the act of slashing wildly down at his adversary. But he turned his head to see who was coming through the door, and, as he brought the razor down, he hacked off the end of his own nose. Then, when he saw that my father was a policeman, he panicked and dove right out the second story window, to the street below, and ran off into the night. Daddy followed the trail of blood for a while, but was never able to find the razor wielding fighter with the stubby nose.

TARRYTOWN'S 'FINEST' in the mid-twenties stand behind new motorcycles. From left to right are Chief William | J. Bowles, Patrolmen Edward H. Martin, Arthur Humphrey, James J. Burns, Edward Briggs, Patrick R y a n, | Charles Schneider, Nicholas Egan, Oscar Purdy, Harry Cregier, Thomas Dwyer a n d Sgt. Allan Delanoy.

Tarrytown Police Department - circa 1919.

~~~

Another time, when my father was still a cop, two deputies were bringing a prisoner down from Sing Sing prison, transporting him to court in White Plains. They were walking up Main Street in Tarrytown when somehow the prisoner got one of the guard's guns, killed one of them and escaped.

My father was on foot patrol, looking for the escaped convict near the railroad tracks, when John D. Rockefeller's chauffeur drove up to him and asked, "Hey Nick, do you need a car?" So they drove down along the railroad, toward Irvington, in search of the killer.

It was snowing, and they would stop at every trestle to see if they could see any footprints in the snow. Then, as they were returning to the car, someone told them that they had seen a suspicious looking character walking toward a nearby root cellar and they should check it out. My father approached it from above with his gun drawn and yelled out, "Come out with your hands up." Slowly, the escaped murderer skulked out from his hiding place, shivering from the cold, and surrendered to Daddy and the chauffeur without a fight.

After my mother and father were married in January of 1911, they lived in an apartment on Wildey Street in Tarrytown, where my oldest sister, Helen, was born later that same year. My sister Mary was born in 1914 and my brother Bartholomew in 1915. But every male child of the Egan families was either born dead or died shortly after childbirth. My brother Bart lived the longest.

Six months.

Then he died.

There was no one left to carry on the Egan name after Bart died of what my mother called "the summer complaint". My mother said that she would walk the floor with little Bart to try to comfort him, but he cried constantly. Even the neighbors would come down and hold him and walk with him to try to give Mother some rest. It was ironic because in the same apartments on Wildey Street there

Nick, Nellie and Helen Mary Egan. 1911.

was another baby boy that had caught the same bug as my brother Bart. The doctor, Doctor Fairchild, wanted to put both babies in the Tarrytown hospital, but my mother refused. My brother Bart died and the other baby lived. The irony of it is that when the other baby grew up he became a criminal. I wonder what Bart might have grown up to be, had he lived.

My mother was always worried about my father and finally persuaded him to resign from the Tarrytown Police Department in 1919. After that he went to work at the General Motors plant and became foreman of the paint department. He would leave the house at 5:00AM every morning to go to the plant and start the drying ovens.

Daddy worked hard. One time he had to walk home from the Chevrolet Plant in a bitter cold snow and wind storm. When he got home he went straight upstairs to bed and was having trouble breathing. My mother had some nitroglycerin in the medicine cabinet, I don't know why, and gave it to Daddy. The doctor later said that it had probably saved his life.

~~~

Mother was thirty-seven years old when I was born and I don't ever remember her or my father having dark hair. They

Nick Egan (on left) at Durante Motors in LIC - circa 1921.

both had salt and pepper gray hair that eventually turned completely white. She always had bad varicose veins, and I can remember one day Mother and I walking down and getting on the train, down by the Tarrytown Lakes, and going into Manhattan, to a store where she could be fitted, and ordered special elastic stockings that would help ease the pain in her legs.

My mother still spoke with an Irish brogue, and some people said that I had picked up a trace of it from her. When I was in college I was the president of the Drama Club, and one day I was auditioning for a part in a play. The drama coach said, "Stop. I'm hearing another language in your accent. Do you have someone who speaks another language?" I told her that my mother had been born in Ireland and that it was her accent that she was picking up on.

Mother was small, about five foot three, and always very frail, but tough as nails. Whenever any of us got sick, she always had her own homegrown remedies that she would use. She would make a mustard plaster and put it on our chest if we had a bad cold. One time I got a case of impetigo rash and she scrubbed it with a stiff brush till my skin was raw and almost bleeding. Then she washed it with Kirkman's soap, a very harsh brown soap, and it cleared up right away.

If we got a sore throat she would make us gargle with hot water, as hot as we could stand it, with lots of table salt dissolved into it. I don't know if these were treatments that she had learned in nursing school or if she had just carried them over from Ireland with her, but they worked.

My father was a pretty big guy, about six feet tall, maybe a little taller, but not fat. He was a very quiet man, and rarely if ever raised his voice. And he never, ever cursed. I suppose it was hard for him to ever get a word in edgewise, between my

Nell (white blouse) and Margaret Horgan.
Tarrytown Hospital, 1918.
Mother had just been operated on.

mother and sisters and myself, but when he spoke you listened. I remember things like when we were in church, if my sisters and I were whispering to each other, all Daddy had to do was look at us. He didn't need to speak. The look said it all. And we behaved.

15

My parents weren't overly affectionate with each other, but I think that was typical of their generation. In those days, people just weren't too prone to public displays of affection.

~~~

One of my mother's cousins was married to Maurice DuPont of the vast DuPont chemical and industrial fortune. Her name was Margaret Mary Fitzgerald. She had been known as "Tottie," and had been working as a barmaid in Ireland when Maurice DuPont

Mother and Father - Mr. and Mrs. Nick Egan.
Tarrytown - October 3, 1920.

saw her and fell in love. Because she was considered by society to be of a lower station in life, his relationship with her nearly caused him to be ostracized from the DuPont family. But he was smitten, so he renounced his position in the family business, married her, and went out on his own. They were married for fifty-two years before his death in 1941. She survived well into her eighties.

~~~

My Uncle Jack Egan married Elizabeth McWalters. He was the Highway Superintendent in Tarrytown for many years and was thought very highly of. During winter storms he would ride on the snowplows all night coming home only to change into dry clothes, and go back out to keep the roads clear.

His daughter Rosemarie never married, but his daughter Dorothy married Bobby Nelson, who was my husband John's first cousin.

I can remember my father and Uncle Jack sitting out on the front porch of our house for hours, smoking cigarettes. Never saying a word. Each just quietly enjoying the comfort of the other.

When my mother was pregnant with me, my Uncle Phil would take care of my sisters, Helen and Mary, and run the house for my mother, as she was on bed rest.

He had been a blacksmith in the Army during the First World War, and had never married.

His twin brother Joe married Margaret Moynahan, from North Tarrytown, but they never had any children. He ran a very successful gambling house, mostly card games, in White Plains. He had several cops on his payroll, or at least he was very good friends with them, and he would always be "notified" if the police were

Philip Bartholomew Egan
World War I Army Expeditionary Force.
Somewhere in France - 1918.

planning a raid on his gambling establishment. I remember one day I was driving on Main Street in White Plains and I saw Uncle Joe walking, so I pulled over into a "NO PARKING" area to talk to him, and he got into the car to chat. A little while later I saw a Cop approaching and said, "Oh oh, I'll have to move my car."

He chuckled, "Oh, don't worry about it Honey," and as the Cop walked up closer to the car, ticket book in hand, poised to write me a summons, he realized who was sitting with me, then he just looked in at Uncle Joe, nodded, and kept walking.

My Uncle Billy was involved with a dairy in either North Tarrytown or Ossining, I don't remember the name of it. He was married to Catherine Coleman, and they had a daughter, Alice, who got married to a man named Patrick Brothers. She and Patrick never had any children, and Alice lived all her life in the house on Union Avenue that had been brought up the hill from the lakes. She died only recently, in 2009.

My Aunt Rose was married to Bill Rogers. They had a daughter named Florence, but after Bill Rogers left them, she and Florence moved in with Uncle Billy, Catherine and Alice. Florence later married Carl Hurrle. She and Carl lived near Pittsburgh, Pennsylvania and had several children. Florence died two years ago, in 2008.

~~~

Daddy was a pretty heavy cigarette smoker, but rarely drank. The most my parents might drink would be an occasional glass of wine if they went out to dinner. I don't recall them even keeping any liquor in the house.

My father enjoyed listening to the radio and would spend hours sitting and tuning in to the old shows like "Amos and Andy", and he loved to hear Kate Smith sing "God Bless America" on the radio.

I remember that when I was about ten or eleven years old there was a radio show called "The Chain Gang" that I used to sit and listen to with him. It was always stories about convicts and prisons, and the sound effects that you could hear were the sound of the chain shackles that the convicts wore, rattling around their ankles.

He also loved to go to the Westchester County Center with my brother-in-law Larry to see the professional wrestling matches. During the staged bouts he would get so caught up in the action that he would mimic some of the wrestlers grunts, groans and grimaces as they beat up on each other. He was missing a couple of teeth, and he liked to kid around and say that if he ever got into the ring with any of the pro wrestlers, they would come out missing more teeth and looking worse than him. Then he would smile broadly, to reveal the gaps in his teeth.

He would sometimes go with Larry to Yonkers Raceway to see the trotters, but he never bet on any of the races. He was always too preoccupied with surveying the crowd for pick-pockets and con-men. Even long after he had retired from the Tarrytown Police Department he still carried on the old habits of a "policeman". Because of his training and all his years as a cop he was always very aware and

Nick Egan - year unknown.

suspicious in crowds, and he constantly had a tendency to appraise the security of a house or a building the first time he walked into it. I remember that after John and I moved into Mrs. McFadden's house in Pocantico, the first time he came over to visit he spent the entire time looking around and commenting that we needed better shades on the windows and locks on the doors, or whatever else he saw that he thought a burglar or peeping Tom might try to take advantage of.

But even as cautious and observant as he was, one night, shortly after my father had resigned from the Police Department, the Chief of Police came up to visit my mother and father. While he was there visiting and they were sitting in the kitchen having tea, someone stole my father's long johns from the clothes line, right out from under the noses of Daddy and the Chief, and they never even noticed till after the thief was long gone.

He wasn't overtly religious, but he always made sure that we attended church every Sunday, together as a family. And he never really had any strong political views one way or another. I don't even remember him having very much to say about the war or world affairs.

Daddy didn't have any hobbies like fishing or hunting or camping. He was pretty much a "home body". He liked to work with his hands and was always very meticulous about keeping the yard and the house looking nice. He would mow the lawn and trim the hedges, and always took pride in it. He had made a brick walkway and driveway out in the front yard, and he converted the old chicken coop that was behind the house into a garage so he could park the car inside.

Nick Egan - October 3, 1920.

20

My parents had a small arbor in the back yard where they would grow grapes. When they would ripen, Mother and I would go out and pick the grapes, then she would boil them on the stove. After they boiled, she would pour the grapes onto a piece of cheesecloth laid over a bowl, and let them drain. Then she would make grape jelly and jam.

She would pour the jelly into preserve jars and then pour melted paraffin on top of it to seal the jars.

Aug. 26, 1933

Mother and Father laughing on the front porch. August 26, 1933.

Sometimes, for the holidays, she would bake tiny loaves of Irish soda bread with raisins, then drizzle sugar icing over them. That was a real treat when I was a kid.

Daddy was a real meat and potatoes kind of man. My mother used to make mashed potatoes, then fry sausages and put them in the pot with the mashed potatoes and a little butter on top, and then she'd put the pot in the oven and let the whole thing brown. She would make a lot of roasts and, once in a while, she would make corn beef and cabbage. That was pretty much a requisite of all good, self respecting Irish Catholic families in those days.

My grandfather, Bartholomew Egan, was stricken blind in his old age by a horse that had kicked him in the head, causing him to lose all his vision. My father and his brothers and sister had an affectionate name for him in his fading years, they called him "The old Gent," and whenever they would go to visit him he would reach out and feel their faces with his fingertips, to identify them by touch.

Somewhere there is a picture of Bart Egan, in a heavy winter coat with a beaver collar, wearing a beaver hat. He is driving a beautiful horse drawn sleigh, and the horse had special rubber horseshoes. They had won a race that day across the frozen Hudson River from Tarrytown to Nyack.

Bart Egan (center of photo) horse racing on the frozen Hudson River.
February 3, 1912.

In later years, my father won a race in a car, across the river. People these days find it hard to believe that the entire Hudson River would freeze so that you could drive cars across it. But it did.

L to R - Joe Egan, Nick Egan, Carle Herrle, Florence Rogers Herrle, Phil Egan, Rose Egan Rogers, Jack Egan, Billy Egan. Taken at Florence and Carl's wedding. - October, 1946.

23

Fifi's great grandparents - John and Elizabeth (McCabe) Egan, and youngest daughter Rose.

Family Tree

Helen, Mary & Kathryn "Fifi" Egan

Nicholas Joseph Egan
(father)

Ellen Horgan
(mother)

Bartholomew Egan
(grandfather)

William Horgan
(grandfather)

Mary Goodman
(grandmother)

Ellen Roche
(grandmother)

John Egan
(great-grandfather)

Michael Horgan
(great-grandfather)

Elizabeth McCabe
(great-grandmother)

Bridget Fitzgerald
(great-grandmother)

Patrick Goodman
(great-grandfather)

Michael Roche
(great-grandfather)

Mary McKenna McGurk
(great-grandmother)

Mary Collins
(great-grandmother)

Lovingly Compiled by Helen Egan Budny

The Egan Family Tree

25

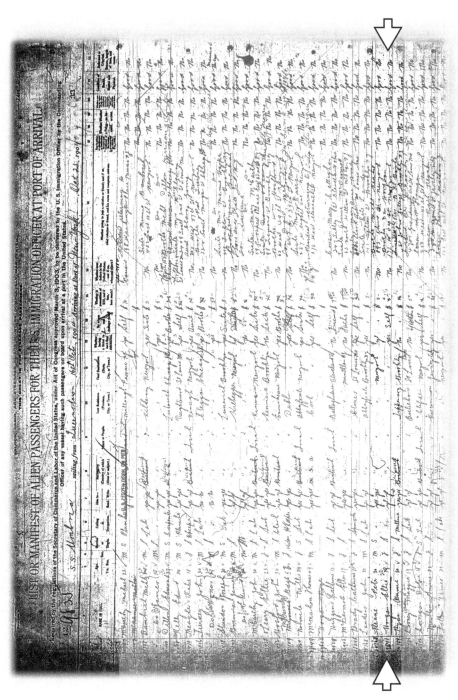

Ships Passenger Manifest - The "Umbria" - arrived NYC - October 24, 1904.

The Horgan family grave - Abbeyfeale, Ireland.

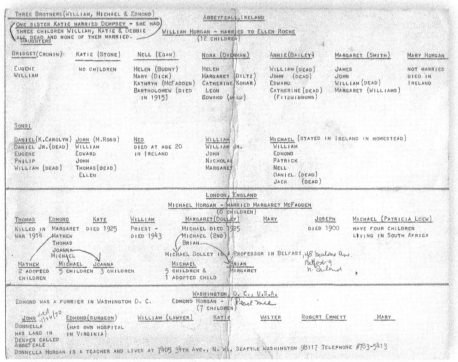

William Horgan and Ellen Roche - Nama Nell's parents and siblings.
Abbeyfeale, Ireland.

Helen and Mary Egan - 1914.

Chapter Two

HELEN and MARY

Both of my sisters were very attractive girls, and were very, very good to me growing up as I was so much younger than the two of them. They were always great to me, and always offered encouragement for anything I wanted to try. They were great sisters.

My sister Helen was always the worrier of the family. She would cry because she thought she might fail a test at school, but end up passing it with flying colors. She was terribly nervous about everything.

She worked as a medical secretary for the X-ray department at Grasslands Hospital (now Westchester County Medical Center) for many years. One of the doctors asked her to come be a secretary at the tuberculosis ward, where one of her jobs was to accompany him on his rounds. She told the doctor that even though she wore a surgical mask and gown, she was worried that she would bring home TB and infect her parents and sisters. She used to get a rash on her hands and legs and, eventually, it was determined that the rash was a product of her stress from worrying about infecting her family, so she left her job at Grasslands.

Fifi with big sister Helen.
May 31, 1926.

She then went to work for the Australian government in Washington D.C. during World War II. She lived in a rented room in a boarding house, and I would often go and visit her in D.C. on weekends.

One night, during the war, she went to a USO dance with Kathryn Morgan, one of her best friends, where she met Walter Budny. Walter was an officer in the Army and eventually got shipped over to Karachi, India. While he was over there, he mailed a diamond ring to my father and asked him to give it to Helen for their engagement. They were married right after the war and moved to Milwaukee, Wisconsin, were he had grown up. Their move to Milwaukee upset my mother very deeply. She missed Helen terribly, and every day she would would pray for them to move back closer to home.

Helen in Washington, D.C.
Labor Day - Monday, September 3, 1945.

30

Helen and Walter Budney - Wedding photo.

Helen and Walter with Eileen and MaryAnn.

While Helen was pregnant with her first daughter, Eileen, our sister Mary and I were also expecting at the same time. Mary's oldest, my nephew Larry Dick, Jr., who was about four years old at the time, got very sick following a baseball game that we had gone to, to see his father, Larry, Sr., play in. During the game I had given little Larry a couple of fig newtons to eat, and afterwards he became violently ill and started vomiting, so we took him to the emergency room.

My sister Mary was pregnant with Mary Ellen at the time, and worn out, so my mother went down to the hospital to sit with little Larry. That night, when Mother left the hospital, she said goodbye to little Larry because he looked so bad that she didn't expect him to last the night. He was so sick he couldn't even recognize anybody.

Helen and little Larry Dick.
Sunday, May 1, 1944.

At the time, Mary and her husband Larry lived in a little house in Glenwolde, near Pennybridge, and Mary spent the night walking around the lake in Glenwolde praying for little Larry. The next morning, when they returned to the hospital, he was doing much better. The nurses told them that the night before, after Mother had left, Dr. Johnston had gone into Larry's room, shut the door and stayed in there all night. In the morning he told the nurses that that during the night he had remembered when he had operated on little Larry for an appendicitis, some months before, and he had noticed some other glands that were swollen and thought that they may have played a big part in his present illness. In any event, Larry was miraculously recovering in the morning.

Helen was so unnerved and unhappy during little Larry's sickness that she persuaded Walter to move back East to be closer to her family. So they moved back to an apartment on Liberty Street in Ossining for a few years, and then lived with my parents for a few years between 1952 and 1957. Eventually they moved to Kingston, New York, where Walter got a job with IBM.

Mother and Father loved little Larry. He was their first grandchild, and the light of their life until the other kids came along a few years later. When little Larry was sick, my father was so upset that he started having chest pains.

It was little Larry that gave them their names "Nama and Tapa". I don't know how that originated, but somehow he came up with those names for them and they just stuck. Helen and Walter, Mary and Larry, and John and I were all "Nama and Tapa" to our grandchildren, and my son Philip carries on that tradition to this day, by having his grandchildren call him "Tapa."

Nama and Tapa Egan with little Larry.
Mother's Day - May 9, 1943.

33

Helen got me a job at Grasslands Hospital while she was working there. I had taken a course in shorthand, and for two summers, when I was in college, I worked as a medical secretary in the X-ray department taking dictation from the doctors. I was a wreck thinking that my shorthand would get confused and I would end up sending someone for an operation that they didn't need or deny someone an operation that they did need.

Helen and I went several times to watch the doctors perform surgery. One time the doctor called me into the X-ray room to see a patient that had undergone major surgery for stomach cancer. He was sitting on the table, looking thin but making progress.

Grasslands was right next to the county jail, and sometimes the prison would send over prisoners for treatment. The guards would bring them in handcuffs. We saw one prisoner who had to have surgery on his hand which had been mangled in a lawn mower while he was mowing the prison lawn.

~~~

I don't know how old Mary was at the time, but when she was

very young she apparently had to have her tonsils taken out. Mother and Father were late leaving with her for the doctor's office and, as they were going out the door, Dr. Fairchild pulled up in front of the house. He told them to go back inside as they were late for their appointment and he had a busy afternoon, and couldn't wait for them. He brought Mary into the kitchen, then he must have given her some type of anesthetic or something, and proceeded to remove her tonsils right there on the dinner table in my mother's kitchen. He must have cut one of them too close or something because, after that, she

Mary Egan - October 3, 1920.

34

always had this peculiar little cough that, even if I was in a crowded church or auditorium, I would always know if she was there or not because I could pick that cough out in a crowd.

~~~

A year or two prior to her meeting her husband Larry, Mary, Helen, my cousin Rosemary Egan and Catherine Morgan went on a cruise to Bermuda. Mary had been seeing a guy named Chuck Gross at the time and he drove her to the ship in New York City.

Helen and Mary - Leaving for cruise to Nassau and Havana, Cuba. Tuesday, July 26, 1938.

On the cruise ships in those days the cruise lines employed handsome young men as "gigolos", whose job was to dance with the single women, have a drink and keep them company so they would enjoy their cruise.

There was a young gigolo on board whose name was Pierre Carnagey. He happened to be the nephew of Dale Carnegie, the author of the famous book "How to Win Friends and Influence People". Upon their return from the cruise, Mary came waltzing off the ship accompanied by Pierre. And that was the end of Chuck Gross.

Mary and Pierre.
Tuesday, July 25, 1939.

Pierre's family had moved to Long Island from Missouri. He had a wonderful mother and father, two sisters; Pauline and Josephine, and a brother named Lew. Lew had the same job as Pierre, only on a different cruise line. He called himself "Lovable Lew of the Corinthian crew." Mary and Helen became very close friends of Pierre and Lew. And Pierre's parents and siblings were all very fond of Mary.

Their uncle, Dale Carnegie, had changed his name from Carnagey, so that he would be more closely associated with Andrew Carnegie, the famous tycoon and philanthropist, for business purposes. Pauline and Josephine ran their uncle Dale's office in New York City, but Josephine and her husband weren't getting along. So one day when he was at work, Josephine, Pauline and their parents moved out of the Long Island house and moved to a house they bought in Tarrytown, leaving Josephine's husband behind.

The Carnageys all loved Mary and she and Pierre had been planning to get married, but Mary changed her mind and called off their engagement due to the fact that Pierre was an atheist. She knew that marrying him would have deeply upset my parents because of their strict commitment to their Irish Catholic beliefs. Pierre was in the Marine Air Corp, and shortly after their breakup he was sent to

Helen. Mary and Lew Carnegey - Northwestern University - Evanston, Illinois - Sunday, July 14, 1940.

Texas with the air corps, then, a short time later, to the Pacific.

He was eventually assigned to a squadron that would later become famous as the highly decorated "BLACK SHEEP SQUADRON," led by Major Greg "Pappy" Boyington. His unit was sent on a night bombing mission over the island of Rabaul on December 23, 1943. They weren't allowed to have radio contact between each other or the American ships below. On their way back from the bombing run, the pilot flying next to Pierre told his commanding officers that he had looked to his right and waved at Pierre. Then he looked and waved to the pilot on his left. When he looked back to his right, Pierre's plane was going down. For the next few nights, as they flew their bombing missions over the very heavily fortified Japanese held territory, they could see a light down in the jungle and they assumed it was Pierre, but after several more nights there was no more light, and Pierre was never seen or heard from again.

N. Y., THURSDAY, FEBRUARY 10, 1944

P. M. Carnagey In Solomons

Maj. Pierre M. Carnagey, a marine pilot, who is the son of Mr. and Mrs. Homer C. Carnegie of 9 Glenwolde, is a member of the Black Sheep Squadron in the Solomons and is reported to be adding to his already high score of 40 combat missions.

His wife, whom he met while teaching at Corpus Christi, Tex., now lives at Corpus Christi. He enlisted in 1940 and received his basic training at Pensacola, Fla., was sent to San Diego, Cal, where he missed Pearl Harbor by the skin of his teeth. He expected daily to be sent to Pearl Harbor. This was before the bombing and he was the only man in his squadron who was not shipped there. From San Diego he was sent to Corpus Christi, Tex., to teach instrument flying, was married and then transferred to Santa Barbara for overseas training.

Major Carnagey graduated from the University of Southern California, where he was a star football and basketball player. He was born in Kansas City, Mo., and has retained the original spelling of his name, which his famous uncle, Dale Carnegie, author of "How to Win Friends and Influence People," changed for his professional work.

Another brother, Lt. Lew James Carnegie, a graduate of Northwestern University, Chicago, Ill., is in the Army Air Corps, and is now stationed in Pensacola, Fla.

Major Carnagey's family have received no word from him since before Christmas.

MAJOR PIERRE M. CARNAGEY, 27, Marine pilot, son of Mr. and Mrs. H. C. Carnegie of 9 Glenwolde is adding to his score of 40 combat missions and 100 combat hours completed in missions over Bougainville in the Solomons Islands.

Both Brothers were lost in W.W.II (dear friends of Helen & Mary Egan)

Article about Pierre Carnegey.

That tragedy became even worse. When his brother Lew, who was in the Army Quartermaster Corp, heard that Pierre was missing in action, he asked to be transferred to the rescue unit. On his very first mission he too was shot down and killed in action.

There was a parade held on Fifth Avenue in New York in honor of Pappy Boyington and the Black sheep Squadron after the war. Josephine Carnagey tried to contact Major Boyington while he was in New York, to find out more about her brothers' fate, but the Major never returned her calls.

~~~

I can remember the fall of 1941, when I was in college at Mount Saint Vincent and was chairman of the junior prom committee, and had to audition bands for the prom. Some of the girls told me that I should audition a band that played at a tea dance on Sunday afternoons at the Good Shepherd Church in the Bronx. So I contacted the band leader and arranged to meet him and his band the following weekend to listen to them play, and I asked Helen and Mary if they would drive me down to the Bronx that Sunday. When we got there I had them come inside with me as it was a bitter cold day. They came in with me and we met the other committee members from The Mount, and I introduced myself to the band leader.

I remember that when we went in to audition the band they were playing a song called "Practice Makes Perfect," and we could hear the foot falls of all the people dancing the "Lindy" to it. When they started to play the next set, my group of girls from The Mount was overwhelmed by all the local guys from the church asking us to dance, much to the chagrin of the local girls. I had told my sisters we would only be a little while, but we ended up closing the place.

The first guy that asked Mary to dance was a handsome young charmer named Larry Dick. Then, while they were dancing, he asked her where she worked, and she told him, "Chevrolet." A few days later, Larry called her there and asked her for a date. And wouldn't you know it, she ended up marrying him.

~~~

Mary and Larry Dick - Wedding photo - March 1, 1942.

Mary and Larry were at a New York Giants football game at the Polo Grounds on December 7, 1941. During the game, an announcement came over the PA system that Pearl Harbor had been attacked by the Japanese, and asked that all military personnel report immediately to their units. Mary told us of how dead quiet it was in the stadium and how so many men stood up and began leaving to report for duty.

Larry was drafted into the Army after Pearl Harbor but was restricted from active duty due to a problem with his eyesight and he ended up being stationed in New Jersey at Fort Dix.

~~~

Something quite serendipitous occurred many years later when Mistrella Egan, Mary's granddaughter, married her fiancee, Sean Murphy. The name of the church where they had their wedding, way upstate in the little town of Red Hook, New York, was "The Good Shepherd Church". The same name as the church in the Bronx where Mary had met Larry, and they had danced together for the first time, so many years earlier.

~~~

Helen and Mary on Orchard Street in Tarrytown - Year unknown.

Egan family photo - circa 1920 (Family friend Mabel Skinner in upper left).

Mary and Helen Egan.
May 31, 1926.

Helen Egan - September 18, 1932.

Mary Egan

Helen, Mary and cousin Rosemary at
the entrance to Hermit's Rest - Grand
Canyon- Tuesday, July 23, 1940.

Mary, Helen and Catherine Morgan - Sea Island, Georgia - August, 1941.

Catherine Morgan, Mary, cousin Rosemary Egan and Helen.
Golfing at Sea Island, Georgia - August, 1941.

Helen and friends sking - Speculator, NY - Sunday, February 22, 1942.

The Egan sisters - Helen, Fifi and Mary with Jerrie - Saturday, May 9, 1936.

Chapter Three

GROWING UP IN TARRYTOWN

The house that I was brought up in was on Union Avenue, number 169. It was one of the original houses that my father and grandfather had moved up from the lakes and it was a lovely, comfortable home. It had living room windows that went from the ceiling to the floor, a modest but elegant dining room and a very big, old fashioned kitchen with two soapstone tubs, side by side, next to the sink that Mother would do the wash in by hand. Daddy made a clothes line, outside the kitchen window, that Mother could hang the clothes out to dry on by leaning out the kitchen window.

Nick and Fifi Egan - 1925.

By the front door there was a hallway adjacent to the stairs, that ran back to the kitchen, with doorways off of it to the dining room and living room. There was a narrow stairway under the main staircase that went down to the basement, where there was a coal bin. The coal man would pull his truck into the driveway and put a chute through the basement window to fill the bin with coal. There was a cellar door access from the back yard down to the basement too. There was a wooden porch out the door, and there was a garage that Daddy had converted from an old chicken coop.

I remember that we always left the doors open so the milk man or the ice man could check the notes my mother would leave for them for what she wanted. The milkman would leave two or three quarts of milk in a box on the rear porch that would sometimes freeze in cold weather. When it would freeze, the cream would come right up out of the top of the bottles. The ice man would come in and put a huge chunk of ice in the ice box, and take the money that Mother had left for him on the kitchen counter.

Fifi Egan - August, 1927.

The kitchen stove was black cast iron, with a chrome edge. There were old cast iron steam radiators to heat the house, and I remember that my sister Mary would always come in from the cold and lean up against the kitchen stove to warm up. We always thought that she would burn herself. Mother would always keep a huge kettle of water boiling on the stove to keep the house from getting too dry, and also for tea. Mother never smoked cigarettes or drank any whiskey or coffee, but she always had the kettle simmering on the stove for the ever essential cup of tea.

Over near the window, where she could lean out to hang the clothes, there was a dish closet where she kept the dishes and pots and pans.

In the front of the house there was a large covered wooden porch. Not closed in, just a roof, and in 1938 there was a terrible hurricane that hit the area. In those days there were no warnings that a hurricane was coming. There was no TV, only radio, so storms like that always caught people by surprise. Daddy had just bought new hardwood planking to put wood floors in the house. He had stored the wood out on the front porch, and it got soaked, and nearly ruined.

I was a senior in high school at the time, and that day, during the hurricane, Mary picked me up at school to bring me home for lunch. When we pulled into the driveway we felt the car jerk violently. We had pulled to the back of the driveway, near the rear porch, and when we looked behind us we saw that a big section of the driveway had collapsed into an old septic tank. We were lucky that the car hadn't gone right down into it. Needless to say, I didn't get back to school, and Mary didn't get back to work that day.

Fifi Egan - circa 1930.

Upstairs in the house, there were three bedrooms and one bathroom. When you came up to the top of the stairs, there were two windows. One on the left, overlooking the driveway and the other,

47

straight ahead at the end of a hallway, overlooking the backyard. To the right was the middle bedroom, where there were two windows looking out to the right side of the house, and a doorway into the front bedroom. There was also a closet and a linen closet between the front and middle rooms. Further back, at the end of the hallway, there was another bedroom in the rear of the house. My father slept in the back bedroom. I slept with my mother in the middle bedroom, and Mary and Helen slept in the front bedroom.

Family outing in Connecticut - August, 1930.

In the front bedroom there were two windows looking out over the roof over the front porch, out to Union Avenue, and a doorway back out to the hall.

At the end of the hall, toward the front of the house, there was a bathroom. That also had a window that looked out to Union Avenue. When you walked into the bathroom, on your right was an old fashioned cast iron claw foot tub. Over the tub was another window overlooking the driveway. There was no shower, as showers didn't exist back then, or at least we didn't have one.

Just outside the bathroom door, between the bathroom and the hallway, there was another narrow flight of stairs, behind a door that looked like a closet, that went up to the attic. There was a window at the front and the rear of the attic. We used the space in the attic for storage of Christmas decorations and things.

In the living room there was an upright piano against the hall wall, and my sisters and I all took piano lessons from the nuns at Mary Mount College. We only had to walk around the corner to Mary Mount, and the three of us learned to read music and play piano but never really became proficient.

Egan family photo - June, 1932.

In later years, to keep all of the McFadden, Dick and Budny kids from going up into the attic, my mother used to say that "Mrs. Brown" lived up there. Mrs. Brown was an imaginary figure that my mother always spoke to the kids about in ominous, hushed tones, as if she didn't want Mrs. Brown to know that she was being talked about. All of the kids were scared to death of ever having the misfortune of encountering the mysterious Mrs. Brown.

Then there were the "CHA-HA-HAs", which were another fabrication of my mother's imagination, that also inhabited the attic. The kids were led to believe that the CHA-HA-HAs were foul tempered little gnomes, akin to Leprechauns, only mean and scary, that had followed her from Ireland and she could never get rid of them. Mother would always glance nervously at the ceiling, in the direction of the attic; dramatically pronouncing "CHA-HA-HAs" with breathy trepidation, and it worked like a charm. Between Mrs. Brown and the CHA-HA-HAs, none of the kids ever dared go up in the attic.

~~~

Uncle Jack bought my cousin Dorothy a shaggy little pony, that she named Sally, when we were about eight or ten years old. They kept Sally tethered in the field opposite my house, in Hackley Woods, and all the Egan cousins would always take turns riding her. She was my first exposure to horses and probably the reason that I was always fond of them and loved to ride.

Sally 1932.

Sally - 1932.

One day when I was only about eight or nine years old, I was walking up Sunnyside Avenue, from the lakes, when a truck, kind of like a UPS delivery truck, pulled up next to me and the driver asked for directions to the house of one of the families that lived near us. I started to tell him the directions but then I figured it would be easier to just show him, so I said, "Why don't I just show you where it is," and I jumped into the passenger side of the truck with the guy. I showed him where to go, then got out of the truck and walked the rest of the way home. Well, I think one of the neighbors or one of my aunts or uncles must have seen me getting out of the truck, and told my mother.

Fifi - early 1930s.

Mother rarely if ever raised her voice, but that time she got very, very angry with me. She was fit to be tied that I had so foolishly gotten into a truck with a strange man, and not only scolded me, but she put me over her knee and spanked my bottom. That was the only time in my life that either one of my parents ever raised a hand to me, and it made quite an impression. I learned my lesson and never rode with any strangers ever again.

Fifi and Jerrie - June, 1932.

Mother was a wonderful seamstress. I remember that sometimes I would wake up in the middle of the night and hear the sewing machine running, and in the morning there would be a new dress for me to wear to school, hanging on the bedroom door. When I was small, my mother would take my father's old suits and make me a coat and hat out of it for the winter weather. Helen's daughters, my nieces Eileen and MaryAnn, used to win sewing competitions and prizes from Singer Sewing Machines, but I can't sew a stitch.

~~~

One night there was a mouse in the house and somebody saw it scurry through the living room. Helen and I had jumped up onto one of the kitchen chairs and my father was down on his hands and knees, on the living room floor, looking for it. There were lace curtains that went from

Nick and Ellen Egan, Kathrine Horgan Stone, Fifi and Helen - June, 1934.

ceiling to floor in the living room, and Helen and I could see that the mouse had climbed up the curtains and was sitting on the curtain rod while my father was crawling around on the floor looking for it. He finally caught the mouse, but Helen and I made quite a picture, standing on a kitchen chair, tightly clutching each other, and shivering in fear of a mouse.

Another time, there was a bat that had gotten between the closed shutters and the glass of the window over the bathroom tub. Somehow my mother was able to open the window and the shutters, and knock the bat down to the driveway below. Then she ran downstairs and got a pot of boiling water off the stove, ran outside and poured the scalding water over the stunned bat, killing it.

~~~

When I was growing up in Tarrytown there were no school buses. I would walk to school with my two cousins, Dorothy and Florence, down Rosehill Avenue to the Frank R. Pierson Elementary School on Broadway in Tarrytown. It was a beautiful school. The building is still there but they eventually made condos out of it some years ago.

When I was going to school there, they had on display, inside the entrance to the building, the original door from the home of Katrina Van Tassel. She was Washington Irving's heroine in the novel "The Legend of Sleepy Hollow," and a real person.

I can remember when I was about ten or eleven, I had gotten very sick and would have episodes when I would be

Fifi - First Communion.

rolling around in bed with intense pain in my legs. The doctor told my mother that I might have polio. Someplace there is a picture of me, as I was getting better, at Rye Playland, and I was very thin. They never actually did come up with a diagnosis for what it was that ailed me, but whatever it was, it eventually passed.

Down in the wooded area, near Rosehill Avenue and Neperan Road, there was a beautiful stone building. It was a private school for girls called "Miss Castle's School for Girls", and young women of high school age would live there in a dormitory that was surrounded by woods.

It must have been the end of the school year because I can remember sitting on the foot of the bed near the open window in Mary and Helen's room, and it was a beautiful spring day. I was looking out the window when my cousins Dorothy Egan and Florence Rogers came running down Union Avenue screaming at the top of their lungs. Of course my mother, and Aunt Rose and Aunt Betty came running out of their houses to see what was wrong. It seemed that as the girls had turned up Rosehill Avenue, near Neperan Road, there was a path coming out of the woods and a young man came out of the path and offered them some candy if they would come into the woods with him. Dorothy thought fast and, glancing up the hill, said to him, "Oh no, we cant, my mother is up there waiting for us."

Fifi and Mabel Skinner with kittens.
Mid 1930s.

With that, the guy turned and ran back into the woods. Aunt Betty hadn't really been waiting for them but thank God the ruse worked to scare the guy away. Anyway, the two of them ran screaming back home and my aunts called the Tarrytown police right away.

The police thought that the young man might be associated with Miss Castle's School for Girls. So that night, my Aunt Rose took Dorothy and Florence down to the school at mealtime. They were to stand in the shadows, near the kitchen where the waiters would bring out trays of food, and if they saw anyone that resembled the man they were to squeeze Aunt Rose's hand. As they were standing there in the shadows, a certain young man came by carrying a tray, and both Dorothy and Florence squeezed Aunt Rose's hand simultaneously. The police arrested the man and took him down to the train station. They put him on a train and told him to get out of town and never come back again. That was the only "punishment" he received, because that was how things like that were handled in those days.

~~~

Mother and Father didn't really do much traveling, but they did take me on a cruise to Bermuda when I was about twelve years old, and we stayed at the Hamilton Hotel while we were there. I had taken one of my sister's gowns to wear to the "Captain's Dinner", and I thought that I was just the cat's meow in that gown.

There are underground caves in Bermuda called the "Crystal Caves", where there are a lot of stalactites and stalagmites. I remember being down in the caves with a tour group, walking on a pontoon bridge over some water with Mother and Father, when someone asked the guide how deep the water under the bridge was. It was so clear that it looked to be only about knee deep, but the guide said, "It's about sixty feet deep. I take my morning swim here every day."

Well, when I realized how deep the water was, I became deathly afraid because I couldn't swim, and I froze. I couldn't walk forward or back, and just held onto my parents for dear life. I was holding up the entire tour group until my parents finally got me to close my eyes and, holding both of my hands, managed to coax me across the bridge.

As we started to come up out of the caves, I put my hand on the railing, and when I looked, there was a big chameleon sitting on the railing about an inch away from my hand. It's throat was pulsing in and out and it's bulging eyes were darting all around, and again I froze in my tracks, shaking in fear, until Mother shooed it away with the back of her hand.

Nick, Fifi and Nellie Egan at the beach - circa 1930.

There was another time when my parents and sisters and I drove to Martha's Vineyard. We drove up and took the ferry over to the island and stayed in these quaint little cottages where they would walk out between the bungalows and ring a bell every morning to let you know that breakfast was being served in the main house.

~~~

There was a train, part of the old Putnam Line I think, that ran along the south side of the Tarrytown Lakes where the parking lot is now. There was a little station house there with a pot belly stove, and we would go in there to warm up when we had been out on the lake ice skating all day. A young man by the name of Fabian Bergeron would sometimes meet me at the lakes to go ice skating when I was about fourteen years old. There was a little island in the middle of one of the lakes, and there would always be a bonfire out there. As you skated across the lake you could hear the ice cracking. That meant that it was getting colder outside, and the ice was freezing even more.

'IT'S NO MORE—This is a picture of the Tarrytown Heights station of the Putnam Division Railroad taken in the winter of 1916. The railroad then as today ran between High Bridge in the Bronx and Brewster, but some years later its course between East View and Briarcliff was changed thereby eliminating Tarrytown Heights, Tower Hill and Pocantico Hills.

The railroad pierced the estate of John D. Rockefeller Jr. To wipe out opposition he purchased almost all of East View. The cost was estimated at more than $2 million with Mr. Rockefeller financing the project.

In the picture left to right are John Harold, Jr., Evelyn Coyle, Susie Melnville, Polly Moscola and 'Charles O'Meara. Also "Pete", the dog owned by Mr. Harold.

Tarrytown Heights train station - 1916.

To the north of the lakes was a huge, huge hill that we called "Buttermilk Hill." On top of it is the Rockefeller mansion, looking down the Hudson River. Unfortunately, when the trains would stop at the little station house, the soot from the smoke stack would rise up toward Buttermilk Hill and the mansion. Mr. Rockefeller became annoyed because the soot and smoke interfered with his view of the Hudson, so he bought that section of the railroad and moved it all the way over to the other side of Buttermilk Hill.

~~~

I remember that some nights, when it was really cold outside, we would be sitting eating dinner and my father would raise his hand and say, "Stop. Listen.", and you could hear the sirens going off down at Sing Sing prison because someone had escaped. Sing Sing prison was what people referred to when they said someone got "sent up the river" because it was right down on the banks of the Hudson River. It was named after the Sing Sing Indians. There were guards up in turrets on top of the prison walls, with machine guns, and you weren't allowed to stop your car on any of the roads that ran past it.

~~~

Everybody knew everybody else in Tarrytown. I can remember a cousin of mine, Ellen Horgan, coming up from the Bronx to visit, and as we walked down Main Street all the shop keepers would know you by name and say, "Hello." Many would ask about your family, especially if someone was sick or something.

Fifi, cousin Ellen Horgan and Jerrie.
Sunday, August 27, 1933.

59

Mr. Undsworth was the owner of what used to be Russell and Lawrie Pharmacy. Next to that was "The Flower Shop" that was run by Mr. Ballard who had lived up on Union Avenue, near us. He had two sons. Everyone asked about your family, and I would ask about theirs. Almost everyone in the town knew each other.

As my cousin and I were walking back up the street, the fire alarm went off, and all the merchants came running out of their stores, yanking off their aprons and running to the fire house. When Ellen saw this she asked, "What's going on? Why are they all running?"

"They're the firemen," I answered, but she just couldn't get over that.

~~~

There were trolley tracks that ran all the way down Main Street. They would divide at the bottom of the hill, past the fire house, and sometimes the trolley would jump off the tracks where they split at the bottom.

There was a store down there named Cartoons Furniture Store, where my mom and dad would buy our furniture. There was an ice cream parlor called Pincus's Ice Cream, and there was a jewelry store at the bottom of Main Street, or maybe it was Orchard Street, called Zimmer's Jewelry Store.

~~~

The old Tarrytown Music Hall was owned by a Mister Harry Goldblatt. My father was a very good dancer and one time he organized a dance to be held at the Tarrytown Music Hall. This was prior to the seats being installed there, and he sold tickets to the dance.

Daddy used to tell a story about the old days, when the music hall would show a motion picture. They were silent movies and there was always a live piano player that would play music to fit the scene of the film. In one scene in "The Perils of Pauline", Pauline is coming through the woods, and everyone in the audience is holding their breath because the villain is hiding, waiting to jump her when she comes by. There was dead quiet in the theater when one of Daddy's friends yelled out, "LOOK OUT, THE SON OF A BITCH IS BEHIND THE TREE." Well, of course that brought down the house.

Harry Goldblatt and Harry Bassett, Uncle Bill Bassett's father, both had bald heads, and one night a week, I think Wednesdays, they would hold a raffle, between the newsreels and the movie. I can remember Larry Dick one night commenting on their two bald heads saying, "If we had one more bald guy we could open a pawn shop," referring to the three big brass balls that adorned the fronts of pawn shops in those days.

The Tarrytown Music Hall

Harry Goldblatt always had giveaways at the movies. They would hand out a tea cup one night or a dinner plate another night, to everyone who bought a ticket to the movie. We got our entire dinner service, one piece at a time, from going to the movies.

I remember when I was young, there was a candy and magazine store next to the Music Hall. I would go down there on Saturdays and my mother would give me twenty-five or thirty cents. I could go buy candy then pay ten or fifteen cents to get into the movies. We would see two movies, the newsreels, coming attractions and a serial, maybe a western like Tom Mix. The serials would always end with the cowboy jumping off a cliff on his horse, or a woman tied to the railroad tracks. This would make you want to come back the next week to see what happened to them. This is where the term "cliff hanger" comes from.

We would sometimes spend all day at the movies. Larry Dick would come pick us up and if we had cried during the movie he would say, "Awww, it must have been a good one, it was a 'four Kleenex' movie." He was always cracking jokes, and was so much fun to be around.

I think when Mary and Larry were on their honeymoon, he sent us a note. In it he said, "I walked down to the ocean and told it a few jokes. You should have heard it roar."

Fifi modeling her dance costumes - May, 1935.

On the corner of Broadway and Main Street, opposite Russell and Lawries Pharmacy, was Graber's Ice Cream Store. That was where everyone hung out after a football game or on a Saturday night. There was a driveway that ran behind Graber's, and at the end of the driveway was an auto repair shop. On the other side of the driveway there was a run down old house, and there was an old man that lived there named Clinky Dutcher. He was kind of a hobo that you would see wandering the streets sometimes, and he was very old. Then one day someone from the garage realized that they hadn't seen him around for a few days, so they went inside and found him dead in the house. He must have been a real pack-rat, because they found stacks of newspapers piled up to the ceiling. They had to maneuver the stretcher in between the rows and rows of piled-up newspapers to get his body out of the house.

Fifi Egan
Sunday, May17, 1936.

There weren't any restaurants in Tarrytown when I was young, but there were a lot of other fine businesses. One of the busiest was a store on Broadway, opposite the Pierson School, named Genungs, were you could buy stylish, good quality women's and children's clothing at modest prices. Everyone in Tarrytown shopped there for their clothes.

As you continued north on Broadway, from Main Street, there was a bank and Dwyer's Funeral Home. Everybody in the family was waked at Dwyer's. My Uncle Jack was so popular in town that he was often asked to be a pall bearer at many funerals. He had helped carry so many caskets in and out of Dwyer's that we used to joke that he should change his middle name to Paul.

Past Dwyer's, on the west side of the street, is the library, and just past the library is a park. There is a statue there of a "Minute Man" dedicated to the local Tarrytown men who had captured Major Andre on that spot.

Major Andre was a Revolutionary War soldier, an American officer at West Point, who became a spy for the British. He worked for Benedict Arnold, the infamous spy, and they had gotten the plans for the American fortifications that protected the Hudson River at West

AUG. 1936

Fifi, Betty, Flo and Margaret at Rye Beach. August, 1936.

Point and he was taking them down to the British Army in New York City. Three woodsmen from the Tarrytown area were in the woods cutting down trees. They had been alerted to look for spies, and they heard Major Andre's horse coming down the trail so they stopped him and searched him, but found nothing. They were just about to let him go on his way when one of them said, "Wait, we never looked in his boots." When they checked his boots they found the stolen plans for West Point. This was an important event in the Revolutionary War, for if Major Andre had succeeded in getting the plans for West Point to the British we might all be British subjects today.

Marymount College was a very well known Catholic girl's school that you could see from my backyard on Union Avenue. It was a beautiful school that was up on a hill overlooking the Hudson.

Next door to Marymount there was a horse stable at the corner of Union Avenue and Irving Avenue, that was owned by a man named George Beck, where some of the girls from Marymount would come to ride. George was from Texas and had a high, crackly voice. He would always call out, "Hey Feefee," mispronouncing my name, whenever he would see me. When it snowed he would come up by my house with a Flexible Flyer hitched to the back of a horse, and yell, "Hey Feefee, do you want to go for a ride?", and he would take me for a sleigh ride behind the horse, up and down Union Avenue. I must have been only about eight years old, but I remember that like it was yesterday.

George had an old man that helped him in the stable, I think his name was Billy, and I used to go down there just to watch them saddle up the horses.

Flo, Harriet, Margaret and Fifi at Rye Beach. August, 1936.

Some days if George was going to take two or three of the Marymount girls out riding, and I was there, he would yell out to Billy, "That white mare needs some exercise. Go saddle her up." Then he would turn to me and drawl, "Hey Feefee, do you want to go for a ride?", and he would take me riding with the older girls from Marymount.

One day my cousin Dorothy Egan and I had gone down to the stable and George asked us if we wanted to ride bareback, both of us on the same horse, and we said, "Sure." Down near the barn there was a big rock that we would step up on to get on the horses, so Dorothy and I climbed up on the rock, then got on the horse, me in front; Dorothy behind me. It had snowed heavily the day before and there were drifts all over the place. We had started up a hill behind the stable when the horse started to buck and the two of us went sailing off, together, into a snow drift. As we went off Dorothy was still holding onto me with both arms around my waist, and we landed in the snow. I was trying to cover my face and head with my hands as I could see and hear the horse's hooves stomping all around us, but he never did actually step on us. George and Billy got us back on the same horse, and this time he didn't buck, so off we rode together. George was very good to me. Now there's a tennis court where the stables used to be.

Fifi and her cousin Dorothy Egan.
May 10, 1936.

~~~

My sisters and I were all married in the Church of the Transfiguration, the Carmelite Church, on Broadway in Tarrytown, near the Tappan Zee Bridge. My mother's and father's funerals were held there too. I think my grandfather, Bart Egan, dug the foundation for the original church back in 1896. The Catholic elementary school was added in 1948, and then the original church was torn down and rebuilt in 1967.

In the original church there was a railing all around the altar where we would kneel to receive Communion or to have our throats blessed, and there was a huge crucifix right behind the railing. People would go up to the railing to pray at the crucifix and kiss or touch the feet of Christ.

Every year when we were very young we used to go to Transfiguration Church on February 3rd. That's the Feast of Saint Blaise, and we would kneel at the railing around the alter to have our throats blessed. The priest would hold lighted candles, crossed under your chin, to bless your throat. One year when we went I happened to glance over at my sister Helen, and I saw smoke. Her hair was on fire. Not really in flames, but smoking. The priest had obviously gotten a little careless with the candles, but he nervously patted her head to put it out. I was probably about ten years old at the time, but I remember Helen getting very flustered by it and was upset for the rest of the Mass.

L to R - Helen, Fifi, Nellie and Mary Egan - Summer, 1938.

The crucifix at Transfiguration had been donated to the original parish by my father's aunt, Rosie McCauley. But then, as the congregation thrived and outgrew their church, the original stone

67

structure was demolished and it was rebuilt in 1967. The new assembly hall was architecturally very innovative because it was built "in the round". During the time that the church was undergoing this reconstruction, my mother and father, and Larry and Mary, paid to have the crucifix cleaned and refurbished. Then, when the crucifix was moved to the new church, it was hung over the altar, where it presides to this day. There is a small brass plaque under the crucifix that tells of its origin at the church.

Eileen and MaryAnn Budny, little Larry, Mary Ellen, Greg and Jimmy Egan, and Jack and Nick all made their first Communions at Transfiguration.

~~~

Behind the church is the Catholic elementary school, and Mary Ellen Dick, Eileen Budny, and Jack and Nick all attended Transfiguration School together. One day, because they didn't understand why everyone in the parish called me "Fifi," one of the nuns called on Jack and asked him, "What is your mother's name?"

"Mommy.", he responded, smiling like a little cherub.

Not getting the information that she was seeking, the nun decided on a different course of questioning. "No no my child," she said piously, "what does your daddy call your mommy?"

"Honey," Jack replied blissfully.

So, seeing that she was getting nowhere fast, the nun called on Eileen and asked her, "What do you call Jack's mommy, my dear?"

Eileen giggled innocently and chirped, "Aunt Fifi."

Jack and Eileen.

68

Well, the poor nun was getting so exasperated that she finally gave up and called me at home to find out what my actual given name was, and why everyone called me "Fifi".

~~~~

One day, many years later when I was teaching at Bethpage, I was talking to my friend Mary McQuillen. She was much younger than I but we had become very close. She told me that her young son, Joe, Jr., was reading "The Headless Horseman" in school, and I started talking about Tarrytown and the fact that the Headless Horseman Bridge is still there. I informed her that Katrina Van Tassel, the story's heroine, was a real person whose family was among the founders of Tarrytown, and that Washington Irving's family burial plot was in the Sleepy Hollow Cemetery and he was actually buried there, not far from my parents and some of my aunts and uncles. One of us suggested that we go up to Tarrytown and tour the area, so Mary, her husband Joe, little Joe and I drove up for a weekend in the fall. I stayed at my sister Mary's, and they stayed at a hotel.

We started out by going to "Sunnyside", Washington Irving's home in Pennybridge. Then we went on a tour of "Lyndhurst", which is a gorgeous old gothic style castle overlooking the Hudson River that had been owned by the Duchesse de Talleyrand.

On Saturday evening I told Mary and Joe that I wanted to go to five o'clock Mass at Transfiguration Church. When we walked into the church I heard someone exclaim, "Fifi, what are you doing here?" It was Anne Doyle, a girl who I knew from my childhood. Another man, Butch Taxter, was sitting behind me, I had known him in high school.

College of Mount Saint Vincent 50 year reunion. June, 1993.

Madeline Byrnes, another girl that I knew from high school, came in and waved to me. Joe and Mary Reilly were stunned by the number of

69

people coming over, hugging and kissing me. It was like "Old Home Week". After church we went for dinner at Horsefeathers Pub, on Broadway, where we ran into even more people that I knew from years before.

On Sunday we went to Philipsburg Manor and up around the

Tarrytown Lakes and Union Avenue where I had grown up. We drove past the statue commemorated to the capture of Major Andre and I explained the story behind it. Then we went through Sleepy Hollow Cemetery. Little Joe knew about the Headless Horseman Bridge from reading "The Legend of Sleepy Hollow", and when we drove across a bridge to the new section of the cemetery, big Joe excitedly fibbed that he saw the Headless Horseman hiding under the bridge. I turned the car around and, as we started back across the bridge, little Joe dove onto the floor in the back of the car, petrified that he might be seen by the legendary Headless Horseman of Sleepy Hollow.

As we were leaving the cemetery, we passed "The Old Dutch Church". There is usually nothing going on there, as the church is normally locked up, but that day there was a wedding ceremony being performed and, after the service, we were able to go inside and look around the old church which dates back to 1685.

After that we drove up toward Ossining and around Sing Sing Prison, then we went up and I showed them where we had lived on Ganung Drive in Ossining.

As we were heading home, Joe Reilly admitted to me that that he had been skeptical about the trip when Mary first proposed it to him, but he had never enjoyed a weekend more and was very glad he had made the trip and seen so many interesting and historic places and things.

I guess I never really gave it any thought while I was growing up, but looking back, I think I must have been a pretty spoiled kid. Although I grew up during the depression years, I never felt like we were poor or wanted for anything, and I always had nice clothes to wear. In fact, at one of my high school reunions many years ago, I was approached by one of my old classmates who confessed that she had been jealous of me, growing up, because I always had nice things. She even remembered a specific poodle skirt and sweater, with small bells down the front, that I had worn to school. I was stunned by her comments because I never considered that my family was any better off than hers or any others in town. But truth be told, I don't think I ever gave it any thought at all. Probably because my sisters were so much older than me, and spoiled me rotten. They and my parents doted on me all the time as a child and I probably just assumed that that was how life was for everybody else that I grew up with.

I know now that I was far more fortunate than many others of my generation.

Helen, her friend Mabel Tierney, and Fifi - circa 1930.

KATHRYN EGAN

Nothing is impossible to a willing heart.

Treasurer Class 1, 2, 3, 4; Girls' Club 3, 4; Dramatic Club 3, 4; "Digging up the Dirt"; Glee Club 4; Cheerleader 3, 4; Latin Club 3; Alhambra 4; G. O. 2, 3, 4; French Club 3.

Kathryn Egan - High school yearbook picture.

Chapter Four

FIFI - A WILLING HEART

I was born on August 2nd, 1922, and was the youngest of three daughters. I was lucky because my parents and sisters were always very supportive of everything I ever wanted to do.

I was named Kathryn after one of my mother's sisters, Aunt Katie. I don't know what year she arrived, but like my mother, she too had come over from Ireland and become a nurse. She married a pharmacist named Ed Stone, but they never had any children. My mother and father are buried in the same plot as Aunt Katie and Uncle Ed in Sleepy Hollow Cemetery.

Aunt Katie had fallen one time and injured her spine. After that she always had trouble walking and would always have to hold on to something for stability. She and Uncle Ed lived on Amsterdam Avenue in New York City, but when I was about ten years old Uncle Ed died, so Aunt Katie came to live with us on Union Avenue. She had a hard time

Fifi and Aunt Katie - Circa 1924.

going up and down the stairs, but she slept in the back bedroom, so Mother would have to run up and down to bring her all her meals.

At one point, she had to go back into the hospital in New York City because of her spinal injury. Her money eventually ran out and the hospital called my mother and told her that if Aunt Katy's bill wasn't paid that they would put her out on the street. So Mother called The Little Sisters of the Poor, in New York, who took her in. I think she was there for about a year when she fell out of bed and exacerbated her spinal injury. She died a short time later.

Aunt Katie Horgan Stone.

~~~

My middle name, Phyllis, was from my father's brother, Uncle Philip. He was a lifelong bachelor and served in the Army as a

Uncle Phil Egan - second from right.

blacksmith during World War I. He was one half of a set of twins, the other was my Uncle Joseph. When Mother was pregnant with me, the doctor insisted that she stay in bed for the last three months of her pregnancy because her varicose veins were so bad. During that time, Uncle Philip helped her run the house and took care of my two older sisters.

74

My Confirmation name is Mary, after Saint Mary, the Blessed Virgin. So my whole name is Kathryn Phyllis Mary Egan McFadden. Is that an Irish name or what?

No one knows for sure how I got the nickname "Fifi", but I have been called Fifi for as long as I can remember. One theory was that my sisters or I had a hard time saying, "Phyllis," and it came out "Fifi," and it just stuck. Everyone I know has always called me Fifi, and I'd bet there are people who I've known for many years, who, if you referred to me by anything other than Fifi, they wouldn't know who you were talking about.

~~~

When I was about ten or twelve years old I enrolled in dancing lessons at The Helen Thorne School of Dance in Tarrytown, and we would meet in the basement of the church on Route 9 in the village. One of the other girls I took lessons with was named Jeanne Trybon.

Jeanne and Fifi in 8th grade - March, 1936.

Japanese dance costume - May, 1935.

She had blond hair and I was a brunette, so Helen Thorne used to like to have us do dance numbers together because she liked the contrast in our coloring. I remember doing a dance with Jeanne where we both wore these exotic Japanese costumes. The dance was called "Cherry Blossom", and my mother made my dance costume for me.

75

Years later, Jeanne became a professional dancer and performed in the Broadway production of "Pal Joey". I went down to the city one day to meet her for lunch while she was appearing in "Pal Joey", and while I was there, she got a call from some friends that wanted to meet us for dinner. Jeanne and I stopped by the theater so she could pick up her paycheck and that was where we met her two friends who wanted to have dinner with us. It turned out that they were two men who were at least twice our age. I didn't like that whole idea, so I backed out of the dinner and went home. I wasn't crazy about the type of people that she was starting to hob-nob with, and I didn't see too much of her after that.

Jeanne's publicity photo.

~~~

I attended Washington Irving High School in Tarrytown, and all through high school I ran for different offices and participated in many of the clubs and activities. I was in the Drama Club, and had the lead in several plays. I was in the Glee Club and was President of the Girls Club in high school.

Washington Irving High School junior play - March, 1938 - Fifi is 3rd from right.

Washington Irving High School

I was a cheerleader during football and basketball seasons, and North Tarrytown was our most bitter rival. Much to my mother's chagrin, if we won a game against North Tarrytown, some of the other cheerleaders and I would ride on the running boards of a car, up Broadway, through North Tarrytown, blowing the horns and doing our W.I. cheers, and basically rubbing it in that we had won. North Tarrytown's cheerleaders would do the same thing to us whenever they were the winners. After games or dances, we would all go down to Graber's Ice Cream store on the corner of Broadway and Main Street. That's where everyone would hang out.

One night we were playing North Tarrytown in basketball at the W.I. gym and the place was packed to the rafters. There was a new cheer that we had been practicing, and another girl and I wanted to do it. But the captain of the cheerleading squad, Madelyn Byrnes, didn't think we knew it well enough and wouldn't let us do it. We kept bugging her and finally she said, "Okay, go ahead and do it."

So, after a few minutes there was a time-out in the game. The teams were sitting on the floor; and the refs were over on the sideline, so the two of us went out onto the middle of the gym floor and did our "Bo Bo Bo Deeton Doton" cheer for the first time. And as we clapped our hands in rhythm to the cheer, it went like this:

Bo Bo Bo Deeton Doton

Bo Bo Bo Deeton Doton

Bo Bo Bo Deeton Doton

SHOO!!!

Dorsey swings it

Red hot and blue.

In the Big Apple

And the Susie 'Q'.

So truck on down

And shag right through.

Come on W.I.

It's up to you!!!

The Big Apple, the Susie Q, the Truck and the Shag were dance crazes that were all the rage during the big band era at the time, and the two of us would be doing those dances as we called them out during the cheer. When we got to the end we'd jump up and down and wave our hands in the air.

Well, we got a standing ovation from not only the crowd in the gym, but all the players, coaches and the referees. We were hot stuff. I think that was the first time that a high school cheer had been done with dancing. That year we won the annual Hudson Valley Cheerleading Competition, and that was our best cheer.

1939 WI chearleading squad - Won cup at Peekskill competition.
Marie Nelson and Fifi are in upper left of photo.

When I was graduating from high school we had our annual "Class Night", and anyone who could sing or dance or had any talent could perform. There was a girl named Evelyn Keyes who sang a very good rendition of "Deep Purple", and I sang "Don't Worry About Me". These were two of the popular songs at the time. My parents and sisters were sitting in the audience in the fifth or sixth row and I could see them as I was singing, and I could see that there hearts were in their throats as they were watching me. I had been practicing at home because there was a spot where I would need to draw a deep breath. But during my performance, I took my breath too soon. I could see the worry on their faces that I would run out of breath too early, but thank God, I was able to pull it off just fine.

Class Night dress - June, 1939.

After I graduated from high school I was unsure what the future held for me. My mother and father both wanted me to attend college even though neither of them had, nor had Helen or Mary.

Helen had a good job in the radiology department at Grasslands Hospital and Mary was the secretary to the General Manager of the Chevrolet plant in Tarrytown. But my parents wanted me to go to college, and in those days you didn't argue with your parents, you did what you were told.

Even though I could see Marymount College from my house and had spent time there when the nuns gave Helen, Mary and me piano lessons, I elected not to go there. I decided I would be a day-hop at the College of Mount Saint Vincent in Riverdale. That meant taking the train from

High school graduation dress and bouquet - June 27, 1939.

Tarrytown to Yonkers, then changing to another train that would take me over to Mount Saint Vincent. Once there I would have to walk over a trestle to the campus.

It was, and still is, a beautiful campus that even has an old castle on it, and there are magnificent views of the Hudson River from the grounds. At the time it was unusual for women to go to college, but it was an all-girl's Catholic college with an enrollment of about three to four hundred women, residents and day-hops combined. At the same time that I was attending Mount Saint Vincent, John McFadden was attending Villanova, in Pennsylvania, but more about him later.

Every year some of my classmates and I would march in the Saint Patrick's Day Parade in New York City, and every year it would rain or snow on us. Sometimes some of us would go down to New York City to see shows and things. I first saw Frank Sinatra at the Paramount Theater in Manhattan. He was so skinny that he wasn't much wider than the microphone stand that he was standing behind.

~~~

I met Shirlee Atwood at Mount Saint Vincent. She was also a day-hop who would come up from the Bronx from a very Irish neighborhood near Fordham. Early in our Freshman year, our Senior Sisters gave a party for us, their Freshman Sisters, and it was supposed to start at five o'clock in the gymnasium. When we got to the party there were some nuns sitting up in the balcony, in their black habits with white collars and their black caps that were tied under the chin, looking down on the proceedings in the gym. We had a juke box playing music, some soft-drinks and cold cuts. It started out as a very quiet gathering, then a group of girls turned up the music and started dancing up a storm in the middle of the floor. Shirlee and her Senior Sister were dancing with them.

Fifi and Shirlee Atwood - Picnic in Hackley Woods - Easter vacation, 1941.

82

The next Monday, all the girls who had been dancing in the group were called down to the Dean's office and reprimanded. A few of the girls were suspended for a week, and a few others were expelled from school. It was the view of all the nuns who ran The Mount that they were preparing us to go out into the world as ladies, and that we represented The Mount at all times and must act accordingly. They didn't consider the girls dancing that day to being conduct becoming of a lady.

Shirlee, Joan, Fifi and Merle - THE MOUNT - March 27, 1941.

Shirlee had a really wonderful sense of humor and, once we got to know each other, we just really clicked. She used to write me notes in class and always ask what I had for lunch. She loved my mother's meatloaf and would always want to trade her lunch for my meatloaf sandwiches. On some of her notes she would write things like;
Dear Sears,
What kind of sandwich do you have today?
If it's meatloaf, I'll trade you my peanut butter and jelly.
Love,
Roebuck
She would always open and close her notes with Sears and Roebucks, Montgomery and Ward, Abbott and Costello or some other goofy greetings.

There was a saying that I picked up from Shirlee while we were in college together. Whenever I would ask her what she was going to wear to a dance or a party, she would always smile impishly and answer, "My purple velour tights."

I don't know where she got it from because she didn't have any purple velour tights, they didn't exist, it was just a joke that she always got a kick out of, the inference being that she was going to wear something shamelessly uninhibited that would obviously provoke the nuns that ruled over us. Over the years, that has become one of my favorite little inside jokes. Whenever John and I were invited anywhere or even if I had to go out somewhere with the kids I'd always say, "Oh, I'll have to get out my purple velour tights," and just like Shirlee, I always got a kick out of it, but I don't think John and the kids ever really got it. They'd just look at me and shake their heads like they thought I was a little strange or something.

Fifi and Shirlee Atwood - College of Mount Saint Vincent - Friday, November 13, 1942.

84

Fifi Egan - College photo.

~~~

Shirlee and I both attended Father Dougherty's religion class, and would always be laughing at each other, so finally Father Dougherty decided to separate us and moved Shirlee to the back of the classroom. But I would always be turning around to wave or smile at her. So after a few days Father Dougherty said, "Shirlee, come back up front. It's easier to control the two of you if you're up here with me."

Father Dougherty considered himself a bit of a comedian, and on the first day of his religion class he told the group, "For every joke you tell me, I'll tell you two." Then one day as class was ending, and we had said our prayers and blessed ourselves, Father told us a very funny joke. We were all laughing and starting out of the classroom with our books when we realized that the girls ahead of us were backing up, back into the classroom. We looked at the door, and there was Father Dougherty bowing and saying, "Good morning Sister," as he walked out. And there, standing in the doorway, was Sister Catherine Marie, Dean of the College, in her formidable black habit and hat. Her hands were folded at her waist and she was glaring at us through her horn rimmed glasses, I can still see her. And for every step she took toward us into the room, we all took a step back.

Fifi and Shirlee.
Class Day - May 31, 1941.

"Be seated," she hissed, and we all sank back down in our desks. She proceeded to chastise us in her stern manner, saying that she, "…had to come down the hall to find out where all the raucous laughter was coming from," and to admonish us, that our "…conduct was not befitting of a Mountie." After about ten minutes of her harsh tongue lashing she finally directed us to, "…leave now, in an orderly and ladylike fashion."

When we went back to Father Dougherty's class the next day, we all yelled at him, "Sure, you got us into trouble and then managed to escape Sister's wrath."

He found it all very amusing and just laughed at us.

During our sophomore year, Shirlee's mother died of cancer, so she had to help her father take care of her younger sister, Caroline. Then Shirlee met Emil Squillante while she was at the Mount and he was attending Manhattan College. He graduated before us, in 1940, before the United States got into the War, and he decided to go to Europe to join the British Air Force and become a fighter pilot to join the fight against the Nazis.

Emil had very dark features; dark hair and olive skinned. He had beautiful brown eyes and long eyelashes. Shirlee used to close her eyes and moan, "Oh luscious lashes," whenever she would talk about him.

I went to visit Shirlee in Myrtle Beach, in 1944. Emil had returned from Europe after Pearl Harbor was attacked and was now stationed down there with the U. S. Army Air Force. The house they had rented was on the beach, not far from the air force base, and every morning she would say to me, "Come on Fifi, we'll miss Em, (short for Emil) he'll be coming by in a few minutes." So we'd go running out on the beach every morning and Emil would swoop down low over the shoreline in his fighter plane. He'd dip his wings and wave to us. A few minutes later, he'd have turned around and do the same things on his way back to the base.

When Shirlee and Emil got married, they had their wedding in Saint Patrick's Cathedral in New York City. I was her Maid of Honor, and one of our Professors from Mount Saint Vincent, Father Halpin, married them. Shirlee was a bridesmaid for me when John and I got married.

After the War Shirlee and Emil moved to Florida, where Emil's family had been in the fruit business. Shirlee began teaching elementary school, and taught for a long time. They had three kids.

Shirlee still lives in Winter Park, Florida, and we still keep in touch with each other on our birthdays, her birthday is four days after mine. She always use to call me "Girlie", and would say to me, "Don't ya know Girlie? All hot numbers are born in August."

Dear Girlie —
I cannot possibly write anything
'cause it would turn out all penitential
and cluchy - there are no words to say
the way we feel & the fun we've had
so I'll say in just a few words - "Lets
be friends for a long, long time and then
for a long time after." Incidentally I don't
mind coming for all your Children that
are to come but I'll only take John every
other day!!

I. SHIRLEE ATWOOD
A.B.

Sodality, 1, 2, 3, 4; A.A., 1, 2, 3, 4; Literary
Society, 2, 3, 4; Epsilon Phi, 4; El Circulo Santa
Teresa, 2.

Josephine
Isabell

Shirlee Atwood's senior yearbook photo from The Mount.

~~~

The time that I went to visit Shirlee in Myrtle Beach, I took the train from Grand Central Station in New York City, and had to change trains at Union Station in Washington D.C. I got on one of the cars going to Myrtle Beach that wasn't too crowded, found a seat and put my luggage in the overhead rack. There were a few people in the car, but I didn't pay too much attention to them. A few minutes later, the Conductor came down the aisle to me and, pointing to the overhead storage, asked, "Is this your bag Miss?"

I said, "Yes."

He took down my bag and instructed, "Would you follow me please?"

We went out of that car, walked down the platform and went into another car toward the front of the train. He showed me to an empty seat and put my luggage in the overhead storage above me. I don't know when, but it finally dawned on me that he had moved me from an "all black car" to a "Whites Only" car.

This all seemed very strange to me because in Tarrytown there was no segregation. I went to school with black kids and had lots of friends who were black. I never gave it a second thought. But once I got further into the South, things were different. It was even more noticeable when I was on the return trip back up to New York and changed trains again in Washington D.C., when I first really noticed the signs for the bathrooms or the drinking fountains that said, "Whites Only." That was my first introduction to racism.

Years before, in high school, there had been a Saint Patrick's Day program and dance at Transfiguration Church. I was scheduled to perform a tap dance in the program and was going to be accompanied on piano by the head of the Music Department at Washington Irving High School. But during rehearsals I had a hard time getting in sync with him, so I asked Father Wholley, at the church, if I could bring my own accompanist, and got his approval.

On the night of the program I arrived with Virginia Conway, a black girl who had accompanied me at a few previous programs at the high school. It had never even occurred to me that there might be an issue with her playing for me, and, just as it had at all our prior collaborations, it all went very well. She was just another kid, and nobody gave it a second thought. That's why it really was a shock when I saw all those racist distinctions being made in the South.

WEDNESDAY, JUNE 2, 1943

MISS KATHRYN P. EGAN

Miss Kathryn Egan Graduated Yesterday

Miss Kathryn Phyllis Egan, daughter of Mr. and Mrs. Nicholas Egan, 169 Union Avenue, yesterday at commencement exercises at the College of Mount Saint Vincent, received the degree of bachelor of arts.

A graduate of the Washington Irving High School, Miss Egan was an English major in college and did her practice teaching at WI. She was in her sophomore year, class secretary; in her junior year, vice-president, and this year was president of the Drama Society, business manager for the Campus Record, college newspaper, and served also as business manager for the Parapet, year book, and was a member of the college publicity committee. She is a member of the Epsilon Phi sorority.

COLLEGE OF MOUNT SAINT VINCENT

Mount Saint Vincent-on-Hudson
City of New York

Account of Miss Kathryn P Egan

Class Sophomore

Date Sept 1940 to Feb 1941

Tuition	$175.00
Board and Residence	~~250.00~~
Room Rent	
Music	
Art	
Commerce Education	
Professional Courses	
Laboratory Fee	
Other Charges:	
	$175.00

Received Payment 9/30/40

COLLEGE OF MOUNT SAINT VINCENT

per *Sister Marie Eustelle .*

Bursar

Tuition bill from Mount Saint Vincent - September, 1940.

L to R - Fran LaSala, Eileen Warren and Fifi - College boat ride - June, 1941.

KATHRYN P. EGAN
A.B.

Class Vice-President, 3; Class Secretary, 2; Sodality, 1, 2, 3, 4; A.A., 1, 2; Epsilon Phi 4; Glee Club, 2; Literary Society, 1, 2, 3, 4; Masque, 1, 2, 3, 4, President, 4; Campus Record Staff, 1, 2, 3, 4, Business Manager, 4, Manager of Junior Issue; Publicity Committee 3, 4; Parapet Staff, 4, Business Manager, 4; Freshman-Junior Party Committee, 1; Sophomore Tea Dance Committee, 2; Co-Chairman of Junior Prom, 3; Junior-Freshman Party Committee, 3.

Fifi's senior yearbook photo from THE MOUNT.

Mount Saint Vincent junior prom - Spring, 1942.

Nick, Ellen and Fifi Egan with John McFadden.
Mount Saint Vincent junior prom - Spring, 1942.

Chapter Five

BRINIE MARLIN

John McFadden was born on June 29th, 1920, in Pocantico Hills, New York. He attended the elementary school that the Rockefeller family had built in Pocantico. He and his sisters, Dolores and Dottie, and his Nelson cousins all attended that school.

His father, John McFadden, Sr., was the first President of the Board of Education in Pocantico and was a Councilman for the Town of Mount Pleasant. He was a wonderful man, and very well liked.

His mother, Laura Foley McFadden, was a very attractive woman with a very reserved demeanor. Unfortunately, she was very sickly

John McFadden - 1933.

in the latter years of her life with a severe form of arthritis.

~~~

I never noticed John until one day when I was about fifteen years old, and I was standing in the doorway of my homeroom at Washington Irving high school before classes started. There was a skylight there on the second floor, and as I was standing there I noticed this young man walking under the skylight. I can still remember the clothes that he had on that day. He was wearing a black knit sweater with a white shirt underneath with black checked pants, and he was carrying books. I thought to myself, "Now there's a good looking guy. Why haven't I noticed him before?" I found out his name and that he had a sister named Dolores in school. He didn't know it yet, but from that moment on, he was a dead duck. He pursued me till I caught him.

I remember that I used to have little get-togethers at our house on Union Avenue, and I had made friends with Dolores and John's cousin, Marie Nelson, and always invited them. That way he could drive Dolores and Marie to my parties and have an excuse to come in for a while and spend a little time. Little by little we got to know each other. A few stolen glances turned to nervous eye contact. And slowly, those early sparks became a steady flame.

~~~

The first time he came to call on me, I was sitting in our living room next to the long windows. I

Dolores McFadden and Marie Nelson - Age 15 - August, 1938.

was reading a magazine and I was facing the hallway by the front door. From where I was sitting I could see the hall window that looked out over the driveway. I don't remember what day it was but it was in the afternoon. I heard someone knocking but I hadn't heard anyone walk up the wooden steps onto the front porch, so I looked out the front windows to the porch, but no one was there. I heard more knocking so I glanced across to the hallway window, and there was John, looking in through the window at me. I thought this odd because

JOHN McFADDEN
French Club 4; Basketball 3, 4.

John McFadden - Class of 1937 ALHAMBRA senior picture.

95

the window was probably eight feet above the driveway. So I walked over to the window to see what he was standing on to be up so high, and that was when I saw that he was on his horse. That was why he could look right into that high window, and gaze right into my eyes.

John (17 years old), John McFadden Sr., and Uncle Johnny Foley.
Pawling, NY - 1939.

That horse had a white face and I think his name was Baldy. John put the horse in our garage then came inside to visit for a while. Later, when my father came home and went to put the car in the garage he was surprised at the smell of the horse that lingered there long after John and Baldy had left.

From then on we were "an item" at school. I was fifteen so it must have been 1937. John was on the basketball team and I was a cheerleader. We would ride on the bus to away games, and he would sit with me and hold my hand.

Sometimes after a date we would go down to Pennybridge, to his Aunt Babe (Dorothy Foley) and Uncle Jimmy Spelaci's, where they had a luncheonette / ice cream store. It was down on Broadway near where the thruway is now.

I remember one time when we had a basketball game against North Tarrytown (which has since been renamed Sleepy Hollow). They were our bitter rivals. The game was at our school, Washington Irving, and the gym was packed to the rafters, standing room only.

John's cousin, Bobby Nelson, also played with him on that team. Bobby's nickname was "Half" Nelson and everybody called him "Halfy". Bobby had another cousin, not related to John, who was also named Bobby Nelson.

John and Fifi - Picnic at Raven Rock.
April 11, 1938.

He played for North Tarrytown and his nickname was "Logger" Nelson. They played opposite each other in the game.

W. I. Defeats N. T., 22 to 18, As 800 Look On

Crimson Upsets Champions; Cooley, McFadden Excel

Refusing to be awed by North Tarrytown High School's impressive record against Hudson River league teams, a scrappy and aggressive Washington Irving High School quintet fought its way to a 22-18 victory over the circuit champions on the winner's court last night.

Ear-splitting cheers thundered through the Crimson gymnasium as Johnny (Red) McFadden, wiry, sharp-shooting guard, dropped in two long-range shots at the psychological moment to halt a desperate last quarter-rally by North Tarrytown which threatened to bring the Orange from behind.

More than 800 spectators watched with admiration and amazement as lithe Irving Cooley played the part of Bob Nelson's shadow, clinging to the famous North Tarrytown captain like a leech as he held him to three points until the closing minutes of the game.

Intense defensive play by both teams forced them to rely on long shots throughout the conflict. Style of play by both teams was identical, the feeders attempting to pass to players cutting through the foul lane. Checked closely, players on neither team were able to receive passes as they cut.

Washington Irving was off to a flying start, running up a commanding and comfortable 9-2 lead at the end of the first quarter. "Halfy" Nelson's foul shot opened the scoring for the evening, but Bob Nelson

(Continued on Page Eight)

W. I. Vanquishes N. T., 22-

McFadden's Set Shots Spark Crimson in Riotous Contest

(Continued From Page One)

put North Tarrytown in the lead, for the first and last time, with a tap-in shot.

McFadden Scores

McFadden scored on a long shot from mid-court, and after Harold Croke made good a charity throw, Cooley pushed the Crimson further in front with a one-hand shot from the foul line climaxing a long dribble, then dropped in a long toss from side-court. As the quarter ended, Art Swanson dropped a foul shot.

As the last quarter started, Washington Irving commanded a 14-10 lead. Paul Danko personally brought the score to a deadlock, scoring twice from the charity line, and adding two more on a tap-in shot. "Halfy" Nelson put the Crimson in the lead once more with a foul toss, setting the stage for McFadden's heroics.

At this point, Washington Irving's play suffered a let-down. Simultaneously, North Tarrytown was staging one of those hard-fought rallies for which the Orange is famous. Virtually every spectator in the closely-packed gymnasium was on his feet, cheering wildly. But enter Johnny McFadden.

The Pocantico Hills lad dribbled down-court, veering toward the side. He stopped and let fly at the basket, and the ball swished through cleanly, as North Tarrytown hopes sagged, and Washington Irving's chances for victory over its bitterest rival boomed.

Apparently disdainful of the adage "lightning strikes twice," North Tarrytown players paid McFadden no heed as he again dribbled down-court seconds later. But "Red" was hot, and he again brought a thundering cheer from the Washington Irving section as he sent the score to 19-15 with a long shot, this time from side-court.

Fighting gamely, Bob Nelson kept North Tarrytown in a threatening position with a lay-up shot on a "sleeper play." McFadden and "Halfy" Nelson, however, added two points to Washington Irving's total from the foul line. Bob Nelson got them back with a one-handed heave from the right-hand corner of the court, and seconds later left the game on fouls. "Halfy" Nelson's last foul shot was superfluous.

Cooley Spectacular

Irving Cooley's spectacular play prevented Bob Nelson from performing in his usual effective manner. Nelson was unable to receive passes from teammates as he spun through the center of the foul lane. Cooley was right on top of him all the way. When Nelson poised the ball over his head to attempt his

EXCEL FOR W. I. IN GAME WITH N. T.

Jack McFadden (left) and Bob Nelson, who, with Irving Cooley, starred in a 22-18 triumph scored by the Crimson over the Orange last night before 800 fans at the Tarrytown floor. The game ended the season for both teams.

WI beats North Tarrytown - Saturday, March 4, 1939.

Season Finale Before 800 Onlookers

Final Standings in Hudson River League

Varsity Results

Ossining 20, Pleasantville 17.
Washington Irving 22, North Tarrytown 18.
Peekskill 31, Hastings 24.

Jayvee Results

Ossining 23, Pleasantville 21.
North Tarrytown 24, Washington Irving 17.
Peekskill 40, Hastings 19.

Varsity Standings

	W.	L.	PC.
North Tarrytown	9	1	.900
Washington Irving	7	3	.700
Ossining	4	6	.400
Hastings	4	6	.400
Peekskill	4	6	.400
Pleasantville	2	8	.200

Jayvee Standings

	W.	L.	PC.
North Tarrytown	9	1	.900
Ossining	6	4	.600
Hastings	5	5	.500
Peekskill	5	5	.500
Pleasantville	3	7	.300
Washington Irving	2	8	.200

After a first-half of apparent inactivity as far as offensive efforts were concerned, Paul Danko suddenly blossomed forth with a half-dozen points which almost turned the tide in favor of North Tarrytown.

Near the end of the third quarter, Danko dropped two foul shots, added two more fouls in the final chapter then midway in the period tapped in the shot that knotted the score.

The difference of four points between the teams may be found in the foul column. Each squad dropped in six shots from the floor, but Washington Irving, with "Halfy" Nelson leading, showed ten foul losses while North Tarrytown had six . . . Croke and Swanson, although ineffective in scoring, played good defensive games . . . Al Daley and Rizzi were the stars for North Tarrytown . . . The former held Croke scoreless from the floor, a job in itself, and Rizzi's long shots featured North Tarrytown's middle-of-the-game offensive drives . . . The Crimson was held to two foul shots during the third quarter, while McFadden's long shots were the only field goals in the last . . . It was the first league defeat of the season for the Orange and Black, and as last year, gives each team a victory and defeat . . . Since Jack Edelson has coached the Orange he shows two losses and two triumphs against Washington Irving . . . The difference in defensive style lies in the use of a "floater" by North Tarrytown, who wandered in the middle of the foul circle, while Washington Irving employed a straight man-to-man defense and a switch . . . Last night's battle, the season's finale for both teams, is the last in the high school career of North Tarrytown's Bob Nelson, Paul Danko and Bill Doherty . . . For Washington Irving, Harold Croke, Red McFadden and Art Swanson played for the last time.

The lineup:

Washington Irving (22)

	G.	F.	P.
Croke, rf	0	1	1
Nelson, lf	0	5	5
Cooley, c	2	0	4
Swanson, rg	0	2	2
Arduino	0	0	0
McFadden, lg	4	2	10
Miller	0	0	0
Totals	6	10	22

North Tarrytown (18)

	G.	F.	P.
Danko, rf	1	4	6
Doherty, lf	0	1	1
Nelson, c	3	1	7
Zastenchik	0	0	0
Daley, rg	0	0	0
Cardwell	0	0	0
Zavica, lg	0	0	0
Rizzi	2	0	4
Moro	0	0	0
Vaszko	0	0	0
Totals	6	6	18

Score by quarters:

North Tarrytown	2	5	10	18
Washington Irving	9	12	14	22

Referee—Dzigian. Umpire—Giangreco. Scorer—Galassi. Timer—Vetrano. Missed fouls: Washington Irving—9. North Tarrytown—8.

WI beats North Tarrytown - Saturday, March 4, 1939.

99

In the closing seconds of the game, John came dribbling the ball to the middle of the court, shot and it went in. Then when they came back up the floor again, he shot from the same spot at mid court and it went in again. That shot put W.I. ahead. The crowd was in pandemonium and we won the game.The next day they had John's picture on the front page of the Tarrytown Daily News. There was an article inside about the game and it went on to say, "Enter Johnny 'Red' McFadden...," and it described how he had tied and won the game in such dramatic fashion.

~~~

I remember in the spring of my junior year, the junior prom was coming up and was going to be held at the high school gym. John and I had been dating for a while but he still hadn't asked me to go to the prom. I don't know why I was so mean to him at the time, but I think it was because I didn't like the fact that he just presumed that I was at his beck and call, and just waiting in breathless anticipation for him to ask me to the prom.

Anyway, one day while I was walking up the steps to class, a cute boy named Frank Cullen was walking behind me. I knew he had a crush on me, so I turned and asked him if he was going to the prom.

"No," he confessed, "are you?"

"No, I'm not," I vamped demurely, and batted my eyelashes at him.

He was grinning nervously and I could see the wheels turning behind his eyes. Finally he swallowed hard and asked,"Would you like go with me?"

So I gasped, feigning surprise, and cooed, "Oh yes, I'd love to," and batted my eyelashes some more.

The next day John called me, and while we were talking he asked, "So, what color dress are you wearing?"

"What are you talking about?", I said, as if I had no idea what he was referring to.

"What color dress are you wearing to the prom?", he repeated.

I don't remember exactly how I said it but it was something like, "If you're asking me to the prom, you're too late. I'm already going with someone else ."

"What do you mean," he demanded, obviously hurt, "I assumed we were going together."

"Well," I countered, "you never asked me."

I knew he felt that way but I didn't like the fact that he just assumed that I would be waiting with bated breath for him to ask me. That's why I got Frank Cullen to ask me.

"Just something to remember me by - John"

The night of the prom, when Frank and I were leaving the gym after it ended, I didn't know it but John was parked outside waiting to drive his sister Dolores and her date home, and he saw me leaving with Frank. School ended a few days later and I hadn't seen John, so neither of us had a chance to talk to the other about that night, and it seemed as if our starry-eyed courtship might have just ended on a sour note.

~~~

As soon as school ended for the summer, John started working at his Uncle Johnny Foley's dairy farm up in Pawling. He would get up very early in the morning to drive up to work in the fields and barns. I was going to summer school to take Shorthand I and Typing I at Ossining High School so that I would be able to take Shorthand II and Typing II in my senior year at W.I.

Then one day I was walking down the stairs in Ossining High School and someone called out my name. It turned out to be Vera Foley, Uncle Johnny's daughter and John's first cousin. She introduced herself to me and said that her Aunt Laura, John's mother, wanted our phone number so that she could call and invite my parents and me up to the family summer house in Candlewood Lake, Connecticut, for a clambake. It was a house that John's father and his uncle, Oxel Nelson, had built together on the lake.

The McFadden house at Candlewood Lake - July 4, 1939.

A few days later, John's mother called my mother and invited our whole family up to a clambake at the clubhouse. I didn't really want to go, as John and I hadn't spoken to each other since the night of the prom, but I went anyway.

When we first got up to Candlewood, John wasn't at the house, he was down at the clubhouse helping to set things up. They were also going to have a swimming meet, and John, his sister Dolores and his cousins Bobby and Marie Nelson were all going to be swimming in several events.

John had told all his friends up at the lake that, "My girlfriend is coming up today," then, after all the swimming events had ended, he and his friends were all lying on the lawn together. I was walking by and, as I passed them, John and I exchanged disinterested glances and we both said, "Hi," very aloofly to each other. His friends all looked cockeyed at him, and scoffed sarcastically, "That's your girlfriend?"

Candlewood Knolls swim team - Summer, 1938.

I remember that day very vividly because somebody brought over a heaping tray of steamed clams with a bowl of melted butter. Mrs. McFadden had been raving about the clams, but I told her I had never had one. She said, "Here," and she dipped a clam in the melted butter and gave it to me. I bit it on the right side of my mouth and it shot over to the left side. I bit again and it shot back over to the right side. So I closed my mouth and just sat there holding it on my tongue. Mrs. McFadden asked, "Would you like another one?", but I just kept my mouth closed and shook my head "No." I couldn't bring myself to tell her that I couldn't swallow it. But she knew.

Later we all went back up to the house and sat out on the porch and talked. As we were leaving, Mrs. McFadden asked if I would like to come up and spend a few days with them after summer school was finished, about a week away. I was still very standoffish but she persisted in asking so finally I said, "Okay."

Dorothy "Babe" Spellaci and Grandma Laura McFadden. Candlewood Lake.

So about a week later I went back up to the house at Candlewood Lake with John's cousins Vera and John Foley, Jr. He was Uncle Johnny's son, and he was always just known as "Junior".

The house at Candlewood Lake had a cinder road and a row of other houses between it and the lake shore. Inside there was a spacious living room with a beautiful, rustic stone fireplace. There was also a big couch and some upholstered chairs, and we would eat meals at a picnic table in there.

Pie eating contest - Candlewood Knolls - Labor Day, 1938.
John is at the bottom right. Mr. McFadden is on the left.

In the back was a kitchen where they did all the cooking. There was a gas stove, a sink, some cabinets and a table to prepare food. There was a back door and a stairway that went down to the basement, where there was a heating unit and a shower. In the front of the house, opposite the living room, there was a comfortably sized bedroom that was Mr. and Mrs. McFadden's. Next to that, going towards the back of the house, there was a bunk-room with two bunk beds where four people could sleep. Continuing back, there was another good sized room with a regular double bed and another set of bunk beds. There was a full size bathroom but everyone took their showers in the basement. The whole house had sheetrock walls but no ceilings, just wood beams above the walls, with clear, open space up to the roof.

That week the sleeping arrangements were; John's parents in their front bedroom, his sisters Dolores and Dottie, cousin Marie Nelson and myself in the two bunk beds of the bunk-room. In the back bedroom was his Aunt Jenny (Foley) and Uncle Oxel Nelson in the bed, and Bobby Nelson and John in the bunk bed. Bobby in the bottom bunk, John in the top.

We had all gone to bed and were sleeping, when suddenly I woke up, startled, to the sound of voices. It was pitch dark, but I could hear Mr. and Mrs. McFadden, speaking in very soft, coaxing voices, saying, "John. John." Then I heard Aunt Jenny and Uncle Oxel quietly imploring, "John. John." Then I heard Bobby Nelson cautiously calling out in the dark, "Hey Red. Hey Red." Suddenly, there was an unbelievable crash and commotion, and then I heard John bristle, "What the hell is going on here? Can't I even get up and go to the bathroom?"

At the same time, Dolores, who was sleeping in the front bunk room in the top bunk, sat straight up in bed and let out a blood curdling scream, then laid back down and went right back to sleep. I was shuddering in my bunk thinking, "What's going on here? Is there something wrong with all these people?"

What I didn't know was that John sometimes walked in his sleep and he had been sleep walking, but that's not half the story. He had been sleep walking above our heads, balanced on top of the sheetrock wall partitions that

John's sister Dolores - Candlewood Lake - Labor Day weekend, 1940.

separated the rooms. The crash that I had heard was when he jumped down off the top of the wall and landed on top of poor Aunt Jenny and almost drove her down into the basement.

Believe it or not, he had no memory of any of it the next day.

There were other weekends that I would go up to Candlewood Lake and my cousin Dorothy Egan would also go as she was dating Bobby Nelson. They too eventually got married.

Bobby Nelson, Dorothy Egan, John, Fifi, Dolores McFadden and Bill Marchese.
Candlewood Lake, 1941.

I remember that Mr. McFadden liked to sit out on the front porch of the house every night and gaze out at the lake. He didn't drink or smoke but he loved to sit and look out at the lake in the evenings. Every night, as all of us kids would be leaving to go down to the clubhouse or somewhere, we would reach out as we walked past him on the porch and he would always put some money in our hands. Not a lot, just enough so we could buy a soda or candy if we wanted. He was a wonderful man.

John always had a couple of horses and we used to go horseback riding all the time up on the Rockefeller's bridle paths in Pocantico Hills. Two of his horses were mares that he had named Brenda and Cobina. They were named after two popular New York City debutantes who were always in the gossip columns of the newspapers.

John J. McFadden, Sr.

One day John had been down at the stables at Sleepy Hollow Country Club and he saw someone who was trying to ride this beautiful mare but was having trouble as the horse kept throwing her head around. John commented on what a beautiful horse it was, and the guy said, "Yeah, but she's gonna be put down tomorrow." John asked why, and the guy said that they had been trying to train her to be a jumper but because of the way she threw her head around and was too high spirited, that no one could ride her. He might have tried to ride her that day, I don't remember, but he asked the guy if they would sell her and he made an offer.

John on Sport - Pocantico Hills, NY - February, 1939.

He went home, and that night asked his father for a loan of one hundred and fifty dollars so he could buy the mare that he had seen. The next day, Mr. McFadden called the groom down at the Sleepy Hollow stable and asked him about the horse. The groom told him that the horse was "impossible" and would be too much for John to handle, and too dangerous. Mr. McFadden tried to talk John out of buying the horse, but John persisted. He proposed that if he could take the mare out to the trails with Bobby Nelson and another horse, run her at a gallop on a long straightaway and then bring her back to a stop and under control, his father would give him the loan. Mr. McFadden knew that John was an accomplished rider, so he agreed to the experiment.

On the day of the trial run, John gave Bobby a big head start, then he let the mare have her head. He went by Bobby's horse like it was standing still, then slowed her down and got her under control in the allotted distance that he and his father had agreed on. So his father loaned him the money and he bought the horse, and named her "Eldorado." He kept her in the old chicken coop that he had converted into a barn behind their house on Dayton Avenue.

John on Eldorado at Uncle Johnny Foley's dairy farm in Pawling, NY.
Fall, 1942.

~~~

One time Eldorado got very sick and had green goop coming out of her nostrils. So John spent three or four nights sleeping out in the barn so he could keep a close eye on her. He made a vaporizer out of a sterno stove and a pot of water to keep moisture in the air in her stall. After a few days she started to recover.

When he finally thought she was strong enough to go out on the trails again, he called me up and asked if I wanted to go out riding with him. My two sisters drove me up to Pocantico, and when we got there the horses were already saddled-up and ready to go. We rode down through the rock cut, which was a beautiful, natural ravine that ran down through the granite rock outcroppings behind the Union Church that the Rockefeller family had built. In the spring you could hear the water from the melting snow running down through it.

But that day it was a very overcast, and we had just gotten through the rock cut when it started to rain. John turned to me and anxiously shouted, "Come on. Eldorado can't get wet." He was worried about her because she was still getting over being sick, so we turned the horses around and gave them their heads.

My two sisters were still at the house talking with Mrs. McFadden when we came thundering up the trail, bent over the horses necks, at full tilt. My sister Helen always said she, "...could never forget the sound of the horse's hooves...," as we came galloping back up to the house.

~~~

There was another time when John went out on Eldorado into the wooded trails by himself. As they were cantering along, Eldorado became very nervous and started prancing from side to side. John couldn't figure out why she was acting so skittish. Then he looked down into a glen near the trail and saw a huge buck looking up at them, snorting and pawing at the ground. The buck started up the hill towards them, so he gave Eldorado her head and took off with the buck hot on their tails. He knew he couldn't get back home in time but nearby there was a large estate owned by the Collier family, who published Collier's Magazine. There was a five or six foot high stone wall around the property, and they jumped right over it. When Eldorado landed on the other side, John could hear her hooves slipping on the loose gravel, but she kept going. They came to a gazebo that was overgrown by rosebushes, and John coaxed her through the thorns, into the gazebo, then pulled some of the branches together so the buck couldn't get in. The buck stayed around for quite a while, still snorting and pawing at the ground, before it finally lost interest and left. It seems almost impossible that a buck would go after a horse but John thought that maybe Eldorado was in heat that day, and that may have been what provoked the buck to chase them.

Then there was the time when John and Eldorado were out on the Rockefeller trails by themselves. They were flying along at a full gallop when John noticed a shovel coming up out hole in the middle of the bridle path in front of them. He knew he couldn't stop in time and, when they got up to it, Eldorado jumped over the hole and the laborer who was down in it digging a ditch. When he looked back, John could see the laborer reaching up out of the ditch and waving his fist in anger at him and Eldorado. They must have scared the poor guy half to death, as they barreled up out of nowhere and flew right over his head.

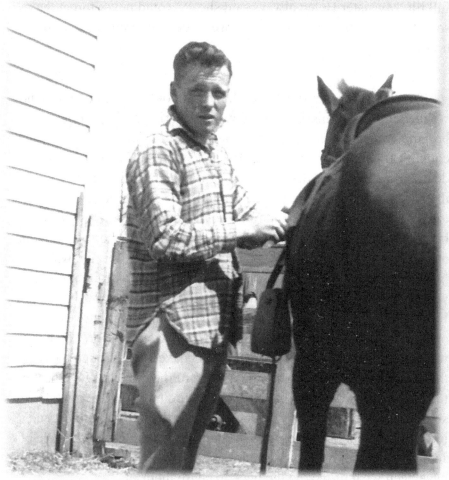

John and Eldorado - 1942.

There were lots of times when John and I would go out riding together on the Rockefeller's property and bridle paths. One time, just after we had slowed the horses down from a gallop, we heard a "jingle" behind us on the trail. We moved the horses over to the right and turned to look. It was Mr. and Mrs. Rockefeller and their groom. John said, "Good morning Mr. and Mrs. Rockefeller," and I smiled at them. Mr. Rockefeller tipped his hat as the two of them nodded there heads and smiled back in silence. They were riding in a lustrously polished carriage, the color of dark burgundy, drawn by a team of magnificent, matching gray horses. Mr. Rockefeller was driving and had a beautiful black top coat with grey suede gloves and a black top hat. Mrs. Rockefeller was wearing a stunning grey fur coat with a matching hat. The groom was sitting up in the back, behind them. He wore a red coat with a white ascot, white jodhpurs, high black boots, white gloves and a black cap, and had his arms folded across his chest. His name was Joe Plick, he was from Pocantico and we knew him very well. We were going to say, "Hi Joe" to him, but he just looked at us and winked, and didn't say a word. John told me later that it was a good thing that Mr. Rockefeller hadn't seen us

John and Fifi -in front of 169 Union Ave., Tarrytown - 1940.

galloping on the bridle paths or he would have forbidden us from ever riding there again.

Mr. Rockefeller had built stone bridges over all of the roads around his estate so that he could take his horse drawn buggy or sleigh out on the bridle paths all the way down to the river without going onto the local roads. They are still there today.

After high school, John applied to Villanova University and was accepted. His first roommate was a guy named Bill Marchese. He was from New Jersey and they stayed roommates for all four years of college, and became close, lifelong friends.

Austin Hall - John's dorm at Villanova.
Junior Prom weekend - Saturday, May 10, 1941.

There was a funny story about a night in their dorm room when John was half asleep in the upper bunk. It was dark in the room, but he noticed a hat go by and someone sat down in the chair. After a few minutes he looked again and saw this "man" sitting in the chair. He thought to himself, "What the hell is this guy doing sitting in our chair," and he dove out of his bunk at the shadowy figure "sitting" in the dark. He shattered the chair, putting a tremendous splinter of wood into his shoulder. When he came fully awake from the crash and the pain in his shoulder, he realized that the figure he had seen was only the hat that Bill had placed on the back of the chair when he had come in earlier in the night. Bill had been asleep in the bottom bunk until his befuddled roommate had shattered the quiet night with his attack on the imagined intruder. This was just one of many times in his life that John would do something crazy in his sleep that he wasn't consciously aware of.

~~~

One time John and Bill came up from Villanova to visit me at my mother's house. Bill was in the kitchen talking with me, and I asked him, "Marchese, what kind of name is that?"

"Wop," was his reply, and he laughed out loud at his own crude remark.

I had asked out of curiosity because he had red hair like John's, and I thought he was Irish. Anyway, I think maybe his mother was Irish.

~~~

The Intramural basketball season is well under way by now. Last year's champs, the Mendel Day-hops, have taken second place. They lost few players by graduation or otherwise, and their new stars have made them top choices for the first half crown. The team which may cause trouble is Austin Hall; John "Red" McFadden is a team in himself. The "Blues" will be hard to stave off.

John played intramural basketball at Villanova. One year they sent out a Christmas card with a photo of the whole team and coaches. John was kneeling in the foreground.

In 1942 there was a prom at Villanova held at The Hotel Pennsylvania in Philadelphia. I drove down with John's parents

John at Villanova.

and his sister Dolores, who went to the prom with Bill Marchese. Somewhere there is a picture of me and John, Bill and Dolores and Ed Reilly and his date Regina. Ed and Regina eventually got married too.

115

While he was away in college John had been keeping his horse, Eldorado, up at his Uncle Johnny Foley's dairy farm in Pawling. While she was there she had been bred with one of the stallions on the farm and was pregnant. John and I had come home for the weekend, following one of the proms at Villanova, and after he dropped me off at my house in Tarrytown he went home to his parents' house in Pocantico. When he got there, there was a message that Eldorado had given birth to a foal, so he immediately took off for Pawling, to the dairy farm, to see his new pride and joy. It took a week or two as John bandied different names around for the filly, but he finally decided to call her "Brinie Marlin."

Brinie Marlin - 6 months old - at Uncle Johnny Foley's dairy farm.
Pawling, NY - Fall, 1942.

The name Brinie Marlin came from a movie that we had seen called "Mr. Lucky", that starred Cary Grant and Lorraine Day. In the movie, Cary Grant plays a character from Australia and in one of the romantic scenes he is trying to explain to Lorraine Day's character what various words and terms from Australia mean in English. He tells her that, "Brinie Marlin means My Darling." After we saw that movie, John and I would always end our letters or cards to each other by signing "Brinie Marlin", and it became our own private little term of endearment for each other from that day on.

But when Eldorado had her foal that day in 1942, John named the new baby Brinie Marlin, and I knew that I finally had some real competition for his affection.

John, Eldorado and Brinie Marlin (6 months old) at Uncle Johnny Foley's dairy farm. - Pawling, NY - Fall, 1942.

John spent his summers during college working at either Uncle Johnny Foley's dairy or at the Chevrolet plant in Tarrytown. Frank Beck was the plant manager and a friend of Mr. McFadden. One summer, some of the Auto Workers Union members were trying to talk John into joining the union, but he didn't want to join as it was only a summer job. On some mornings there would be organizers who would taunt John, and even kick his lunch box out of his hand on his way into the plant.

There was a railroad siding next to the plant where a lot of material; parts and tires and things, would be brought to the plant by freight train, and one morning John was down in one of the box cars, unloading tires. He was by himself, standing on a stack of tires, when he looked down and in came this big, burly guy into the boxcar. The guy was one of the union organizers, and started to climb up on the stack of tires, and grabbed at John's ankle to pull him down. They ended up down on the floor of the freight car and started to fight. John gave the guy a

John in my parent's backyard - April, 1940.

good shot that sent him sprawling back against the wall of the boxcar. When the guy hit the wall, he just threw his arms out, gasped, and collapsed face down on the floor with blood spurting out of a hole in his back. It seems that there had been a big spike sticking out from the wall of the boxcar that had punctured his back. The guy finally got up and staggered out of the car, and the union organizers never bothered John again.

That night John and I had a date and I noticed that he had a cut on his cheek. I asked him what had happened and he said, "Oh, I just cut myself shaving." I didn't find out the real story until he was finished working for the summer and went back to Villanova.

~~~

The Japanese attacked Pearl Harbor on December 7th, 1941. It was John's junior year at Villanova. The day after the attack, John and some of his friends, including Jake Mauche, went down to the Marine Corps recruiting office in Philadelphia to enlist. But when the recruitment officer found out that they were all college students he told them that they should stay in school and

John and Fifi - circa 1941.

finish their education, and get their degrees. He said that they "….were just the type of men that the Marine Corps would need as officers," so he stayed in school and graduated in the spring of 1943. But within two or three days of his graduation he would go back to the recruitment office and enlist in the Marine Corps.

TELEPHONE 767-768

WASHINGTON DAIRY
J. J. FOLEY, PROP.
MILK FROM OUR OWN FARM
282 N. WASHINGTON ST.
N. TARRYTOWN, N. Y.

MILK
CREAM
BUTTERMILK

ORANGEADE
CHOCOLATE MILK
BUTTER – EGGS

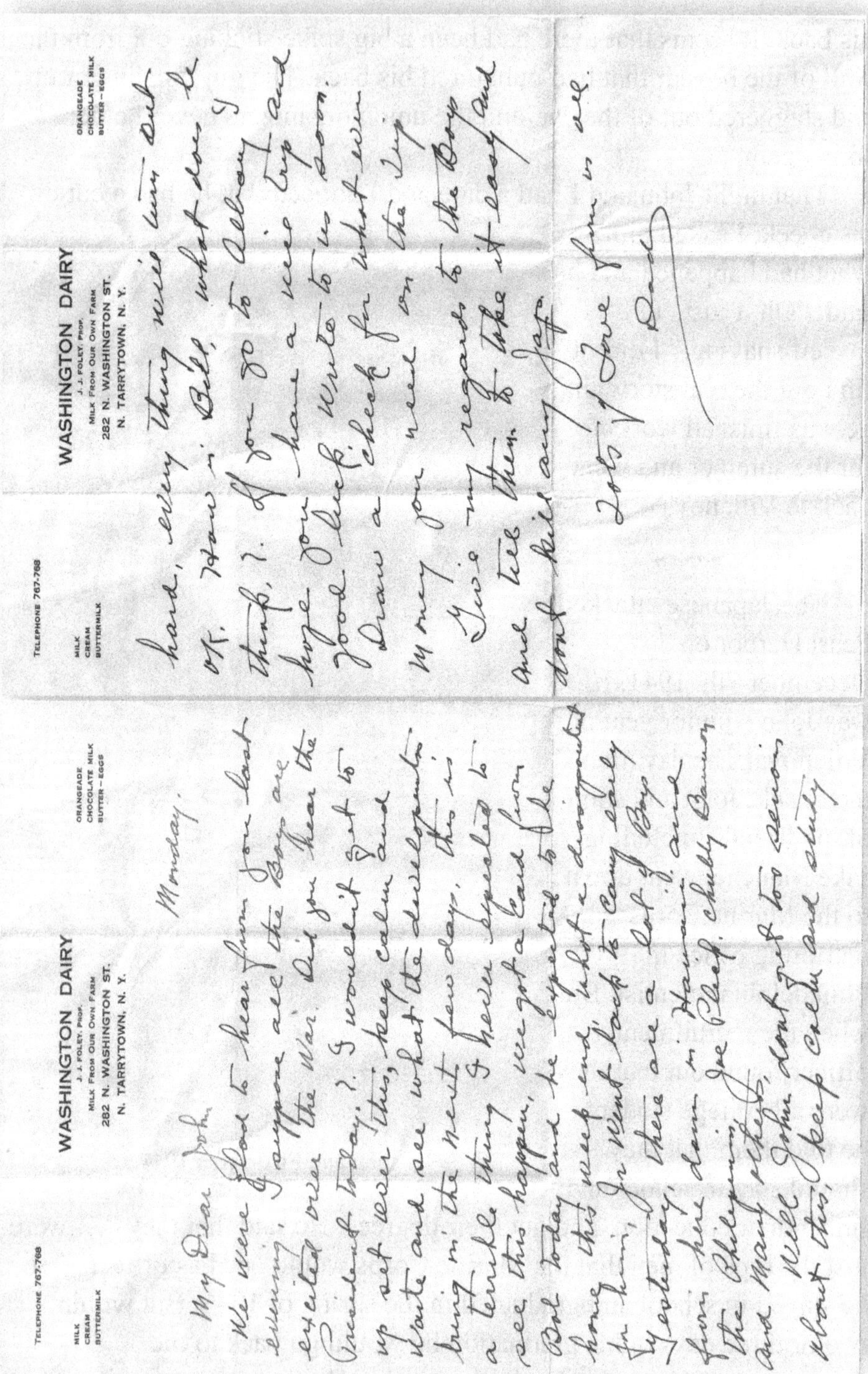

Monday.

My Dear John

We were glad to hear from you last evening. I suppose all the Boys are excited over the War. Did you hear the President today?. I wouldn't get to up set over this, keep calm and waite and see what the developments bring in the next few days, this is a terrible thing I never expected to see this happen, we got a card from Bob today and he expected to be home this week end, what a dissapointment for him, Jr went back to Camp early Yesterday, there are a lot of Boys from here down in Hawaii and the Philippinis, Joe Pleck, chubby Bannon and many others,

Well John dont get too serious about this, keep calm and study

TELEPHONE 767-768

WASHINGTON DAIRY
J. J. FOLEY, PROP.
MILK FROM OUR OWN FARM
282 N. WASHINGTON ST.
N. TARRYTOWN, N. Y.

MILK
CREAM
BUTTERMILK

ORANGEADE
CHOCOLATE MILK
BUTTER – EGGS

hard, every thing will turn out OK. How is Bill, what does he think?. If you go to Albany I hope you have a nice trip and good luck. Write to us soon.

Draw a check for what ever money you need on the Trip

Give my regards to the Boys and tell them to take it easy and dont kill any Japs.

Lots of Love from us all.

Dad

Letter from John's father to John - Dated December 8, 1941.

4415 FIFTH AVENUE · IN THE SCHENLEY PARK DISTRICT · PITTSBURGH · PENNA.

Jan. 12, 1942

Dear Dad,

Everything is fine here. It is still pretty cold and the snow is still here but outside of that everthing is O.K.

Bill passed his Navy Reserve physical the other day so he is all set. Thats not the air corps but just the regular Navy, the V-7 class. He has to take a special Math course that they are starting here to qualify and when he graduates, which they are supposed to guarantee, he will go in training period for three months, then he will receive his commission as an Ensign. He will also have to go in training during the summer. When he is commissioned he will go on active duty with the fleet. I could try for it too but I wouldn't want to get stuck on a ship, Bill thinks he'd like it, I know I wouldn't.

Bill also wrote home to get the address of that friend of his in the cavalry, and then I will write to him about it.

Try and get those three letters of recommendation as soon as you can, I'd better do something soon. I think I would like the Army Air Corps better than the Navy, you don't have to land on any carriers etc..

I will send my laundry to-day. I might come home this week. Tell Dotty I will write when I get a chance.

love John.

John.

Jan. 15, 1941.

Dear Dad,

Everything O.K.,

Naval air corps.

officer at school

to-day. donna

Pretty good, till

you all about it

future I can't tell

love you.

love

John

Notes from John to his father about enlistment in the
armed forces, shortly after Pearl Harbor.

121

In February of 1943, John's father had been sick. John knew that his father hadn't been feeling well, but no one knew the extent of his illness. Then one night, John was in his dorm room sleeping when a knock came on his door. It was one of the Augustinian Brothers and he asked John to come out into the hallway. When they got out in the hall, the Brother, without any lead up to soften the terrible news, said, "John, your father died." John was shocked and fell back against the wall, as he was not expecting anything like that. Certainly not to be so callously told that his father was dead. Mr. McFadden was only forty-nine years old, and it was just too unexpected.

John took the death of his father very hard and never forgot the brusque manner that the news was told to him, but it was his senior year so, after the funeral, he went back and finished school at Villanova.

SERIOUSLY ILL—John J. Mc-Fadden of Pocantico Hills, president of the Board of Education there and associated with John J. Foley in the operation of the Washington Dairy, was removed to the Tarrytown Hospital early yesterday, suffering from a heart attack. His condition was reported at the hospital today as fairly good. Mr. McFadden is one of Mount Pleasant's best known citizens and a former member of the Town Board.

John J. McFadden, Sr.

122

Within days of his graduation from Villanova, in May of 1943, John enlisted in the Marine Corps. But before he left for basic training there was going to be a celebration in Pocantico to honor all the young men who had joined the armed forces. He had always had his horses, and they were very important to him, but around that time Uncle Johnny Foley had been thinking about selling the dairy farm up in Pawling, and John didn't know what to do about Brinie Marlin. Somehow, Mr. Rockefeller got wind of this and came over to John at the celebration and said, "John, I understand that you have a beautiful foal."

John replied, "Yes Sir, I do."

Mr. Rockefeller continued, "I also understand that your uncle is selling the farm. What are you going to do with the foal?"

"I have no idea." John confessed, "I don't know where I'll be or how long I'll be gone."

Mr. Rockefeller then asked, "Would it be all right with you if I bring your foal down from Pawling and keep her here at my stables till you return?"

Well, John was overwhelmed. "Oh yes sir," he enthused gratefully, "that would be wonderful."

Sometime after he got to Saipan he got a letter from Mr. Rockefeller that stated, "John, as of this date I have taken the liberty of sending my van up to Pawling to get your foal. I will keep her at my stable until your return."

Brinie Marlin at the Rockefeller's stone barn.
Pocantico Hills, NY - Spring, 1944.

I don't know how long Brinie was kept at the Rockefeller's stable, but while she was there, John Hughes, who was the son of the president of the bank in Tarrytown, and a friend of John's, was training her and breaking her to a bit and saddle. Brinie was kept there until after John returned home from the war.

~~~

When John and I started dating, back in high school, he was the typical All-American guy. He had a lot of friends from the basketball team and from Candlewood Lake, and he was fun to be around. He was a fun loving guy, but always on the quiet side.

We'd have parties, and the first time that I let him kiss me was when we were playing "spin the bottle" at one of our parties. Sometimes we would double date with his cousin, Bobby Nelson, and my cousin, Dorothy Egan.

Right from the start, I was always the outgoing one, not him. He never wanted to draw attention to himself. When we would dance together, I would always feel his hand pressing on my back, as he didn't want me getting too animated or flamboyant. He didn't want me to, "... make a scene."

While he was in Villanova he used to listen to a radio station in Philadelphia that played a song called "I Bought You Violets for Your Furs", by Frank Sinatra, that he liked to sing. Another song that we use to sing,

John napping on the porch at Candlewood Lake.

in harmony together, when driving back and forth to Candlewood Lake was called "East of the Sun and West of the Moon". We loved to sing them to each other, and sometimes, even to this day, whenever I hear those songs I get the feeling that John is near.

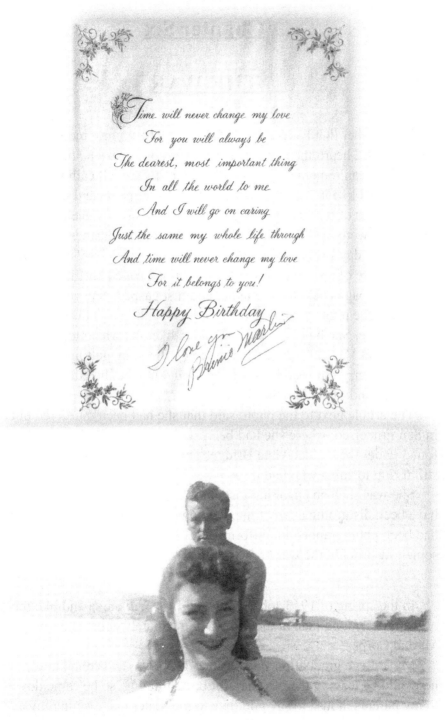

Time will never change my love
For you will always be
The dearest, most important thing
In all the world to me
And I will go on caring
Just the same my whole life through
And time will never change my love
For it belongs to you!

Happy Birthday

I love you
Bernie Marlin

Fifi and John - Candlewood Lake - August, 1941.

125

Chapter Six

THE WAR

I remember that I was standing in the kitchen of my mother's house when I heard the news that Pearl Harbor had been attacked, on the radio. I can remember hearing President Roosevelt calling it, "A day that will live in infamy," but I really didn't understand the ramifications of it at the time. I guess I had led a pretty sheltered life. John and I were in college and life went on, almost business as usual.

But one day I was on the train reading the New York Times and saw a picture of a young woman. At first I had paged past it, but then I flipped the page back, looked again and just gasped. The young woman in the photo was in a Navy uniform, and I recognized her as Mary Dunne. She had been a day-hopper, like me, who attended Mount Saint Vincent, who I used to see on the train, getting on and off at Dobb's Ferry. She had been a year behind me, but had dropped out of college and joined the Service.

The article next to the photo said that she had been murdered out in San Francisco, where she had been stationed, and her body had been found under the Golden Gate Bridge. The Navy and the police where still trying to solve who had thrown her from the bridge.

She was such an engaging girl, and very pretty. I know it would have been disturbing at any time, but something about the fact that she had been photographed in uniform, and I knew her well, really somehow brought the war home to me.

~~~

In the spring of 1943 John graduated from Villanova and like most of the other young men at the time he immediately enlisted in the Marine Corps.

My college graduation was on June 1st, 1943, and John knew that he would be leaving the next day for basic training, so he came down to my parents' house to say goodbye to me. Later that evening my parents were up in bed and Helen was in the kitchen reading the newspaper. John and I were sitting in the living room talking when he excused himself to go to the bathroom, and walked upstairs. It seemed like he was gone an awfully long time. When he came back downstairs he said, "I have to get going, but I want to give you your graduation present." Then he took a small box out of his pocket, and handed it to me with a look of nervous anticipation on his face.

When I saw the look on his face I thought to myself, "Wow, this must be a pretty good present," and quickly opened it. But it was more than just a present, it was a diamond ring. An engagement ring.

Fifi and John - Villanova junior prom weekend - Saturday, April 25, 1942.

The reason he had been upstairs so long wasn't that he was in the bathroom, he had gone up to ask my parents if he could marry me, and asked for their blessing. They gave it, and I was in shock when he gave me the ring.

Their Will to Win is Stronger than Ever

These six husky U. S. Marines in training at Parris Island, S. C., are all former Villanova College students. From left: John J. McFadden; Jacques Mauch, former basketball manager; Joseph McEvoy; Leo Jago, former football player; Steve Pritko of football fame, and Robert Kelty, former basketball star

Villanova's Marines - THE EVENING BULLETIN.
Philadelphia - Friday, July 9, 1943.

128

But not everyone was happy with John and the decisions that he was making at that point in his life. His mother and her brother, Uncle Johnny Foley, were both upset with him when he gave me the ring, as they both thought that it was too soon after the death of his father, only four months earlier.

And I'm sure that his enlistment in the Marine Corp, right out of college, was also a grave concern to his mother and sisters, along with his paternal aunts and uncles. He was

Uncle Johnny Foley and Aunt Dorothy "Babe" Foley Spellaci. Candlewood Lake, 1933.

the only male of child rearing age, and thereby the only one that could carry on the family lineage. If he were to be lost in the war it would have meant the end of the line for the McFadden name.

~~~

John with Mrs. McFadden

That summer John was in Quantico, Virginia for basic training and Officer Candidate Training School. I remember that the first time that I saw him in his officers' uniform was when he called me from Quantico and asked me to meet him in New York City. He told me to meet him under the big clock in Grand Central Station at six o'clock that evening. When I got to Grand Central, I went to the clock, but he wasn't there. As I was waiting I started thinking that maybe we had missed each other and he had taken a train up to Tarrytown. There were men in military uniform coming and going in all directions, and I couldn't find him. But then I looked up and saw him walking toward me. I'll never forget it. He looked so handsome, he took my breath away.

John in Quantico - 1943.

~~~

My sister Helen was living in Washington D.C., working for the Australian government during the War. I used to go down and visit her in D.C. and John would come up from camp on weekends, when he could get leave, and meet me. John would stay at the Y.M.C.A., and I would stay with Helen at her rooming house. On the collar of his uniform he wore a gold "O.C." pin which stood for Officer Candidate, and as we would walk around D.C. he would be saluted by other Service personnel thinking that he was already a Marine Corps officer. "Those guys would die if they knew they were saluting an officer candidate instead of a real officer," he confided.

John's roommate at Villanova, Bill Marchese, had enlisted in the Navy, and another of his close friends, Jake Mauche, had enlisted in the Marines. I don't know where Jake went through basic training or Officer Candidate School, but he ended up in San Diego with John prior to shipping out to the Pacific.

We had talked about getting married and we knew that John would be a Second Lieutenant when he finished Officer Candidate School, so we decided that we would get married after he received his commission, which would be right after Thanksgiving of 1943. We picked December 5th as our wedding date. Bill Marchese was going to be John's Best Man. My sister Helen would be my Maid of Honor.

NEWS, TARRYTOWN, N. Y., THURSDAY, SEPTEMBER 23, 1943

J. J. McFadden Is Lieutenant

John J. McFadden, Jr., son of Mrs. Laura McFadden of 11 Dayton Avenue, Pocantico Hills, and the late John McFadden, has been commissioned a second lieutenant in the U. S. Marine Corps after successfully completing Officer Candidates Course at Quantico, Va.

He will enter advanced officers' training, also at Quantico, immediately, and expects to be graduated again in December as a first lieutenant.

A basketball star in both high school and college, he graduated from Washington Irving High School and Villanova College, Villanova, Pa., where he majored in business administration and pre-law. Enlisting on Mar. 17, 1942, he remained in the reserve until graduation last May, when he entered basic Marine Corps training at Parris Island, N. C. He is now 23.

LT. JOHN J. McFADDEN, JR.

Article about John recieving his officer's commission.
Tarrytown Daily News - September 23, 1943.

We had sent out the invitations, booked the Carmelite Church at Transfiguration in Tarrytown and the reception dinner at the Roger Smith Hotel in White Plains. Mary and Larry were to drive us to the Park Central Hotel in New York City after the wedding, for our honeymoon.

131

Lt. John McFadden-Kathryn Egan
Wed in Ceremony at Carmelite

Miss Kathryn Phyllis Egan, daughter of Mr. and Mrs. Nicholas Egan, 160 Union Avenue, became the bride of Lt. John J. McFadden, USMC, son of Mrs. Laura Foley McFadden of Pocantico Hills, in a ceremony performed by the Rev. Father John A. Wholley in the candle-lit Carmelite Church of the Transfiguration before some 200 guests last night.

Mr. Egan gave his daughter in marriage, and the couple was attended by the bride's sister, Miss Helen Egan, as maid of honor, and Lawrence James Dick, who was best man. The bridegroom's sister, Miss Dolores McFadden, and Miss Shirlee Atwood of New York City, a classmate of the bride at the College of Mount St. Vincent, were bridesmaids.

The bride wore a gown of white satin with a full skirt an dtrain and a bodice and sleeves of net embroidered with seed pearl sprays. Her three-quarter illusion net veil was sprinkled with clusters of lily-of-the-valley, and was draped from a juliet cap of tulle with pearl trim. She carried a white prayer book with an orchid marker and sweet pea streamers. The maid of honor wore blue brocaded satin in princess style, with a sweetheart neckline and three - quarter sleeves. Fuschia pom-poms were clustered on each side of her deep blue velvet Dutch cap, and she carried a matching bouquet of pom-poms. The bridesmaids were gowned similarly in pale yellow brocaded satin, with amber velvet caps and amber and yellow pom-poms. Mrs. Egan wore a teal blue ensemble with an orchid corsage, and Mrs. McFadden wore black, also with an orchid corsage.

Miss Pauline Cattano, also a classmate at Mount St. Vincent, sang two solos, "Because," and during the ceremony, "Ave Maria." She was accompanied by organist Giovani Camajani. A reception for 70 was held at the Hotel Roger Smith in White Plains, and following it, Lieutenant and Mrs. McFadden left on their wedding trip.

Lieutenant McFadden will leave on Dec. 26, for San Diego, Calif., for a special course of instruction at the Marine Base there. Mrs. McFadden plans to join him later.

Mrs. McFadden was graduated from the Washington Irving High School in 1939, and last June received her degree from the College of Mount St. Vincent. She was active in the school publications; in the Dramatic Association, and in class activities. She has been employed at the National Industrial Conference Board, Park Avenue, New York. Lieutenant McFadden, son of the late John J. McFadden who for many years was a member of the Town Council of Mount Pleasant, and president of the Pocantico Hills Board of Education, is also a graduate of the Washington Irving High School. He received his B. S. degree last June from Villanova College, where he was studying law and was called into service on June 3.

Mr. and Mrs. Nicholas J. Egan

announce the marriage of their daughter

Kathryn Phyllis

to

Lieutenant John Joseph McFadden, Jr.

United States Marine Corps Reserve

on Sunday, December the fifth

nineteen hundred and forty-three

Tarrytown, New York

Fifi and John's wedding announcement.
Date had to be changed because of John's orders.

132

John was scheduled to leave on December 26th, for Camp Elliott in California, but at the end of November he called me from Quantico. He sounded a little dejected on the phone, and when I asked him if he was okay, he muttered, "We can't get married next week."

Well, when I finally stopped hyperventilating I asked, "Why, what's wrong?"

He said he had gotten orders that he had to report on December 4th to Newport News, Virginia, to learn how to load tanks onto transport ships. He didn't know when he would be coming back, so we couldn't even set a new date for the wedding. So off he went to Newport News, leaving me and our wedding plans in limbo.

Then, at about seven o'clock, on the morning of Monday, December 13th, I got an unexpected phone call from John saying that he had arrived home during the night. He asked me, "When are we getting married?"

"It has to be next Saturday," I told him, "so I have time to contact everybody and call the Roger Smith Hotel and the Park Central and the church."

"That's no good," he said, "either we get married tomorrow night or we don't get married till I get back from the Marine Corps."

Well, everything fell into place and we got married the next night, December 14th, 1943, at Transfiguration Church. The only one from our original plans who couldn't make it was Ensign Bill Marchese. He had shipped out earlier that week, so my brother in law, Larry Dick, stood in as John's Best Man. Everybody else was able to attend.

Ensign Bill Marchese

I remember that on the night of our wedding, my parents and sisters and I were all running around the house getting ready to go to the church. Mary, Larry and little Larry were living with my parents at the time as they were waiting to move into their new house they had bought in Glenwolde. Little Larry was only about a year old and was lying on my mother's bed, crying his eyes out, but Mary was busy trying to get ready for the wedding. I was already in my wedding dress, with my hair done and all, but I couldn't bear to hear little Larry crying, so I picked him up and started giving him a bottle and burping him, to calm him down. But then everyone started yelling at me to put him down before he spit-up all over my wedding gown. Thankfully, the babysitter showed up and took little Larry, and we all ran off to the church.

Shirlee Atwood, Larry Dick, Helen Egan, Fifi, John and Dolores McFadden.
December 14, 1943.

Just after John and I got married, Mary and Larry let us use their new house in Glenwolde. Their furniture was there but they hadn't moved in yet, so they told us to use the house till it was time for John to leave for the Marines.

I had never cooked a meal for John before we got married, so I decided that I'd better show him that I knew how to cook, before he left to go overseas, or he might start wondering what he had gotten himself into.

So one night, I made him a delicious steak dinner with baked potatoes and a couple of vegetables. To complete the scene and add a little ambiance, I had put two candles on the table so that we could have dinner by candlelight. It was all very romantic.

After dinner we cleaned up the dishes and drove up to my mother and father's house to visit for a little while. Mary and Larry were still living there, and once we got there, I was telling them all about the wonderful candlelit dinner that I had prepared for John. Well, I guess my parents never did anything romantic like that, because my father just couldn't understand why we would eat

Fifi at Mary and Larry's house in Glenwolde.

dinner by candlelight when we had a perfectly good light fixture in the kitchen. He looked at John and me and joked, "What did you do, blow a fuse?" Well, we all got a good laugh out of that.

John left for California on December 26th, 1943. He called me in the middle of January and told me that he would be stationed at Camp Elliott, in the El Cajon Valley, not far from San Diego, for a few months while he was training on tanks out in the desert, and asked me to come join him out in San Diego.

Because we were at war, there were no airplanes to take. You couldn't just go down to the station and get on a train, you had to make a reservation. And I didn't really know what I would need, so I just loaded up a steamer trunk with clothes. I was only twenty-one years old and had never been away from home before, so my mother insisted on coming with me as she was so worried about me traveling alone. She had never been out West either, but it was good to have her with me.

First we went by train from New York to Chicago where we had to change trains. The train out of Chicago was called "The Silver Meteor" or something. When boarding, they always had the Servicemen board first, then, if there was room, you could get on. When Mother and I got on The Silver Meteor, it was packed with Servicemen and a few other civilians, but we found two seats. I can remember the train stopping in the middle of the night, and when I raised the window shade to look out, I could see a young woman holding a baby, running along next to the train. I don't know if she was running to catch the train to meet her husband in California or if he had shipped out and she was going home. The whole trip from New York took about three days, and I can remember seeing orange groves when we finally reached California.

Fifi and Mother - Balboa Park, San Diego. Sunday, January 30, 1944.

On the way out in the train, Mother and I would play cards with some of the Marines on board. As we were approaching Los Angeles through the orange groves, one of the Marines went to the dining car and managed to wrangle two ham sandwiches for us.

The Silver Meteor took us to Los Angeles but we still had a long ride on another train to get to San Diego, and had to wait for a couple of hours in the station for that train. We had shipped the steamer trunk ahead earlier, but Mother and I were both carrying suit cases. When we went down to the gate for the train to San Diego there were maybe two other couples standing at the gate. But as the time for departure got closer, people started to gather and it soon got very crowded. As we were standing there I overheard a woman standing behind us say, "I hope we get on this train tonight."

I turned to her and asked, "What! You mean we might not get on?"

"Don't count on it Honey," she exclaimed, "this is my third night down here trying to get to San Diego."

Well, that didn't sound too promising, and the thought of being stuck in Los Angeles started to make my mother and me very nervous.

Two of the Marines that we had been playing cards with on The Silver Meteor were standing close to us and overheard the conversation. One of them pointed down the platform and said, "Listen, they'll probably be opening the other gate over there for all the Servicemen. If there's room for civilians they'll open this gate here for you to board. Give us your suitcases and we'll get them to San Diego, just in case you don't get on, then we'll check them into the baggage room at the station there." Things were different in those days, and besides, we didn't have too many other options, so we trusted them and gave them our suitcases. He said, "If they open your gate, run like hell and we'll be watching for you on the platform."

So finally, they opened the first gate and all the Servicemen went through to the train. Then, a few minutes later, they opened our gate, and Mother and I ran like hell up the ramp to the platform. Quite a distance away, I could see one of our Marine friends frantically waving his arms for us to come down by him, so we ran down the platform to him. His buddy was standing up on the landing that you would normally go up the train's steps to, but the steps had already been retracted as the train was getting ready to pull out and we couldn't get up, so he reached down and grabbed both of my wrists and pulled. The other Marine, still on the ground, put both hands on my fanny and pushed. And just like that, I was on the train. Mother, God bless her, got on the same way.

Because it was full of Servicemen, there were no empty seats on the train, and Mother and I had to sit on our suitcases, on the little platform between the cars, all the way to San Diego.

~~~

When we finally arrived in San Diego, John was waiting for us at the station. Then we got a cab and went to a house that was owned by another Marine that John had met. His elderly parents and his young daughter lived there. I have no idea where his wife was, but we were going to live there too. Our "home" there was going to be the back porch of the house.

Inside, there were two big soapstone tubs with a cover over them, and we had to go up the back steps to get in. At the top of the steps, before you went inside, was our "bathroom," which consisted of thin corrugated metal walls with a shower and a toilet inside, but no sink.

There were two windows that looked out from the main house into our living space on the porch, and my mother slept on a couch under those windows. It felt like we had very little privacy. In fact, one night while Mother was sleeping, she happened to look up at the windows above her and catch the old lady peeking out the window over the couch into where she was sleeping. We never said anything, but it was certainly something that made Mother and me uncomfortable.

There was a small closet that had a window in it, and an electric hot plate. This was our "kitchen", and we had to wash the dishes in the soapstone tubs next to Mothers "bed". If anybody ever came over to have a cup of coffee they would have to sit in the doorway next to the two tubs. I think we paid fifteen dollars a month rent for the privilege of living there. Anybody in San Diego who had a spare room was renting it out because people were all just clamoring for living space.

Fifi with John and her mother.
San Diego - Sunday, February 13, 1944.

In our bedroom there was a double bed and a bureau, and there was just barely enough room between them to open the drawers to put clothes in. There was a window in the wall about three feet from the foot of the bed. After a few days of living there I looked up one morning and noticed a tear in the window shade, but I didn't think too much of it at the time.

Every night, the twelve year old daughter of the Marine who owned the place would start jumping rope in the house, in the room right next to where Mother slept. Then the young girl and her grandmother would start to argue. Then once the old lady and the granddaughter got fighting you'd hear the grandfather yell out at the top of his lungs, "JEEESUSSS - KEEE - RIST," in his coarse bellowing voice, and then all three of them would be fighting and screaming at each other. Gracious living, it wasn't.

~~~

John, as he had done for as long as I had known him, would sleepwalk sometimes. Usually when he did he would let out a yell just before he got out of the bed. I had gotten into the habit of reaching over, with my arm across his chest, and holding him down as soon as I heard him yell, to keep him in the bed. One night he let out a yell and I instinctively reached over, but he was already bolting upright in the bed. I grabbed the back of his pajamas, then heard the feint "pop, pop, pop" of the buttons popping off his pajama top, but I was able to pull him back into bed. As usual, he looked at me and growled, "What the hell's going on?", as if I was the one acting crazy in the middle of the night.

~~~

My mother stayed with us for about a month and then went back home to Tarrytown. But after she left I had a lot of time on my hands, so I decided to get a job. I got hired at Grayson's' Department Store which was a very upscale, women's clothing store in San Diego. I worked in the credit office, processing forms for people who wanted to set up credit lines. Most of the people coming in were Mexicans. One man, when I asked him his name, told me his name was "Yayzoo."

140

Since I had never taken any Spanish in school, I smiled at him and asked, "How do you spell that?"

He looked back at me, very annoyed, and indignantly exclaimed, "YAYZOO," and spelled out, "J.E.S.U.S."

Grayson's was in the main area of downtown San Diego. Near the first floor entrance was a store, kind of like Dunkin Donuts, where they made fresh pies all day long. The woman who was my boss at Grayson's would take one of us girls from the credit department for coffee and a piece of pie every afternoon. The first time she took me, she kept up a steady stream of conversation. But through the entire exchange I kept looking up and down in disbelief, from her face to her plate because, oddly, she was covering the whole top of her pumpkin pie with table salt. Yuck!

Grayson's had a lot of Sale days, and whenever they did they would allow the employees to come in early and buy things at special discounts. I bought so much new clothes that it was a wonder that I was able to

In front of our first apartment in San Diego. Laughing at John struggling with the camera. Tuesday, Febuary 1, 1944.

close my suitcases when I finally returned home to New York.

141

Every morning, when I would leave the house for work, I would lock the door into our living space as I left. But one morning I was lying in bed and I looked up at the window and I noticed that the tear in the window shade had been sewn and repaired. I sat straight up and gasped as I realized that the old lady, the mother of the Marine who owned the house, had come into our living space unannounced and uninvited, and that bothered me. I decided right there and then to move out, even though we didn't even have another place to live lined up.

I spoke to a friend of mine at Grayson's, Dolores McDermott, and she told me that there might be a room available where she lived, at the El Patio Hotel in downtown San Diego.

El Patio Hotel - 1515 Front St., San Diego, California.
Mr. and Mrs. George Tatgenhorst; Prop.

So we moved into the El Patio, which got its name from the central courtyard patio that had a huge palm tree growing in the middle of it. It was a fairly standard hotel room, but it had ample closet space and a real bathroom where everything worked. It was very comfortable, and a hundred percent better than where we had been. We were on the first floor, and there was a balcony on the second floor that overlooked the central courtyard patio. John and I became friendly with Dolores and her husband, Oscar, who was a sailor. I think they were from somewhere in the Midwest. I remember they had really twangy voices.

We lived in the El Patio Hotel from the beginning of March, 1944, till that June, and one day, not long after we had moved there, I wanted to go for a ride on one of the trolley cars to go shopping in San Diego. John told me, "Go up to the corner to get the El Cajon trolley."

When I got to the trolley stop, there were lots of other trolley's coming in and out and people coming and going. I had been waiting there for about fifteen minutes when a woman walked by and I asked her, "Is this the right stop for the El Cajon trolley?"

John with Dolores, & Oscar - El Patio Hotel.
San Diego - Sunday, May 21, 1944.

"Yes," she answered, "it just left here a minute ago."

"No," I corrected her, "the sign on that one said, 'El Ca-<u>john</u>.'"

Well, she got a big kick out of that. "Sorry Honey," she laughed, affably setting me straight, "it's pronounced, 'Ca-<u>hone</u>.'"

At that point I had to laugh with her, at myself, for my ignorance of how some of the Spanish words were pronounced.

There were many times while John had been going through tank training out in the dessert that he had to spend the night out at the camp, and I would be all alone at our hotel room. Our room was on the first floor of the El Patio and all night I could hear sailors walking by on the street outside our window, drunk out of their minds, on the way back down to their ships. I would be scared to death.

But on some nights, John would send a guy by the name of Marvin Barnes, in a jeep, to come pick me up at the hotel or at work. He would bring me out to the camp so I could have dinner with John in the officers' mess. If I had to use the ladies room out at the camp, all

143

they had was an outhouse. So John would walk me out to it with a flashlight because I was petrified that there would be snakes or rats or something out there in the dark. After dinner we would watch a movie, and then Marvin would drive me back to the El Patio.

~~~

One day, back when John had been going through basic training in Quantico, he had given the group he was leading the wrong command and caused them to march into the water. His Drill Sergeant punished him by making him do what they called "Riding the Range." He had to put on asbestos gloves and kneepads and boot covers, then

Fifi and John - El Patio Hotel.
San Diego - 1944.

climb up on top of the big stoves in the kitchens of the mess hall and clean the cooking surfaces with steel wool. Later, after he got out to California to Camp Elliott, new men would often come in for tank or artillery training. One day, John was "Officer of the Day" and he recognized one of the new guys as the Drill Sergeant that had ordered him to ride the range back in Quantico. He thought that the guy might have recognized him too as he gave him a funny look at first. As John was now a Lieutenant and outranked the guy he could have vindictively given him some lousy duty as payback for making him "Ride the Range," but he didn't retaliate. He decided to let bygones be bygones, and that was the end of that.

Although most restaurants were very crowded and you had to wait in long lines to get in, we ate out a lot because we had no place to cook or to sit down to eat even if we did cook.

One night, John and I were going out on the town with Jake Mauche. We had a favorite bar in San Diego called The Saratoga, where the food was pretty good. As we were waiting for the trolley, Jake was hopping on and off the curb, again and again, and he was singing "Mares eat oats and does eat oats and little lambs eat ivy…," I don't know why, but I remember that like it was yesterday.

Another night, we were with Jake and Joe McEvoy, who was another Marine who had also gone to Villanova with John and Jake. We went to the movies to see "Cover Girl" starring Rita Hayworth. There were always long lines to get into the movies or restaurants, so often you would miss the beginning of a movie. When we finally got into the theater, I was sitting between John and Joe McEvoy, and Joe started talking up a storm to the guy sitting next to him. I said, "Joe, how do you know that guy?"

John and Jacques Mauch - San Diego. Sunday, Febuary 13, 1944.

He said, "Oh I don't know him, I just want to find out what we missed."

Then one day in the beginning of June, I came home from work and found John's sea bag on the floor, all packed and ready to go. I knew that meant he was going to have to leave to go overseas, and I was crying when he came in the door. The next morning as he was leaving the hotel, he said that if he could get home that night, he would, but he didn't know if he would be able to. He did get home that night, and the next morning he told me the same thing. It was day to day like that for two or three days. I would go to work each morning not knowing if I would see him that night or ever again.

In those days you weren't allowed to talk about it if you were shipping out. Secrecy was very important regarding troop movements, but that morning there were rumors going around that the Second Marine Division was getting ready to ship out any day. Jake Mauche called me at work that day. His unit had the job of loading equipment and supplies on the troop transport ships in San Diego harbor. All he said when I picked up the phone was, "Fifi, tomorrow's the day." He could have been court marshaled for having told me.

When I got back to our apartment that night, John was already

2nd Lieut. John J. McFadden, USMC.
Taken in San Diego in early 1944, just before shipping out to Siapan.

there, and of course he knew that he and his unit would be shipping out early the next morning, and he was very upset. It was strange the next day, because all of the previous mornings, as he was leaving, I had been crying. But that morning John was crying. I can still hear the sound of his footsteps as he left our apartment and ran up the block to meet the jeep that was picking him up to take him down to his ship.

~~~

Before he left, John had told me that the wife of one of the other officers that was shipping out with him would be coming to stay with me as she was also going to be returning to New York, and she stayed with me for a couple of days. I was able to make a reservation on the train back to New York for June 7th.

But on the morning of June 6th, we were awakened by the sounds of sirens and horns blaring outside. The two of us jumped up and ran out onto the porch to see what was going on. All I could think of was that John's convoy had been attacked at sea, and sunk. Instead, it was D-Day, and people all over town were celebrating the news that the Allies had landed on Normandy.

~~~

When I returned to New York I stayed with my mother and father and sister Helen at our house on Union Avenue, and I got my job back with the National Industrial Conference Board and continued to work in New York City.

Like everyone else, my mother and father both contributed to the War effort during those years. The General Motors plant in Tarrytown, where my father was a foreman, had been enlisted by the War Department to produce "Avenger" torpedo bombers for the Navy. My mother did volunteer nursing work at the local hospitals, for the Red Cross, due to the shortage of qualified nurses during the war.

Mother in nursing uniform - volunteering for Red Cross during World War II - Fathers Day - Sunday, June 21,1942.

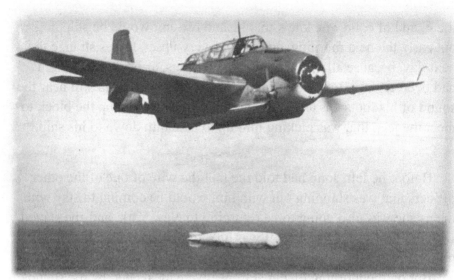

AVENGER torpedo bomber - built by Eastern Aircraft.
A division of General Motors' Tarrytown plant.

Helen with Mother and Daddy - Mother in nurses uniform as she was doing
volunteer work for the Red Cross during World War II.
Father's Day - June 21, 1942.

Front side of John's Marine Corp ID.

Backside of John's Marine
Corp ID.

V- Mail Christmas Card from John.
1944.

I would get letters from John, but he couldn't say anything about where he was or what was going on. All the mail went through military censors and sometimes there would be words or even whole sentences cut out of a letter. These letters came in what was called "V-Mail", the "V" standing for "VICTORY".

Earlier that year, my sister Mary and her husband Larry Dick had moved into their new house in Glenwolde, and Mother, Father and Helen and I had made plans to spend Christmas Eve at their house with them. The plan was to go there and exchange gifts, and then go to midnight Mass.

John had sent a letter to Mary and told her what he wanted to get me for Christmas that year, and asked her to get it for him. So that Christmas Eve, 1944, Mary gave me a box from John, and when I opened it there was a beautiful watch inside. It was made from "Rose gold," with four diamonds and three rubies on each side. On the back, he had asked Mary to have the jeweler inscribe the words,

<u>"Not for just an hour"</u>

<u>John</u>

These words were part of a verse from the song "Always" by Irving Berlin that goes;

I'll be loving you,

Always.

With a love that's true,

Always.

Not for just an hour.

Not for just a day.

Not for just a year,

But Always.

When I opened it and read the inscription, I dissolved into tears. I loved it, but I hardly ever wore it because I was so afraid I might lose it.

I gave that watch to my grandson, John Philip McFadden, in 2008 after he got engaged; and he gave it to his wife, Kelly, on their wedding day, August 8th, 2009. The day I gave it to him and told him the story behind it, he sat quietly on the bed in my room, admiring it, then professed reverently, "Thank you Nama, I'm honored."

150

I can't remember how it got started but I had a group of girlfriends that I had grown up with in Tarrytown that I spent a lot of time with during the war. There was Ebba and Vera Chickachee, Bette Myers, my cousin Dorothy Egan, Harriet Dudley, Edith Gross, Jean Jones, Eileen Fox, Marion Primps, Pat Kinane, Flo Bradley, and myself. All of our husbands, fiancés or boyfriends were away in the War. We would meet once a week at one of our houses with the intention of knitting a scarf or making something to send to our husbands or the other troops overseas. But invariably we would just end up laughing and drinking coffee, and talking till late at night. Then get up and go to work the next morning.

CLUB - Circa 1944.

We called our group "Club." We would all put money into a kitty and once a month or so our Club would get all dressed up and go out to dinner or go to the city to see a show.

If somebody's' husband would get home on leave, the rest of us would be so excited for them. Ebba Chickachee would later marry Artie Kadish. He was a Sailor on the "USS MOBILE" which was a light cruiser seeing action in the Pacific. Anytime one of the other boyfriends or husbands got home, Ebba would ask, "Has anybody seen it?", meaning Artie's ship. Artie Kadish actually did bump into John while they were both on Saipan.

~~~

John and his unit ended up in the thick of it on several of the islands in the Pacific during World War II. In June of 1944, while on Saipan, they had attacked a Japanese outpost in a small village. After they thought the fighting was over, he and another Marine were sitting against one of the tanks having a "C" ration and talking. They got the order to move out and as John started to climb back into his tank, the other Marine was shot and killed by a Japanese sniper. John saw the whole thing. He wrote a letter to the Marine's parents, but never heard back from them.

Another day on Saipan, John got orders to move his unit out. He had a "runner" who was a guy from the Blue Ridge Mountains in Kentucky and was only eighteen or nineteen years old but was already married. Because there was no way for the drivers of the tanks or half-tracks to communicate with each other, the "runner" had the job of carrying John's orders to the drivers; whether it be to move forward, or left or right, close ranks, or whatever. That morning, as they started across a field of high sugar cane, an enemy machine gun position opened fire on his unit. They could see the machine gun fire cutting the cane all around them. As he saw the cane getting mowed down, John yelled to the kid to, "Get down." John dove to his left, the runner dove to the right. His unit fired back and killed the Jap machine gunner. When he looked for his runner, he found him lying on his back with blood gushing out of his throat. He yelled for a Medic, but the boy was too badly hit and died right there.

After the shooting and the chaos stopped, John gathered the men from his unit around him and asked for a volunteer to replace the fallen runner. He told them that he didn't want to, but if no one would volunteer, he would have to appoint one of them. There were no takers, so he picked out one of the men, then told the rest of them that they would all have to be ready to move out at daylight. But when daylight came, the young man that he had picked out was nowhere to be found. He had run off into the jungle during the night.

At that point John decided he would do the running himself. But as they started to move out, the young Marine appeared from the jungle, his fatigues all tattered and torn, his face and arms bloodied from having spent the night in the jungle. He apologized to John and told him he was ready to assume his duty as runner. Nevertheless, upon the first command that John gave him to carry out, he fell to the ground in a convulsion. He was subsequently put on a hospital ship and sent home due to a nervous breakdown.

~~~~

There was another day that John's commanding officer ordered him to have the tanks in his unit fire phosphorescent shells into the caves that pock marked the mountainous terrain of Saipan. Initially John balked because, when he looked up at the caves through his binoculars, he could see that there were many women holding tiny babies, along with children and old men in the caves. His C.O. told him that he had to fire, asserting it, "…was an order." John insisted that there were women and children in the caves, but the commander maintained that there were also Japanese soldiers in the caves that were killing fellow Marines, and warned him that he would be court marshaled if he didn't carry out the orders. So, reluctantly, John gave the order to fire.

Later they saw some of the women and children coming down from the caves. The women carried small tea kettles with long thin spouts. They couldn't believe it when the Marines would give them food and water. They would fill their kettles with water from the Marines' canteens, and then feed their babies with the long spout in the baby's mouth.

~~~~

Marpy Point was a high cliff overlooking the ocean at one end of the island of Saipan. The Japanese soldiers had told the natives and civilians on Saipan that if they were captured by the Americans, the Marines would rape and torture the women and bayonet their babies. As a result, the women chose to commit suicide by throwing their children off the cliff at Marpy Point and jumping off after them, to the rocks several hundred feet below. Some would jump off with their babies in their arms. Even entire families were seen, holding hands, as they jumped off the cliffs to their deaths.

~~~

Towards the end of the fighting on Saipan, there would be sporadic gun fire sometimes as some of the Japanese soldiers would try to sneak into the Marine's camps and steal food. The Marines, not knowing their intentions, would shoot them.

One morning John was outside shaving, and, as he was looking at his reflection in his small hand held mirror, he noticed a movement in the brush behind him. Then he saw a piece of white cloth come out of the brush, attached to the end of a stick. He was by himself and realized that he didn't even have his sidearm on, so he tried to act nonchalant. He dumped the soapy water out of his helmet, put it on and headed back toward the other tents. Then he got some of his men, went back and took the hapless Jap conscript into custody as a prisoner of war.

That Japanese soldier couldn't know it at the time, but that was probably the luckiest day of his life, to have stumbled into John's camp, rather than some of the other more trigger happy Marines.

~~~

After Saipan was secured, John's unit loaded up and joined the main task force at sea. They didn't know it at the time but they were heading to the island of Tinian. On July 24th, 1944, the morning that the Marines assaulted the beach at Tinian, the Navy attack bombers would fly in very low over the ocean and release their bombs well behind them. The bombs would come flying in over their heads and explode out in front of their position on the beach. He could hear the bombs whistling in over his head, but then the next thing he knew, he was waking up, lying flat on his back. He didn't know how long he had been unconscious but his helmet had a big dent in it, and the half-track he had been in had a huge chunk missing out of one of the solid rubber tires.

Aug 2, 1944

My darling –

I've only a few minutes honey but I just wanted to write a few lines to let you know that I am alright. I suppose that you have guessed where and what I have been doing and your probably right. Thank God for your prayers and those of the rest of my family. I have come through the battle for Tinian without a scratch. It's almost all over now darling so please don't worry. Write first chance I get – I love you more than ever Fifi and will be glad to get back home. Give my love to all. I love you – John

Letter from John to Fifi on her 22nd birthday - August 2, 1944.

155

That night, John and his men were trying to sleep in the foxholes they had dug under their tanks and half-tracks. There was a stretch of beach between them and the Japs that the Marines called the "No man's land", and they had strict orders not to raise their heads out of their foxholes. Suddenly, all hell broke loose. There were tracer bullets flying in all directions. The Japs were shooting at them and the Marines were returning fire, back and forth across that deadly ground. Then, a few minutes into the firefight, a Marine came staggering towards them, out of the kill zone, back toward John's unit, and crawled back in his foxhole. Some of the other Marines quickly scrambled to his side, thinking that he most certainly had been wounded and would need urgent medical attention. But, to their amazement, he wasn't bleeding anywhere.

What they discovered was that he had been sleep walking and had wandered out into the No Man's Land to relieve himself, and miraculously returned without a scratch despite all the bullets flying all around him. The next morning he had no recollection of his close brush with death, but he took plenty of razzing from his fellow Marines about it.

~~~

John would send me letters when he was overseas and occasionally he would mention, "Carl will be coming to see you." Then in another letter he'd say, "Carl will be calling you." But I didn't know who he meant, I didn't know anyone named Carl.

Photo of Dottie, Dolores and Fifi that they had taken and sent to John in 1944, while he was in the Pacific.

Then one day at work, I had been back from lunch about half an hour and the receptionist called me and said to come out to her desk which was right by the elevators. As I approached her desk, a man sitting on a bench stood up and stepped forward as if to greet me. He was in a Marine Corps uniform, and as I looked at him my eyes kept going up, and up, and up. This was Carl Doll. He had been John's tent mate on Saipan. He was very tall, about six foot four, and very thin. I sat and talked with him for a while but then had to go back to work, so we made arrangements for him to come up to John's mother's house in Pocantico for dinner the following night.

The next night, after dinner, we were sitting around the table and he started talking about his military experiences. He had joined the Marines before the war, when he was only eighteen years old, and had been at the Battle of Guadalcanal. He wasn't an officer but I think he was a Sergeant or something and was in charge of about thirty men. It was their job to establish communication lines between the ships and the Marine units on the beaches.

During one of their landings, as his unit was approaching the beach, their landing craft got hit. Only he and one other guy survived. They lay in the water for hours, with the bodies of their buddies floating all around them, and didn't move. They tried to play possum because their weapons had jammed from the sand and seawater and if the Japs had come down to them, they were sitting ducks, and they'd have been shot like so many fish in a barrel. After darkness fell he and the other Marine swam back to their ship that was anchored offshore. We were sitting in the safety of my mother-in-law's house in Pocantico Hills, New York, several years and thousands of miles removed from that night on Guadalcanal, but as he told us the story his hands were shaking.

He had been sent home for some "R and R", but was going to have to return to his unit in the Pacific soon. Before he went back though, I went out to dinner one more time with Carl and his fiancée, Mary. That night he told me that before he had left his unit for the states, they were preparing for a major offensive. They all speculated that they would soon be heading to invade the mainland of Japan, and they knew there would be a lot of Marines killed when they did.

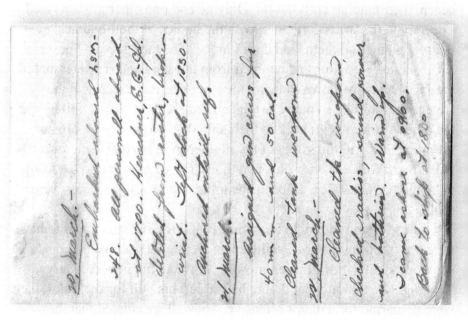

Pages from John's war diary leading up to the inavasion of Okinowa - 1 of 3.

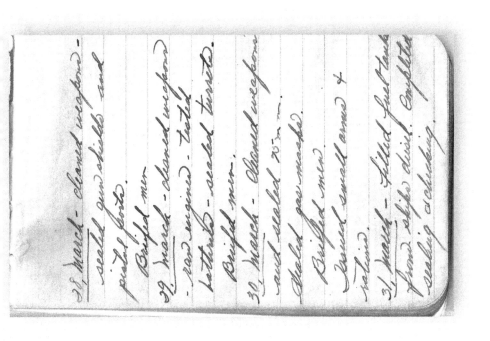

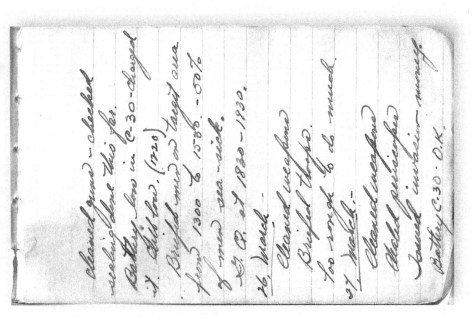

Pages from John's war diary leading up to the inavasion of Okinowa - 2 of 3.

Pages from John's war diary leading up to the invasion of Okinowa - 3 of 3.

On Easter Sunday, April 1st, 1945, John and his unit were stationed off the coast of Okinawa with the rest of the U.S. invasion fleet. The Captain of the troop transport ship that they were on asked around if there was anyone who knew how to operate the forty millimeter gun on the L.S.M.s, which were the amphibious landing craft that they deployed to spearhead the beach invasions. He was looking for someone who could train some of the green sailors who had recently come aboard as replacements. John said he knew how to operate the gun and offered to train the men.

They could just see the silhouette of the island off in the distance when suddenly they spotted a Japanese kamikaze plane flying just above the tops of the waves, coming straight at the L.S.M. they were in. John started firing the forty millimeter gun at the plane, but at the last second the kamikaze climbed slightly, flew over them, and crashed explosively into the ship right next to them. John said that the plane was so low that he could see the twisted grimace on the pilot's face as it flew over them, and he could have jumped up and grabbed its landing gear.

Saipan, 1944 - John at bottom right.

The ship that got hit was on fire and men started jumping off into the ocean. Suddenly a voice came over the ships' public address loudspeakers and boomed, "Who the hell gave the order to abandon ship? Get back on board and save the ship." So the men in the water started climbing up ropes and cargo nets and got back on board. But they weren't able to save the ship. It sank after about a half an hour.

While John was with the invasion fleet at Okinawa his unit took part in some diversionary attacks against the Japanese but I don't think he was involved in any of the main battles that were fought there, and eventually returned to Saipan.

Saipan, 1944 - "The end of a perfect day".

~~~

The United States dropped the atomic bomb on Hiroshima on August 6th, 1945, then another one on Nagasaki three days later, on August 9th. Japan surrendered on August 14th, 1945, and, sometime after they gave up the fight, John was transferred to be part of the U.S. occupation force in Japan. He lived in a house with two other Marine Corps officers, on a bay not far from Nagasaki. His job there was to try to find the records of the American prisoners of war that the Japs had captured.

It was a real Japanese house with paper walls and sliding paper doors. They had a Japanese houseboy named Abei and a maid named Suki, but when their Commanding Officer found out they had a maid, he made them get rid of her. Abei stayed.

One day John was sitting in the kitchen, leaning his chair against the wall, when he heard Abei struggling up the stairs, trying to lift a case of beer into the kitchen. John went out to him and said, "What's the matter Abei? Let me give you a hand." He reached down and picked up the case of beer with one hand, and swung it up onto the kitchen floor. Abei, who was small in stature like many Japanese men, was amazed that John could lift the case with one arm, and started feeling John's muscles and commenting in broken English on John's strength. He called John, "Misto Mikkifondo," which was his broken English way of pronouncing "Mr. McFadden."

John in tub - Japanese house outside Nagasaki.

John and his fellow Marines would ask Abei to tell them what it was like on the day that the atomic bomb was dropped on Nagasaki, and Abei would act out what happened. He would sweep his hand through the air, mimicking what he called the "Melican plane" (American airplane), and imitate the drone of the bomber's engines, "zzzzzzzzzz." Then he would yell "**BOOM**," at the top of his lungs, and throw himself on the floor, reenacting how he had been knocked down by the shockwave of the bomb. I don't know how far Abei was from Nagasaki the day the bomb was dropped, I think it was about seventy-five miles, but he told John that he could see parts of ships and buildings and things flying through the sky from the force of the blast.

Abei told the Marines that he had one brother who had been trained to be a kamikaze pilot, but told them that his brother had luckily never gotten to go on his suicide mission. "He not pilot anymore. He a merchant in Tokyo," he said happily.

John and his housemates also had a little old Japanese man who would leave a basket of fresh prawns that he had caught, each day on their doorstep. They were probably loaded with radiation, but nobody knew anything about radiation at the time.

On the day that he left Nagasaki, John had his unit at attention on the pier, as they were to undergo inspection prior to boarding their ship. As they were lined up at attention, John heard a familiar voice coming down the pier toward him, yelling, "Misto Mikkifondo, Misto Mikkifondo." It was Abei, and he threw himself at John's feet, begging him to take him back to the United States with him.

John had to stay at attention and just whispered down to him, "Abei, let go! Let go!"

He had grown very fond of Abei during their time together, but had to leave him behind in Japan that day. He would often wonder aloud, even years later, about what ever might have become of Abei and his brother.

~~~

When John finally returned home from the Pacific he brought several souvenirs from the War back with him. There were two Samurai swords, a pistol, and a silk kimono.

One of the Samurai swords and the pistol had belonged to a Japanese officer that had charged his tank during a banzai suicide attack on Tinian. It was unmistakably the dress sword of an officer, as it had a shiny, polished blade and an ornate handle. The other one was a sword from a Japanese soldier that had quite evidently been used in combat. It was not as fancy, and there were nicks in the edge of the blade. Most notable about it though was that it still had dried blood stains on it.

The pistol was a Japanese copy of a German Luger and it had a hard leather holster with it. I don't think he ever had any bullets for it but, a few years after we started having kids, John took it down and threw it into one of the Tarrytown Lakes because he didn't want the boys ever getting a hold of it.

I think he bought the kimono while he was stationed near Nagasaki. It was pink colored silk, partially embroidered with flowers. I don't know where it is anymore. I would put things away for safe keeping and then forget where I had put them. I hope somebody in the family has it now.

~~~

Towards the end of the war I was working in New York City for the National Industrial Conference Board at the John Powers Building. John Powers was the head of a well known modeling agency in Manhattan at the time. I could take the train from Tarrytown into Grand Central and then just walk to my building. I would always leave Tarrytown thinking I was well dressed, stylish and attractive. But after I would get into the elevator with one or two of the John Powers' models, I would want to

Fifi (lower right) and some of the girls at the National Industrial Conference Board - Circa 1945.

go home and start over again. If you got onto the elevator with John Powers himself, he would practically undress you with his eyes. It wasn't a leering look, he was just trying to decide if you had any "model qualities".

My Job at the National Industrial Conference Board was to do a survey of clerical salaries all across the country for companies that subscribed to our services. When all of the surveys had been returned to me I would make up a spreadsheet that indicated what the median salary should be for various regions across the country. My boss was a man named Avery Rabbe, and he was a snappy dresser. Every now and then he would ask some of us young girls, about ten of us, if we would be hostesses at the various seminars that they held at the Waldorf Astoria.

His secretary was a good friend of mine. Her name was Sheila Tunney. My desk was near hers, so we would always talk to each other during the day. We were both dyed-in-the-wool Brooklyn Dodger fans and loved to gossip about the Dodgers. Leo Durocher was the manager at the time, and he was married to a movie star named Lorraine Day.

Well, one morning Avery came out of his office and handed Sheila some money and said, "Will you two go out to Ebbets Field and see the game so I don't

Sheila - by the Tarrytown Lakes on the way to see Brinie Marlin. March 11, 1945.

have to listen to you anymore today?" This really took us by surprise but we weren't going to make him say it twice, or give him time to reconsider. We grabbed our hats and coats and ran out of the office. And off we went to see the Dodgers' game.

I think John was still on Saipan when he and Carl Doll wrote a song called "Once Around the Moon". He sent it to me in a letter and asked me to try to call around to see if anyone might have some interest in having it published.

My friend, Sheila Tunney, had seen an article in one of the gossip columns that said that Dick Haymes was going to be appearing at the Paramount Theater in Times Square. Dick Haymes was a very popular singer and actor at the time, second only to Frank Sinatra. The name of his press agent was also in the article and it said that he had been seen staying at one of the swanky hotels in New York City. So Sheila and I got this wild idea. I don't remember how, but we were able to get the phone number for the press agent, and contacted him.

I told him that my husband was overseas with the Marine Corps and had written a beautiful love song, and I wanted him to look at it to see if it had any potential. He graciously agreed, so I took it to him.

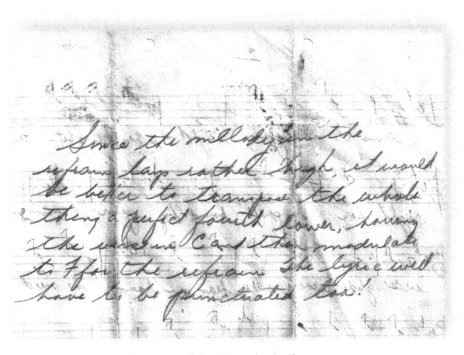

Once Around the Moon- back of page 2.

167

Once Around the Moon - page 1 of 2.

Once Around the Moon - page 2 of 2.

When I arrived at his hotel room, he quietly looked it over and had someone play it on the piano for him. However, after he listened to it all the way through, he took my hand and politely told me that it was very nice but, unfortunately, it sounded like a lot of other songs at the time and he didn't think he could do anything with it.

~~~

More than year later, after the War was over, John called me after he had finally landed back in California. He and a few other Marines had bought a used car and were going to drive it cross country, dropping members of the group off at their homes as they came. A few days later he sent me a telegram from the road, saying he would be arriving back in New York the next evening and told me to book a room at the Park Central Hotel in Manhattan, and he would meet me there.

CLUB - 1945.

So I called the Park Central but there were no rooms to be had, they were booked solid. I didn't know what to do but, somehow, Sheila came up with the crazy idea of calling the press agent for Dick Haymes again, to see if he could help.

I called him up and reminded him that I was the girl that had brought "Once Around the Moon" to him. I told him my husband was returning from two years in the Pacific, and would be home the next night. I explained my plight, that the Park Central had no rooms, and that I had no way of contacting John. He listened quietly, and I was thinking to myself, "He must think I'm out of my mind,"

But then, unexpectedly, he said, "Let me see what I can do."

Amazingly, he called me back about a half an hour later and told me to, "Get down to the Plaza right away, they'll have a room for you."

So I left work and hot footed it down to the Plaza Hotel and paid for the room he had gotten us, it was a suite. After that I marched over to the Park Central where I told the concierge at the desk my name and asked them that if John came in asking for me, could they tell him that I would be at The Plaza. Then, filled with anticipation, I walked all the way back to The Plaza. But through all this, I don't think my feet ever touched the ground that whole afternoon.

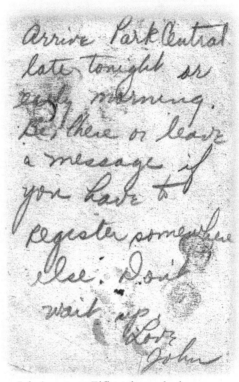

John's note to Fifi - telegraphed on way back to New York after the War.

At about four o'clock in the morning I heard a knock on the door. It was John, finally home from the War. I hardly recognized him he was so thin, and he had grown a bushy mustache to protect his lips from the sun while at sea. As he had walked down the hallway toward the room, he eagerly took his bags from the porter, gave him a handsome tip and urged candidly, "Get Lost Mack, I haven't seen my wife in two years!"

It was Sunday, January 27th, 1946.

L to R - Doug Kent, John McFadden, Dick Sowdor and Joe Plick Jr. - Pocantico Hills, 1946.

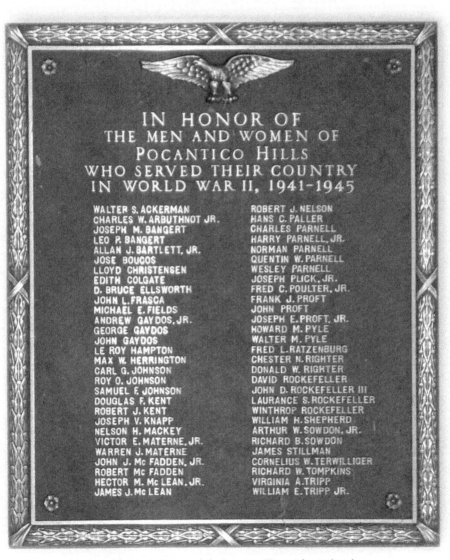

IN HONOR OF
THE MEN AND WOMEN OF
POCANTICO HILLS
WHO SERVED THEIR COUNTRY
IN WORLD WAR II, 1941-1945

WALTER S. ACKERMAN
CHARLES W. ARBUTHNOT JR.
JOSEPH M. BANGERT
LEO P. BANGERT
ALLAN J. BARTLETT, JR.
JOSE BOUCOS
LLOYD CHRISTENSEN
EDITH COLGATE
D. BRUCE ELLSWORTH
JOHN L. FRASCA
MICHAEL E. FIELDS
ANDREW GAYDOS, JR.
GEORGE GAYDOS
JOHN GAYDOS
LE ROY HAMPTON
MAX W. HERRINGTON
CARL G. JOHNSON
ROY O. JOHNSON
SAMUEL F. JOHNSON
DOUGLAS F. KENT
ROBERT J. KENT
JOSEPH V. KNAPP
NELSON H. MACKEY
VICTOR E. MATERNE, JR.
WARREN J. MATERNE
JOHN J. Mc FADDEN, JR.
ROBERT Mc FADDEN
HECTOR M. Mc LEAN, JR.
JAMES J. Mc LEAN

ROBERT J. NELSON
HANS C. PALLER
CHARLES PARNELL
HARRY PARNELL, JR.
NORMAN PARNELL
QUENTIN W. PARNELL
WESLEY PARNELL
JOSEPH PLICK, JR.
FRED C. POULTER, JR.
FRANK J. PROFT
JOHN PROFT
JOSEPH E. PROFT, JR.
HOWARD M. PYLE
WALTER M. PYLE
FRED L. RATZENBURG
CHESTER N. RIGHTER
DONALD W. RIGHTER
DAVID ROCKEFELLER
JOHN D. ROCKEFELLER III
LAURANCE S. ROCKEFELLER
WINTHROP ROCKEFELLER
WILLIAM H. SHEPHERD
ARTHUR W. SOWDON, JR.
RICHARD B. SOWDON
JAMES STILLMAN
CORNELIUS W. TERWILLIGER
RICHARD W. TOMPKINS
VIRGINIA A. TRIPP
WILLIAM E. TRIPP JR.

World War II Memorial plaque at Pocantico school.

173

Chapter Seven

THE AMERICAN DREAM

After John's return from the war, we went back to Pocantico and moved into Mrs. McFadden's house on Dayton Avenue. Our bedroom was the sun porch on the first floor, but over the following year John converted the house next door, also owned by his mother, into a two family house. His Aunt Jenny (McFadden) and Uncle Martin Neubauer and Uncles Bill and Bob McFadden lived upstairs.

Fifi, John and Mrs. McFadden.

John and I moved into the bottom floor of that house on February 24th, 1947. I was pregnant with our first baby at the time, and Mrs. McFadden couldn't understand why we were moving when I was so close to my delivery date. I told her that I just wanted to spend our first night in our new home and get settled in. Little did I know how short our time to settle in would be.The next day, February 25th, 1947, Jack was born.

Fifi, John and Jack - April, 1947.

~~~

One day, shortly after his return from the war, John was sitting in the living room and his mother was in the kitchen talking with one of the neighbors. He overheard the neighbor ask, "What is John going to do with himself now that he's home?"

"I don't know," his mother answered, "I think maybe he's toying with the idea of going to work for his Uncle Johnny, at the dairy."

"Oh, he should go into real estate," the woman suggested, "he should go see a man by the name of John Streb. He has an office in Dobbs Ferry and I understand he's looking for salesmen."

So, a day or two later, John went down to Dobbs Ferry and introduced himself to John Streb. They talked for a while and seemed to hit it off pretty well. John Streb explained the business to him and how he would be paid; how the commissions worked and so on. Streb offered him a job and John took it.

The next day John started work. When he returned home that evening, he strode in through the kitchen door and, with a flourish, threw his fedora across the kitchen and proudly announced that he had sold not one, but two houses that day. From then on he was hooked on the real estate business.

John J. McFadden - Circa 1948.

I remember John telling me about a house in Dobbs Ferry, that he brought a customer to look at, that was owned by a movie actress named Ruth Gordon. There was a large stone stairway leading up to the house, and when John got to the top of the steps and rang the doorbell, a maid answered the door. He introduced himself, and the maid called into the house that, "Mr. McFadden is here with a client."

Ruth Gordon called down, "Oh, just tell him to come on up."

When he got inside the house and reached the first landing of the stairs up to the second floor he was confronted by a full length, life size portrait of Ruth Gordon, in the nude, and he heard his female client gasp when she saw the portrait. As they continued upstairs, they found Miss Gordon in a bedroom, lying across a bed, clad only in a sheer black bra and panties, casually reading a manuscript.When she stood and started walking toward them with her hand extended to greet them, John's client gasped again, even louder.

"Oh,"sighed Miss Gordon, looking down at herself, "excuse me," and she disappeared into a closet. She reappeared, smiling broadly, a few minutes later, this time wearing a sheer black negligee that didn't cover much more than what she had changed out of. I don't think John ever did make the sale of that house.

A few weeks later John Streb came into the office looking very tired and haggard. He told John that he had spent a good part of the night down at police headquarters with Ruth Gordon. It seems that she and her husband were having a huge argument and he had started beating her up. She tried to leave the house but as she opened the door he kicked her and caught her "….right in the ass," and sent her flying down the stone steps. All she had on was a nightgown or a slip but, when she got up, she ran all the way down to police headquarters in her bare feet. Because she really didn't know anyone in Dobbs Ferry, she had called John Streb to come get her and bring her home after her husband had been arrested and charged with assault.

~~~

I don't remember how long John worked for John Streb but he had been very successful because there was such a demand for houses after the war, and after about a year he wanted to open his own office. He had an amicable parting with John Streb and left to go out on his own.

He opened an office on Broadway in Tarrytown, across the street from the library, in a new group of storefronts right next to Dwyer's Funeral Home. He had two or three salesmen and two secretaries. The office looked right out onto Broadway.

View of North Broadway in Tarrytown from John's office window.

~~~

After John had been in his office in Tarrytown for a while, and was becoming prominent in the real estate business after the war, he was put in charge of the local "COMMUNITY CHEST" charity drive. One day he said to me, "Fifi, I'm going to be busy today, would you mind going up to the Rockefeller mansion and pick up all the donations collected by the head housekeeper?", and I said, "Okay."

So I drove up to the mansion gates and even though they knew me, they stopped me and asked where I was going and why. I told them I had to go up to the mansion to pick up the donations, and then they called up to the main house to see if I was expected. I parked the car, walked up and rang the bell of the front door that was solid brass, and massive. The butler answered the door and let me into the foyer. On the left side, on a raised dais, was a huge pipe organ. The pipes went all the way up to a balcony on the second floor.

A woman came out smiling and introduced herself as the head housekeeper. We got into an elevator and went down two floors, and then she led me along a white tiled hallway into her beautiful, warm, chintz office. Her desk faced a window that looked all the way down the Hudson River to New York City. She gave me the envelope containing the donations and then, as I was leaving, she asked if I had ever been there before. When I told her that I hadn't, she asked me if I would like a tour. Of course I gladly accepted her offer.

The housekeepers were all busy covering the furniture with white linens, as the Rockefeller family was away at their summer home. As we walked along she would point out a painting or a beautiful glass bowl and say, "Oh, this was a gift from the Shah of Iran" or "This was a gift from the Queen of so and so…." She showed me the whole house before I left. It was all very impressive.

~~~

John would always have to work on Sundays with his real estate business, and one Sunday morning, while Jack was still an infant, I was going to leave to go to early Mass at the Church of the Magdalene, just down the block from the house. I woke John up and asked him to watch Jack while I was gone. He said, "Okay," and off I went.

After Mass, as I was walking back up to the house, I could hear Jack crying and screaming in his bassinet. When I went inside I found John, still asleep, so I picked Jack up and put him on top of the changing table and called out to John. I heard him behind me saying, "Shhhhhhh, Shhhhhhhh," and when I turned and looked, he was reaching over from the bed, with one arm, and rocking Jack's bassinet, not realizing that I was there and had picked Jack up.

I called out his name a little louder, "John, John.", and when he looked up at me through his sleepy eyes, I just pointed to Jack, who was on the changing table with me, and shook my head in exasperation. Eventually he woke up, showered and went off to his office, and Jack survived.

~~~

There was a gravel driveway that ran all the way out to Dayton Avenue, behind Mrs. McFadden's two houses in Pocantico Hills. On the other side of the driveway, opposite the back of the two houses,

179

was a three or four car garage. Next to the end of the garage was an old chicken coop that John had converted into a barn for his horses. I think he had as many as four horses there at one time. There were the twin horses; Brenda and Cobina, Eldorado and Brinie Marlin.

I remember that the day after Christmas, 1947, there was a huge snowstorm. I was pregnant with Nick, and we couldn't get out of the house for days. The roads were impassable, so Uncle Martin had to walk all the way down to Washington Street in North Tarrytown, to his job at the Foley dairy, through snow up to his knees.

~~~

On February 3rd, 1948, Nick was born. There was less than a year between them, and he, like Jack, weighed nine pounds, two and a half ounces. Boy, talk about "Irish twins". Whenever neighbors or relatives would walk up the gravel driveway behind the house, they could see in through the windows, and they would knock on the glass and wave for me to hold up the boys so they could see them, and I loved to show them off.

~~~

One night, in March of that year, John was out of the house on business. I had put Jack to bed and was just finishing giving Nick his ten o'clock bottle. It was windy outside and I could hear the sound of the tree branches tapping against the windows. As I was sitting on the couch with

Jack and Nick.

Nick, I suddenly got the strong sensation that someone was watching

me from one of the windows. I didn't dare turn around to look at the window, I knew that if it was anyone that I was familiar with they would have knocked on the glass and waved. I was petrified, but I picked Nick up and, while trying to act calm, walked into our bedroom and put him in the bassinet. Then I got the feeling again, that whoever it was had walked around the side of the house, and was now watching me through the bedroom window. I was standing there in the dark thinking maybe I should call Aunt Jenny and Uncle Martin upstairs and ask them to look out their window and see if they could see anybody outside. Just then I saw John's headlights coming up the hill and turning into the driveway. When he came inside I told him about the creepy feeling that I had been having, so he went outside and walked around the house. When he came back in he said he didn't see anyone or any sign that someone had been out there.

The next night, I went out to play bridge with some of my friends, and John stayed home with the boys, but the night after that I was home alone with the boys again. John was next door at his mother's and his cousin Bobby Nelson was there too. I was sitting next to the bay window in the living room, reading a magazine, when suddenly I heard some rustling in the bushes just outside the window, and again got the feeling that someone was watching me. So, once again, I tried to act very casually, and went over to the phone and called next door and told John. He ran out the back door, and Bobby ran out the front door of his mother's house, and they both ran around our house from opposite directions, but again found no one.

Aunt Jenny, Aunt Lilly and Mrs. McFadden were all standing by the door with Rosary beads in their hands, and I overheard them saying, "Oh poor Fifi, she's so overtired from taking care of the two little babies. The stress must be getting to her, she's starting to imagine things."

But John was there too and said, "Wait a minute, I thought she was imagining things too, but the other night when I was here alone with the kids I went to bed early, then I heard someone walking on the front porch. I jumped up and went out the front door, and could hear someone running through the tall grass down in front of the house."

The next night, John was down the block at the firehouse. At about ten o'clock I was in the kitchen pouring myself a glass of milk, and I heard someone walk up the steps onto the front porch. I thought to myself, "Oh my God, he's gonna walk right in tonight." I picked up the phone and called John at the firehouse, and he came sprinting back to the house. He searched all around, but again found nothing. When he came back inside he announced, "That's it, tomorrow I'm going to get a dog!"

The following evening, John came racing into the driveway with a huge Boxer, its front legs hanging out of the car windows. He was panting like crazy and had a chain collar around his neck. We brought this big dog into our little four room apartment and then stood there in numb disbelief as we watched the dog run around the apartment, leaping over the furniture. He leaped over the chairs, the couch, the coffee table, and everything else in the house, like they weren't even there.

When it came time to go to bed, I told John to tie the Boxer to the radiator in the living room, but the dog didn't like that and whined and carried on so much that, finally, John went out to the living room, moved the couch over close to the dog so he could lay down and reach his arm over to calm him, and spent the night on the couch.

During the day, when I would tie the dog outside, he would constantly bark and whine for attention. He was a real pain in the neck but I had to admit that as soon as we got him I felt a lot safer and stopped having the feeling that I was being watched at night.

The dog carried on so much, when he was tied in the yard, that after a few days I let him run loose, and he'd be racing all over the place. But one day, shortly after, we got a call from the groundskeeper at the Rockefeller estate, telling us that we would have to keep the dog tied up. It seems that Lawrence Rockefeller's wife and children had been out horseback riding on their bridle paths and the Boxer had run up and scared them and spooked their horses. We tried tying him up again but he barked incessantly, so I let him loose again. This time we got a call from the Rockefeller estate saying that the dog would be shot if it was spotted running loose again. So we decided we had to get rid of the big Boxer, and John gave it to one of his friends.

~~~

Around the same time that I had been having all these feelings of being watched, there was a rash of burglaries going on around Tarrytown, North Tarrytown and Philips Manor. The burglar had become known as the "Pants Burglar" because his M.O. was to burglarize houses in the middle of the night, while the occupants were home but sleeping. He would always take the man of the house's pants with him when he left so it would slow the owner down if he tried to give chase. He would always leave the pants on the lawn of a neighbor, three or four doors down from the house that he had victimized.

My sister Mary had a friend who lived in Philips Manor, who woke up one night and thought she smelled a strange odor in the house. When she opened her eyes she saw a black man, standing by her dresser, looking through her jewelry box with a flashlight. She didn't wake her husband because she was afraid of a confrontation. Then the burglar walked past her toward the hallway, where her two young sons were sleeping in a room just down the hall. She was praying they wouldn't wake up. After the burglar left the house she woke her husband and told him what had gone on, but he didn't believe her. She said, "Check and see where your pants are." When he looked, his pants were gone. The burglar had taken them with him. When they went to check the rest of the house, they found the window in the downstairs bathroom open where the burglar had come in, and their little dog lying dead on the bathroom floor. It had been chloroformed. That was the strange odor that she had smelled when she first woke up.

Then one night, another woman in Philips Manor woke up to the sound of a ladder being put up against the side of her house. She called the police and they arrived in just a couple of minutes, in time to catch a black man on the ladder. After they had him in custody he started to confess to all the burglaries he had committed. So they drove him around and told him to point out the houses that he had broken into. They drove him around Philips Manor, Tarrytown and Pocantico Hills, and he pointed out all of the houses that he had robbed. As they drove

183

past our house, he pointed to it and told the police that he been casing it, but he didn't rob it because we "…had gotten a big brown dog."

~~~

When Nick was about two months old we had another big snowstorm in Pocantico. The next morning I was making breakfast. Jack was in his high chair and John was getting dressed for work, when I heard a knock on the front door. When I opened the door, there was this nicely dressed man standing there on the front porch. I said, "Yes, can I help you?", and when he started to speak I could smell the liquor on him.

Jack and Nick - Pocantico - January, 1949.

"Good morning," he said, "could I please use your phone?", and he went on to explain that he had, "…taken a wrong turn and been stuck in a snow drift, up behind the house, all night." He wanted to call his wife and admitted, "She'll be mad as hell."

He looked harmless, so I said, "Okay," and he stamped the snow off of his feet on the porch and came in. I showed him the phone on the wall between the kitchen and our bedroom, then I went in and told John, "You'd better come out here. There's a guy here who says his car is stuck in a drift behind the house."

As the guy was walking over to the phone, he walked past Jack, sitting in his highchair, and then he looked in the bedroom and saw Nick, and did a double take at the two baby boys, and started to laugh.

He called his wife from our kitchen but she was angry and wouldn't talk to him other than to say that if he didn't get home fast, she would, "…throw a hammer through the TV."

So John called a tow truck to pull the guy's car out of the snowdrift then drove him down to the garage where the car had been towed. Then the guy asked John to come into the luncheonette so he could buy him a cup of coffee. As they were having coffee, he called his wife again from a pay phone, but she was still mad, and as she had threatened, she threw a hammer at the TV. John could hear the glass shatter, right through the phone. After that they left the luncheonette and he had John follow him into the toy store, where he bought a stuffed teddy bear. That was Jack's first teddy bear.

Jack - Pocantico Hills, NY - March 17, 1949.

Jack, Nick and Blackie - Pocantico - Winter, 1950.

~~~

I remember one day that Uncle Martin was working on the roof of the house and had put a ladder up to the roof. As he was working, he heard a noise behind him, and when he turned to look at the ladder, there was Jack, smiling at him over the edge of the roof. Martin didn't want to startle Jack so he just spoke softly to him as he moved close enough to grab his hand. Then he took Jack up on to the roof and handed him in through a window to Aunt Jennie. When he went back to the ladder, he looked down, and there was Nick, who could only have been maybe three years old, starting to climb up the first few rungs of the ladder, looking for his big brother up on the roof. So Uncle Martin called into the house, and I came out and rescued Nick.

186

After his return from the War, John's filly, Brinie Marlin, was still being kept at the Rockefeller's stable in Pocantico Hills. But John felt that he couldn't impose on Mr. Rockefeller's good will anymore so he moved Brinie down to the stable at the Sleepy Hollow Country Club. Soon though, John was so busy with his business and the boys that he rarely had time to spend with Brinie. That, coupled with the fact that it was very expensive to keep a horse at Sleepy Hollow's stables finally convinced him that he should give up Brinie, so he decided to sell her.

Somehow David Rockefeller heard that John was going to sell Brinie, and he decided to buy her for his wife. John had told David that Brinie was a very high spirited horse, but David decided to buy her anyway.

A day or two later I was home with Jack and Nick, and it was getting near suppertime. Women didn't wear slacks in those days, so I was wearing a skirt, my saddle shoes and an old sweater. The boys had run me ragged that day as usual, so my hair was a mess and I didn't have any make-up on, and I looked like I had been shot from a cannon when John came roaring into the driveway. He strode quickly into the house and announced, "Fifi, David's going to be here in about twenty minutes."

I couldn't think of anyone we knew named David, so I looked at him and asked, "David who?"

"David Rockefeller." he answered, as he gave me a look that insinuated, "Who else would it be?", as if David Rockefeller were a regular at our house.

Well, I looked at him like he had three heads and challenged, "What's HE coming HERE for?"

"He's coming to get the saddle and bridle for Brinie," John explained.

So, sure enough, there was David Rockefeller in my little kitchen about a half an hour later, dressed in a brown leather jacket and denim pants. John introduced me to him and we made some small talk. Then he took the saddle and bridle, said, "Goodbye," and left. He was a very pleasant man and it was nice to meet him, I just wished that John would have given me a little notice so I could have at least straightened up the house, brushed my hair and put on a little lipstick.

~~~

John had made some good friends in the real estate and insurance business, and one of them mentioned one day that he was going to play poker that evening with a guy named Duke Fullerton. So John went and played poker with them that night, and got to know Duke Fullerton, and they got to be pretty good friends.

Duke Fullerton had been in the Army during the war, and had been captured by the Japanese and forced to endure the Bataan Death March. He told John how he and the other POWs had been taken on what looked like fishing boats, and just piled on top of each other. Many of the men had died just from being crushed to death under the weight of their comrades. When they heard planes flying overhead, they would pray that they would be American planes that would sink the boats, kill the Japs, and put them out of their misery. They all had dysentery and would vomit all over each other, they were so sick and overcrowded. When they got to the POW camp, they would eat dirt or charcoal, anything to try to stop the diarrhea. One morning they realized that there were no guards around. Then they heard a noise that sounded like something ramming against the prison wall, and they tried to move as far away from the wall as they could. Suddenly, the wall crashed down and a tank came rumbling in. The poor prisoners were terrified at first, then a guy stuck his head up out of the tank and yelled, "Would anybody like a cigarette?" It was the U.S. Army that had advanced, and come to free them. They couldn't believe it. They were all so weak and sick that they all had to be taken out in stretchers. Duke weighed only eighty-five pounds when he was brought back to the states and he had to be treated for tuberculosis. When he got back to Westchester, a friend of his gave him two Boxer puppies and told him that maybe he could make some money by breeding and raising Boxers, and so he did.

John was impressed by one of Duke's Boxers that was a fawn colored female with a diamond shaped patch of white on her neck. Her name was Diamond Lil. He was so impressed by her that he wanted to get one of her puppies, and he bought one of the females from her next litter.

One morning I let the new puppy out, and a little while later Uncle Oxel Nelson came knocking on the door. When I answered it he said, "Fifi, do you have a little brown dog?"

"Yes," I acknowledged.

"Well, it just got hit by a car out on Bedford Road," he said.

I ran into the bedroom and threw on some shoes, and John and I jumped in the car and raced down to where the puppy was. She was lying in the road, her sides heaving, and she was having trouble breathing. So I ran back to the house and grabbed a blanket off one of the boy's beds. We wrapped her up in the blanket, and John picked her up, put her in the car, and took off towards the Vets office in White Plains. On our way there he was speeding, and a cop waved him down and demanded, "Where the hell do you think you're going so fast?" John explained that the puppy had been hit by a car and we were on our way to the Vet. The Cop said, "Don't you see your driving through a school zone?", but then he saw the injured puppy on the seat of the car and let John go with a warning. But when we finally got to the Vet's office the puppy was already dead, and I cried and cried for weeks.

Then one day, a few weeks later, Duke Fullerton called again and said, "Fifi, I've got another dog for you."

At first I declined, saying, "No way Duke, I couldn't stand it if something happened to another dog."

But he persisted, "Fifi, it's a really great dog, but I have to be honest with you, the family that had this dog returned her to me because she was butting their son in the face. But I really think the boy must have been doing something to provoke her."

"Oh no," I protested, "I couldn't take a chance like that with my boys."

"Why don't you just try her for two weeks?" he appealed, "She's been spayed and has had some training. If you don't like her, you can give her back to me."

I'm not sure why exactly, but finally I relented and said, "Okay."

The next day, John and I took Jack and Nick to Duke's place. When we got there, there were these two beautiful Boxers running around his yard. Duke called them over and told them to, "Sit." They immediately dropped down and sat looking up at him, at attention. The one that he wanted us to take was sitting right in front of Jack, when suddenly it jumped up and, BOOM, it butted Jack right in the face.

Jack screamed and grabbed his face, and I almost passed out.

Duke shouted, "Sit," and the dog sat and snapped to attention again.

Frightened and angry, I yelled,"Duke, I couldn't possibly take this dog."

John was attending to Jack, who was crying, but when he moved Jack's hands away from his face, we saw that there were no marks. Jack was more frightened than actually hurt.

Duke was apologetic, but determined. "Please take her," he implored, "I promise she'll be all right."

Finally, after some coaxing from John, I relented, although I was still very leery of the dog. Duke told us not to ever hit her if she misbehaved, "Just roll up a newspaper or magazine, and she'll get the message."

So we took her home and named her Suki, which was the name of the Japanese house maid that John had had while he was stationed in Nagasaki. That night when we were getting ready for bed I told John to tie the dog up in the kitchen. But he didn't like that idea, he wanted to give her the run of the house, and as usual, when it came to animals, John prevailed.

During that first night, I awoke with the feeling that someone was watching me. When I opened my eyes, Suki's face was just inches away from mine, resting on the mattress. I started to try to back away from her very carefully, as I was still very nervous with her and didn't trust her. Then I realized that she was looking me right in the eye and wagging her tail. So I got up and let her out in the backyard. She went and did her business then came right back in. No problem.

Suki turned out to be the most wonderful dog. She was like my alter ego. If she saw me putting on lipstick, she would know that I was getting ready to go out, and would stand by the front door, waiting to go with me. And she was great with the kids, and very protective of them. If she didn't follow the boys out the door when they went out to play, she would sit quietly looking out the window, then back at me, then back out the window until I would let her out, then she would

Mary Ann, Philip and Eileen with Suki.
In front of my parent's house.
Saturday, May 23, 1953.

stay with the kids all day. If I couldn't find the boys at lunchtime, all I had to do was whistle for Suki, and she would come running. I knew that whatever direction she had come from was where I would find the boys.

We had Suki till she was about fifteen years old. She had developed arthritis, and eventually it got so bad that she couldn't go up and down the stairs anymore. When we finally had to have her put to sleep, none of us could bear the thought of it, so we had to have one of the neighbors sons take her to the Vet to do it.

~~~

After John's office in Tarrytown had been up and running for a while, he became connected with a developer named David Bogdenoff, and the first big development that he exclusively handled the sales for was called "Tarry Crest", which was near my parent's house in the area that had always been known as the Hackley Woods.

Then one day John came home to our apartment in Pocantico and very casually, as if he were talking about a pack of cigarettes or a loaf of bread, said to me, "Oh Fifi, I bought a house today." He had bought the house that was the "builder's model" at the Tarry Crest development, which had been beautifully furnished by a professional interior decorator. The address was number 52 Barnes Road, and John had bought it lock, stock and barrel, with all the furniture and décor included.

It was a small, three bedroom, one bathroom ranch, at the top of the hill. There was no basement and the kitchen was at the front of the house. There was a large living room / dining room combination with a big picture window that looked out into the back yard, onto a patio. When you entered the house, there was a hallway on the right that went down to the bedrooms. The first bedroom that you came to, down the hallway, we used as a den, and we had a daybed, a TV and a desk in there. Hanging above the desk was a big mirror that my mother had given to me.

There were bunk beds for Jack and Nick in their room, which they were delighted about because they could play all kinds of games in there. They quickly became adept at arranging their pillows and

192

blankets so that their bunk beds could easily be converted into a hideout, a fort, or a castle, for imaginary games of cowboys and indians, or knights of the roundtable.

The house was furnished and decorated beautifully because it had been the builder's model. The dining room had an elegant cherrywood dining room table, chairs and hutch, and there was a painting of some native fishermen on some lush Caribbean island, hanging on one of the walls. The living room couch backed up to the drop leaf of the dining room table.

Our first house - 52 Barnes Rd., Tarrytown.

~~~

I remember that, as it got close to the holidays that year, we decided to have an egg nog party on New Year's Day. Then, a day or so before the party, John asked me, "How many are coming?"

"I really don't know," I answered, "but I've been seeing people in town and asking them to drop by for egg nog."

"I've been doing that too.", he said, so we really had no idea how many people were coming to our little get together.

John had set up a bar on one side of the dining room for those that didn't like egg nog, and both the egg nog and the bar were doing a great business. There were lots of hors d'oeuvres and stuff to eat too. I remember Nick came to me and wanted to help with something, so I gave him a little dish of cheese and crackers to hand out. As he went to pick it up it slipped out of his hands, and broke on the floor. You should have seen the look in his eyes, he was so upset.

We had told people to, "Drop in…," but it seems that they came and wouldn't leave. I had to go back down to the dairy on Washington Avenue, and buy up all the egg nog that they had left.

John and Fifi dancing in the living room.
Circa 1950.

Needless to say, the party was a huge success.

One day I was doing some cooking, when Jack and Nick came tearing through the kitchen and almost knocked me down. I threw my paring knife down on the countertop and yelled, "Jesus Christ, will you kids slow down?"

John was sitting at the table and looked up at me and said dryly, "You seem a little stressed, why don't you take a vacation?"

"Really," I snapped, "who's gonna watch the kids if I take a vacation?"

"I will," he replied smugly.

Jack and Nick wrestling - Pocantico - 1951.

Well, that was a novelty, so I immediately picked up the phone and called our old friends, Bea and Jake Mauche, in Bryn Maure, Pennsylvania, near Villanova. They were happy to hear from me, so I went and visited them for the weekend.

The first night that I was there, the phone rang and it was John. He said that Jack and Nick wanted to say goodnight to me, so he put the boys on the phone and they said, "Goodnight."

Then John got back on the phone and, with an air of self-contented superiority, said to me, "I don't know what you do with all your spare time." He gloated that he had had time to do a load of wash, took a nap, and, "...even had time for a martini." I knew right away that this was the real reason for his call, he just wanted to nudge me.

I took the train and a taxi home a few days later, and I was so eager to see John and the boys that I ran into the house as fast as I could, but no one was there. I looked out the window into the backyard, and there was John with Jack, Nick and Suki, chopping up some fallen branches from one of the trees. I called out to them and waved excitedly, but they just turned and gave me a very blasé wave. Suki didn't even come to me, she barely even wagged her tail. It was a very disappointing welcome, and I almost wished I hadn't let the taxi go.

~~~

For Easter, in 1951, we bought two rabbits for Jack and Nick, and they were overjoyed. We told them that they would have to keep the rabbits in a little cage out in the garage. The morning after we got them, I heard a loud knocking on the door, and when I looked I saw Nick standing there. At first I thought he was laughing, but, when I opened the door, he was crying hysterically. His rabbit had died during the night, and he was devastated.

Jack's rabbit survived and kept getting bigger and bigger, but he soon got tired of taking care of it. Somehow it would get out of its cage once in a while, but I swear I didn't let it loose. I would get a call now and then from one of the neighbors, saying, "Fifi, do you have a big white rabbit?", and I would have to send Jack and Nick to go get it. It got so big that eventually John took it up to the stable near Briarcliff and let it loose, and that was the end of the pet rabbit.

Jack and Nick - Circa 1951.

Philip was born in October, 1951, but in the weeks before he was born we didn't know what we were going to name him, so we asked Jack and Nick to help us pick out some names. I didn't know if I would have a boy or a girl, so we asked them for some suggestions for girls' names. John had suggested "Honora," which had been his maternal grandmother's name, but Jack and Nick rolled on the floor, laughing hysterically, when they heard that.

Then I suggested "Meredith", because I liked names that were euphonious, and I was picking a few names that started with "M". Again they laughed hysterically.

Then I remember Jack sitting there with his little hand pressed thoughtfully against his cheek, proclaiming seriously, "I have a good name. How about 'Clementine'?"

Well, then John and I laughed hysterically. Jack was referring to the song that I used to sing with him, "Oh my darling, Oh my darling, Oh my darling Clementine," and he thought that would be a good name for a baby sister, but that turned out to be a bridge that we wouldn't have to cross.

In the delivery room, when I saw that we had a third boy, I named him Philip after my Uncle Phil and myself. My mother had given me the middle name of Phyllis, after my Uncle Philip, because he had taken care of my older sisters while she was pregnant with me.

Fifi and Philip - March,1952.

Tarrytown Hospital Association

21 WOOD COURT, TARRYTOWN, N. Y.

Mrs Kathryn Mc Fadden
52 Barnes Road
Tarrytown, NY   23 October 1951

ADMITTED: OCTOBER 17, 1951 - 10:20 AM   DISCHARGED: OCTOBER 23, 1951 - 11:00 AM

BED AND BOARD FROM OCT 17 TO OCT 23 INC. 6¼ DAYS @ 20.00			
BED AND BOARD NURSERY OCT 17 TO OCT 23 INC. 6¼ DAYS @ 5.00		32	50
OPERATING, DELIVERY OR CYSTOSCOPIC ROOM		22	00
LABORATORY		8	00
X-RAY			
DRUGS, MEDICINE ETC.		6	60
PHYSIOTHERAPY			
EMERGENCY			
BLOOD OR BLOOD PLASMA			
SPECIAL NURSES BOARD			
AMBULANCE			
MISCELLANEOUS Telephone			10
	TOTAL	2 06	20
SPACE BELOW RESERVED FOR MESSAGE	LESS BLUE CROSS ALLOW	80.00	
	BALANCE DUE	$ 1 26.	20

Bill from Tarrytown Hospital from when Philip was born.

Philip was different from his two older brothers. He was only eight
pounds when he was born and I can remember hearing him crying
down the hall from my room in the hospital at night. I remember
hearing the nurses, out in the hallway, commenting to each other, "Oh,
that's the McFadden baby," when they would hear him crying so loud.
In fact, when I was getting ready to leave the hospital with him,

198

Doctor Taylor explained to me that Philip had gotten a hernia from crying so hard. He told me that when Philip got old enough to understand, I should sit him down and explain to him that if he ever felt any pain in his abdomen, that he should sit down and have someone come get me. Whenever the hernia flared up, as it often would, I would put him in a warm bath to help alleviate the pain. He would eventually have surgery to repair the hernia when he was nine years old, but it never really slowed him down.

Jack, Philip and Nick- 1952.

Philip's hair was very blonde and very curly. He was the only one of my boys with curly hair. When my mother would come over to the house, she liked to curl his hair around her finger and let it fall down the back of his head. When John would get home from work he would take one look at Philip and say to me, "Oh, I see your mother was here today."

Nama Nell with Jimmy Dick and Philip.
February, 1952.

~~~

We were already in our house on Barnes Road when John sold one of the houses across the street from us to a couple named Harry and Carol Minnick. They also had two boys, Jimmy and Tommy, who were about the same ages as Jack and Nick. John and Harry hadn't known each other prior to them buying the house but they quickly became good friends, fishing and drinking buddies.

John had wanted to learn how to play the guitar, and so did Carol Minnick, so they used to have a guitar teacher come to our house and give them lessons, but John's fingers had been broken too many times playing basketball, and it was difficult for him to play.

At some point, Mr. Minnick, Harry's father, turned over the presidency of Tensolite Corporation to Harry, and he was very successful with it and became very wealthy. They eventually bought a farm up in Yorktown. There was a barn on the property, and Carol loved horses, so they had several of them. There was a swimming pool there too, and we could sit up by the house at night and watch all the boys playing in the pool.

Carol Minnick also raised gladiolas and Siamese cats, and she had an old man that helped out with the property, the barn and the horses. He lived out in the barn, next to the hayloft above the stalls.

John was doing very well in his new office in Tarrytown, and after a while an old friend of the McFadden family came to see him. His name was Peter Critchley and he had owned a real estate agency in Hawthorne for many years, where his two sons, Frank and Joe, both worked for him. He told John that he thought it would be a good idea if they merged, and his son Frank worked with John. So, after some discussion and negotiation, they formed a partnership, and John's firm became known as "Critchley and McFadden". Frank worked mainly out of the Tarrytown office with John.

Know Your Local Businessmen

August 28, 1952 By MARION GROSS

John J. McFadden, Jr. and Francis P. Critchley of Critchley and McFadden, Real Estate and Insurance, 420 Commerce St., Hawthorne.

—*One-Minute Polaroid Photo by The Townsman*

John J. McFadden and Francis Critchley, both in their early thirties, are two of the youngest established brokers in Westchester County. The firm, founded in 1951 with the merger of the Critchley Agency and the McFadden Agency, was the outgrowth of a friendship which began in school days and included several years of operating as friendly competitors.

Peter Critchley, the third member of the firm, now retired, has been a resident of the Town of Mount Pleasant for more than forty years. The firm has offices at 420 Commerce St., Hawthorne and 106 N. Broadway, Tarrytown.

Both Mr. Critchley and Mr. McFadden were born in Pocantico Hills and attended the Pocantico Hills Grammar School. Mr. Critchley attended Hakes Business School and Pace Institute in New York City. He served with the Army Air Corps during the war and following his release from active duty with a Captain's rank, went into the real estate and insurance business with his father. He resides in Hawthorne, is married and has two children, 8 and 5 years of age.

Mr. McFadden is a graduate of Villanova College in Philadelphia and holds a BS degree in Economics. He served with the Marine Corps during the war and was also released with the rank of Captain. A resident of Tarrytown, he is also married and has three children, age 6, 5 and 10 months.

The firm handles real estate in Westchester County and all forms of insurance. They are the regional agents for two of the largest insurance companies in New York. They are currently acting as sales agents for Crossroads and Long Hill developments in Briarcliff Manor and for a 215 cooperative apartment house, the Half Moon Apartments, in Irvington.

201

In the meantime, David Bogdenoff had bought land in Briarcliff Manor, on Route 9A. That development was called "The Crossroads", and they, Critchley and McFadden, did very well selling off the houses in that development.

Local ad for Critchley and McFadden.

~~~

Early in 1952, Nick and Philip came down with a very bad case of the mumps. John had been having a problem with a tooth, and one morning he got up and said, "Geez, it's not bad enough I've got a toothache, now I've got swollen glands too."

I looked at him warily, and said, "Maybe you should go back to bed."

"Why," he asked.

"Because," I cautioned, "I'll bet you're coming down with the mumps too,"

So I called Doctor Taylor, and he came over and examined John and told him he should stay in bed. A day or two later, on Sunday morning, Doctor Taylor came back to check on John. When he left, he told me that if I needed help his wife would be able to contact him. I thought it was curious that he would say that to me, but that afternoon

I took John's temperature, and it was up to 105 degrees. So I called Doctor Taylor's office, and they got his wife. She said that he was up at Marymount, tending to the sick nuns, but soon after he showed up at our house. By this time, John was becoming delirious with the fever.

Doctor Taylor needed to start an IV on John, so he had someone bring a coat rack up from John's office so he could hang the IV bottle from it. After he got the IV going and showed me how to change it, he told me that he would be going out to Tappan Hill that night, and if I needed to get him, to call there. Then, at about nine o'clock that night, I was watching the IV bottle, and it was almost time to change it, when I heard a knock on the door. I opened the door, and, wouldn't you know it, it was Doctor Taylor. He had come from the party at Tappan Hill, and said, "I thought you might need a hand."

Jack and Nick's birthday party.
February, 1952.

He checked John and changed the IV bottle, then he looked at me standing there holding Philip. I must have looked very tired because he took Philip from me and said, "Where's this kid's snowsuit?" He looked at Jack and Nick and said, "You guys go get your coats too." Then he called his wife, Anne, and told her, "Tell the girls I'm bringing home a couple of kids for them to watch." He turned to me and said, "When do you want them back? We'll keep them overnight if you want."

203

I slept on the couch that night, and I could hear John talking in his sleep. In his delirium, he was reliving the war. He was drenched in sweat and mumbling things like, "Come in 'A' company, come in 'A' company, this is 'C' company." Then he'd scream, "Look out for that son of a bitch in the trees."

When Doctor Taylor brought the boys back the next day, he had Philip, sound asleep, draped over one arm. He told me that his two daughters had had a ball curling Philip's hair that day.

By the next day John started to improve, and by the weekend he wanted to go down to his office. So I called Doctor Taylor and asked if it was okay for John to go into work. He said, "Fifi, he's a thick Irishman. If he wants to go out for a little while, let him go."

So John got dressed, and I was going to drive him to the office, but when he got in the car he said, "I changed my mind. I don't want to go to the office, take me up to the horse farm in Chappaqua." I asked why, and he said that his horse, a horse he had named "Gentleman's Folly", hadn't been out of its stall for a few days and needed to get outside. So I drove him to the stable, and he let Folly out into the paddock to get some exercise. I remember it was a cold, windy, March day.

We stayed at the stable for about an hour, then left. I said that I wanted to pick up some groceries while we were out, but John asked me to drop

TARRYTOWN NORTH TARRYTO IRVINGTON

April 10, 1

McFadden, Realtor, Has Recovered

John J. McFadden, a member of the realty firm of Critchley and McFadden, of North Broadway, has returned to his office after being ill for five weeks at his home in Barnes Road, Tarry Crest.

In a few years' time, from a small start in Main Street, Mr. McFadden has grown to be one of the most aggressive operators in this section. His first big assignment was the selling of the new homes in Tappan Hill for Morris and David Bogdanoff and when that firm developed the Cross Roads in Briarcliff Manor, the firm of Critchley and McFadden was engaged to do the selling job.

Mr. McFadden's biggest job—one that many thought was an impossibility—was in getting the Village of Tarrytown to rezone Broadway from McKeel Avenue to Wildey Street for business. As a result the A. and P. Company and nine other stores were located on the block. In addition a large tract of land exempt from taxation was added to the tax roll and the assessed valuation increased by almost $200,000.

Newspaper article - April 10, 1953.

204

him off at the house first. By the time I returned from the store, John was already back in bed, feeling lousy again. He had a serious relapse and almost died from the mumps. That episode really set him back a lot, and it took a long time for him to fully recover.

John and Philip - 1952.

~~~

One day my father had to drive my mother to the doctor's office, Doctor Milton Johnston, for her chronic indigestion problems. On the way to the doctor's, Daddy complained that his stomach was bothering him also, so after Doctor Johnston finished examining Mother, he told my father to lie down on the gurney.

As he was listening to my father's heart with his stethoscope, he told my mother to put her ear down by my father's chest. She could hear his breathing and his heart beating, but she could also hear a feint "swooshing" sound. So the doctor told my parents that he wanted Daddy to go into the hospital for some tests, but Daddy didn't want to go because it was coming up on the 4th of July weekend. They agreed that he would go in for the tests right after the long holiday weekend.

Daddy entered the hospital on Sunday, July 6th. The doctor ran his tests, then told my mother that Daddy had a very large aneurysm in his chest, which had been source of the strange "swooshing" sound that she had heard when she put her ear to his chest the week before. He said that they would have to keep my father in the hospital for a while longer, for observation, and warned that when they did release him, he would have to be extremely limited in any future physical activity. He wouldn't be allowed to drive a car, mow the lawn or climb stairs, because the doctor was afraid that the aneurysm might burst.

Mother and Father with Jack and Nick.
Mothers Day - May 8, 1949.

The weather was very hot that July, and I remember that they had my father in a bed out in a screened-in porch in the back of Tarrytown Hospital. There was only one other bed out there with him. John had tried to bring down an electric fan to help cool off his room, but the nurses said he couldn't leave it, due to something to do with the oxygen supply in the room. I think they were afraid that it might cause a spark and set the oxygen on fire. When I went down to see him one night after supper, he was sweating profusely, and he kept telling me to go back home to the kids because it was so hot.

My sister Helen and her husband Walter were living with my parents at the time, and every night Walter would drive Mother to the hospital. She would sit and talk with Daddy for an hour or two before bed, and then help him wash up and put on his pajamas.

One night, as they drove around to the screened porch at the back of the hospital, they could see inside, and there were several doctors and nurses around the bed, working on my father. When they went inside, Doctor Johnston told my mother that the aneurysm had burst and he didn't expect my father to survive very long.

When we got the news at home, Mary came and picked up Helen and me and we all drove to the hospital together. I can remember my sisters and me sitting with my mother, on the back steps of the hospital, when Doctor Johnston came outside and told us that Daddy had died.

We knew that he had the aneurism and that he was going to be very restricted, but it happened very quickly, and we just weren't prepared for his death.

I don't remember when any of my uncles died, but I do remember when my father died. It was on July 24th, 1952, and he was waked in the living room of our house on Union Avenue, which was pretty much customary at the time.

Nick Egan

~~~

In 1953 I was pregnant again with our fourth son, Brian. Doctor Taylor figured that I would go into labor somewhere around the beginning of August, so I asked him if I could have Brian on my birthday, August 2nd. But, overstating the obvious, he smiled and pointed out, "That's not up to me."

Doctor Taylor told me that he would be on vacation with his family at that time and asked me if there was another doctor that I would be comfortable with. I didn't know of any other doctors, so he suggested another one that he had a lot of confidence in. I can't remember the other doctor's name, but Doctor Taylor called him and asked him if he would be able to handle a delivery in early August while he was away. The other doctor said he would be around and would handle the delivery for him. So Doctor Taylor left for Long Beach Island, New Jersey, to take a rare, well earned vacation with his family.

Then, on July 27th, Frank Critchley had come over and he and John had gone downtown to get a pizza, or as John used to call it, "a hot pie." Anyway, I was standing in the kitchen doing some ironing, when suddenly I realized that my water had broken. I called John down at the Italian restaurant, and he and Frank came right home.

A few days before, John had asked me if I knew the name of the doctor that Doctor Taylor had left in charge of the delivery, and I said, "No."

"What are you gonna do," he wisecracked, "introduce yourself on the delivery table?"

So we called the new doctor but got no answer. We called a few more times and still got no answer, so John drove by his house but there was no one home. At that point we started to get a little concerned, so John called Doctor Taylor down in Long Beach Island and told him what was going on, and asked him if he could recommend another doctor. I could overhear John talking to Doctor Taylor, saying things like, "Oh that's okay Doc, we'll find somebody else," but I was getting nervous and somehow the doctor must have sensed it.

Doctor Taylor said, "Let me speak to Fifi," so John handed me the phone and Doctor Taylor said to me, "Fifi, do you want me to come up?"

"YES!!", I blurted out tearfully.

"Okay," he said, "get down to the hospital and see Nurse Bushell, and I'll see you in four hours."

So Frank Critchley stayed with Jack, Nick and Philip, and John drove me to the hospital. We kept watching the clock in the delivery room, and, as the time got closer and closer to four hours, we were getting antsy. There had been a set of twins born that day, and Nurse Bushell was busy keeping an eye on them too.

John had gone out and fallen asleep in the car when, at about four o'clock in the morning, he heard tires screeching on pavement as Doctor Taylor roared into the parking lot. His two young daughters jumped out of the car with their dog, and he ran into the hospital while his wife, Anne, stayed outside with the girls.

Nurse Bushell and I heard the elevator doors open, and we knew it was him. He examined me and said, "It'll be a little while longer." He said he was going to take Anne and the girls back to their house to let them get settled, then he would be back to the hospital shortly. His house was right up the street from Tarrytown Hospital.

He came back at about 4:30 a.m. and said, "Okay, Lets get this show on the road." He told Nurse Bushell to give me some "Pit", and when she gave me the shot, my right arm contracted so hard it broke the board that they had taped it to. It didn't take long, and Brian was born a short time later, on July 28th. He weighed nine pounds even.

Brian - one year old - July, 1954.

The next morning, Doctor Taylor came in to check on me and Brian. "You and the baby are doing fine," he assured, "so I'm going back to Long Beach Island. I'll see you in a week."

And off he went.

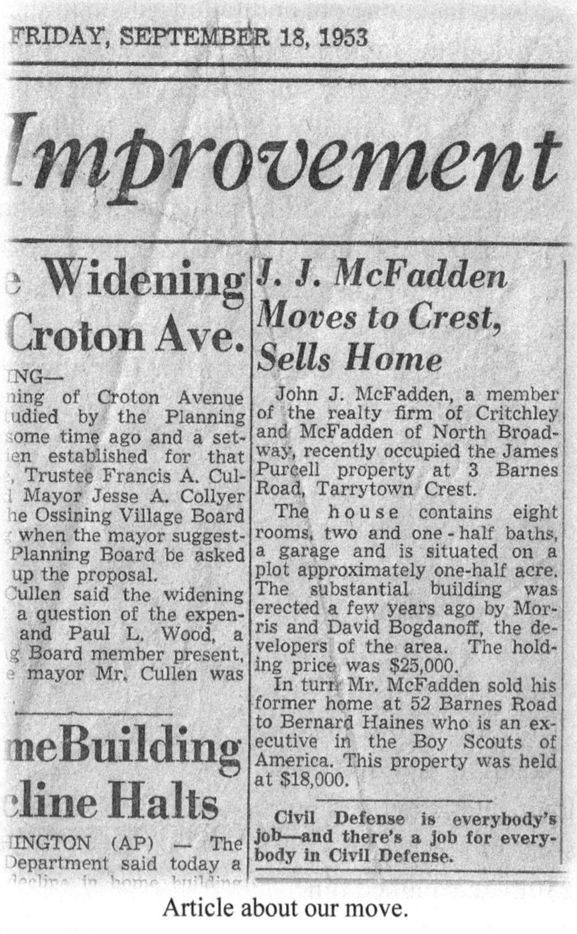

~~~

We lived at number 52 Barnes Road from 1950 to 1953, and Philip and Brian were both born while we were living there. But, as I was expecting Brian we decided that we needed some more room, and about three weeks after he was born we moved around the corner to a "garrison colonial" on the corner of Barnes Road and Crest Drive.

Our new home had a white picket fence and the garage was attached, as part of the house. It was surrounded by rose bushes and had four beautiful peach trees in the yard. They were "Freestone" peaches, and delicious. If there was ever a forecast of a storm, I would call up the neighbors and invite them to come pick the peaches before the storm could knock them off the trees and they would be wasted. And people would stop their cars on the road to look at the many lush rose bushes in our yard, when they were in bloom.

Article about our move.

210

John with Jack, Nick, Philip and the Minnick boys.
Jones Beach - July, 1954.

John had hired a local moving company whose insurance he wrote. The man who owned it told me, "Don't worry about a thing Mrs. McFadden. Just sit and take care of the baby, and we'll take care of everything." I just had to sit there and direct them where to put things.

The house had four bedrooms upstairs. One of them was a huge master bedroom and bath. The other rooms were all a comfortable size too.

The first night in the house, I asked John to feed the kids, "Just give them soup and a sandwich," I said.

211

I could hear him out in the kitchen opening and closing cabinets, then he came in and asked, "Where are all the pots and pans?"

I said, "They must still be in a box or something." Well, we looked high and low but couldn't find them. We finally realized that the movers had left all of the pots and pans and even some of the dishes back at the other house. Thank God we had only moved around the corner and the truck wasn't on its way to California. John had to go back to the old house and get everything. Some of the dishes and things hadn't even been packed and were still in the old kitchen cabinets.

Brian, Philip, Nick and Jack - Christmas, 1953.

One day John was in his office in Tarrytown, and he got a call from this Irish guy named Bill, who was a friend of his who was also in the real estate business and had an office in Irvington. He had called John because he had a client who was looking for a specific type of house, and didn't have anything among his own listings that his client liked. John told him that he thought he had a house that would satisfy what he was looking for, so Bill said he would come up that afternoon with the client so that they could look at the house.

When Bill arrived that afternoon he was accompanied by a white haired, older gentleman that he introduced to John as a retired Navy Admiral. John shook the older man's hand and said proudly, "I was in the Navy too sir."

"Really," inquired the Admiral, giving John the once-over, "what part?"

"The best part," John asserted, "I was in the Marines."

Well, with that established as common ground, they started to talk about some of their experiences in the war when the Admiral said to John, "I can remember one day, it was April 1st, 1945, and we could just see the silhouette of Okinawa off in the mist. All of a sudden, out from the shoreline, just above the tips of the waves came a kamikaze. It was headed right for one of the LSMs …."

John interrupted him and, finishing his sentence, blurted out, "And it skipped over the LSM and hit the ship right next to it."

The Admiral looked at him skeptically and demanded, "How the hell did you know that?"

"Because Sir," John boasted, "I was on that LSM, shooting at that son of a bitch."

It turned out that the Admiral was the one who had called out over the loudspeakers "Who the hell gave the order to abandon ship? Get back on board and save the ship." I don't remember if John actually sold him the house, but it was certainly a strange twist of fate that he would meet that same Admiral, years later, well after the war was over.

Several years went by, and we were living in the garrison colonial when, somehow, John found out that his horse, Brinie, was being kept in a stable in White Plains after she had apparently been sold there by David Rockefeller. And every few weeks John would come home from work and tell me that he had stopped by the stable in White Plains to visit her. On several occasions, he mentioned that he didn't think she was being very well cared for, and was being neglected by the present owner.

Then, one evening as it was getting close to Thanksgiving, in 1954, John came home from work and was reading the paper in the living room by the fireplace. The boys were all in bed, and I was folding some laundry in the living room with him. He was even more quiet than usual until he finally looked up from the paper and casually said, "Oh, by the way Fifi, I want to tell you something."

But I didn't wait for him to finish. I turned towards him and concluded, "You bought Brinie back, didn't you?"

He was flabbergasted "How did you know?", he chuckled.

I smiled wryly and taunted, "Who are you trying to kid? I knew as soon as you started visiting her in White Plains that it was only a matter of time till you would want to buy her back again."

So John rescued Brinie Marlin from the barn in White Plains and moved her to the stable in Chappaqua. Then within several weeks he decided to buy another horse for Jack and Nick, so that they could learn to ride. This would be their Christmas present. So he bought a little palomino that they named "Ginger," but she would constantly yank her head down and John worried that the boys would get hurt. So he got rid of Ginger and bought another palomino that they named "Dusty." At some point John moved the horses from the stable in Chapaqua to our friends Harry and Carol Minnick's farm up in Yorktown, where they stayed for years afterward. This was where the boys and some of my nieces and nephews learned to ride.

After John and Frank Critchley sold off The Crossroads development in Briarcliff, the builder, David Bogdenoff, started another new housing development a little further north off 9A. This one was called "Torbank".

Then one day John came home and told me that he wanted to buy one of the new houses being built in the Torbank development. He told me that I would be able to pick out all of the carpet, tile, and the appliances. Everything, even the color scheme.

John had chosen the plot at the top of the hill on Ganung Drive. I went to see the house before it was completed, and even

Fifi and Frank Critchley - circa 1950.

then I knew it was going to be beautiful.

The layout of the house was such that when you went in the front door, you would walk left into the living room which had an eighteen foot high ceiling and a bay window looking out onto the front yard. In the left-rear corner of the living room there was a fireplace that was open on two sides, the front and right side.

When you went to the right, from the front door, you went into the dining room, and then off that, at the front of the house was the kitchen, which had a door out to the side yard. There was a window over the kitchen sink that brought the sun inside, and allowed me to look out to the front yard of the house, right out to Ganung Drive.

If you walked straight in from the front door, there were two sets of stairs. One went upstairs to the bedrooms, and the other went downstairs to the playroom and den.

Upstairs there was a balcony that ran all the way across the back wall of the living room. To the left of the stairs was the master bedroom and bath. I had picked green tile and a green sink and toilet for that bathroom. Turning right from the stairs was another full bathroom and two bedrooms for the four boys.

Downstairs, on the right, was a huge twenty-two foot by twenty foot playroom. The whole back wall was sliding glass doors that looked out to the backyard and gave us an amazing view out to the Hudson River. To the left there was a half bathroom. Beyond the bathroom was a den with a big leather chair, a couch / daybed and a TV. Across the hall from the den was the utility room with the clothes washer and dryer, and the oil burner.

When you went out the sliding glass doors to the backyard, there was a concrete patio, and the yard sloped down away from the house. You could see the MaryKnoll Seminary, and hear the Angelus bells toll every day at 9:00 a.m., noon and 6:00 p.m.. As you looked out to the North, you could see all the way up the Hudson River Valley, and you could see the red flashing light on top of Bear Mountain. If you looked to the West, you could see across the Hudson to Rockland County and New Jersey. If a storm was coming, you could see the line of the rain moving down the river from miles away.

The PINK PALACE
Suki and Philip in the playroom.

To the right of the patio was a stone wall that marked the boundary of an old estate on the other side of it. That property had been sold to make room for another development. There was a beautiful old mansion on that property that people had gone into and stolen all the plumbing and lighting fixtures, and anything else that was of value.

On the sides and the back of our house there were eight apple trees that always bloomed in the spring. It was a gorgeous piece of property.

The PINK PALACE
View of the Hudson from the back patio.

~~~

When I first saw the house it had white shingles on the roof, and that's when I decided that the exterior should be painted either "salmon pink" or aqua. But John didn't want either of those colors. He said, "How about we paint the house charcoal gray and make the shutters either pink or aqua?", but I wouldn't agree with him. We bickered about it, but I wouldn't change my mind.

Then one day a woman who was one of John's salespeople called me and said, "Fifi, come up to Ossining, they're painting the outside of your house." She wouldn't tell me what color, John had sworn her to secrecy, so I put the boys in the car and drove up to Ossining. As I drove up Route 9A, I could look up and see the house at the top of the hill. And it was spectacular. It was "salmon pink" with a white roof, shutters and trim.

I went inside, and the living room had been painted mauve. The dining room had a chair-rail all around and was painted the same mauve from the char-rail down. Above the chair-rail was beautiful wallpaper which was decorated with a woodlands scene with varied, muted shades of green.

The kitchen walls were also a salmon pink, and the counter top was light beige. The refrigerator, stove, dishwasher and sink were all aqua. The oven was mounted flush with the wall, which was something new in those days.

While the men were still painting the outside of the house, I walked diagonally down across the street to one of the models that was being used as a sales office. When I got inside, Mr. Bogdenoff, who was the father of David Bogdenoff, the developer, approached me and said in his thick Jewish accent, "Why do you want to paint your house that color? Why don't you paint it white or a nice green or something a little more conservative?"

The PINK PALACE
The view from our front door, note the Hillman "Minx" in the driveway.

I got a little perturbed with his question and replied, "Mr. Bogdenoff, everybody's house is an expression of the owner's personality." I pointed up the hill to where my house was being painted pink and said, "And that's my personality up there." He knew I was annoyed at his comment, so a little while later he approached me and asked if I would like to go to lunch with him.

"No thank you," I replied curtly.

After we moved in, and the rest of the development was completed, a lot of the neighbors would use our house as a landmark when giving friends directions to their own houses. They would say, "…go five houses past the pink house…," or something like that. But from the day that I looked up from Route 9A and saw it being painted, I just always referred to it as my "Pink Palace".

~~~

There were a few weeks that August of 1955, between the time that the garrison colonial in Tarry Crest was sold and the date that we would be able to move into the new house in Torbank, so we moved all of our furniture and belongings, and stored them in the playroom of the new house. In the meantime, John and Harry Minnick had arranged the rental of two cottages out at the extreme east end of Montauk Point, for the weeks while we waited for our new house to be completed.

John drove out to Montauk in his Packard, and I drove out in the Hillman "Minx" that he had bought for me. It was quite the "chic" little car to have at the time. I had Jack, Nick, Philip, Brian and Suki all with me out there, and it was great. I could watch the fishing boats going out past the light house every morning, and then see them returning in the afternoons. My four boys and Jimmy and Tommy Minnick could play in the sand dunes and fly kites all day. John and Harry would drive out on Thursdays and spend the

Philip in Montauk - Summer, 1955.

weekends with us, then go back up to their offices in Tarrytown on Monday mornings.

219

Brian, Nick and Philip - Montauk Point - Summer, 1955.

One Saturday, John went down to Gossman's Dock in Montauk Point and bought a huge lobster. When he put it in the big pot that we had gotten to cook it in, it kept trying to climb out of the boiling water. I remember all of the boys screaming, and running around the kitchen, in fear of that big lobster.

~~~

There was a house, right next to ours on Ganung Drive, that Vic and Annarae Cordy bought. They had met when they were both in the Army in Lei, New Guinea, during the war. They had three kids; Bobby, Christine and Steve. We didn't know them before we moved in next to each other, but they were great neighbors and we became close friends.

Chris and Rosemary Lennox bought a house right around the corner on Ganung Drive. John had known Chris most of his life and I had known Rosemary since just after high school. I know it's not true, but one might think that Chris had a thing about the names of the women in his life. His mother's name was Rosemary, his sister's name was Rosemary, and he had married a girl named Rosemary. It's a wonder that he didn't name his daughter Rosemary too.

Chris and Roe were hysterical. Chris would always be lying around on the couch, smoking cigars and drinking beer. I remember one time, Rosemary came to the top of the stairs and asked in her low, husky voice, "Chris, would you go up in the attic and bring down the baby scale?"

Chris, recumbent on the living room couch, looked up and asked, "What for Rosemary?", in his goofy, Ed Norton voice.

"I want to weigh the baby.", she rasped impatiently.

Barely opening his eyes, Chris lazily pulled the cigar out of his mouth and protested, "For Christ sake Rosemary, wouldn't it be easier just for you to take the baby up to the attic?"

~~~

I remember the day that a traveling salesman knocked on our front door and said that he had a great oven cleaning product, and asked if he could demonstrate it. "Sure," I said, so I let him in and he proceeded to clean my oven with his miracle oven cleaning product.

When he was done cleaning the oven, he was obviously pleased with the results of his labors and he turned to me and asked proudly, "Well, how many would you like?"

"Of what?", I asked, disingenuously.

"Of the oven cleaner, of course," he scowled.

"Oh," I said, feigning naiveté, "I don't need any, you just cleaned my oven."

Well, he couldn't believe it and just shook his head in disgust as he left. It was a terrible thing to do to him when I think back about it now, but my friend Rosemary Lennox and I had laughed hysterically when I told her about it back then.

One spring day Rosemary called me and asked, "What did you get for Mother's Day?", and I told her that John had gotten me some flowers and a card from all the boys.

"What did you get?" I asked, knowing that her level of expectation wasn't very high when it came to getting gifts from Chris for things like anniversaries and such, but I still held out hope that he had come up with something somewhat romantic, even if it was only superficial, just for Rosemary's sake.

"You won't believe what Chris gave me.", she confessed, trying to sound up-beat about it, "He gave me a new lawn mower."

After a long silence, I growled, "Rosemary, if I ever see you pushing that lawn mower around your yard, I'll never talk to you again."

Well, wouldn't you know, a few weeks later, on Sunday afternoon, John and I were driving past their house, and there was Chris, sitting on the top step of their front porch, smoking a cigar and drinking a beer. And there was Rosemary, mowing the lawn with the new lawn mower. As we drove past I just waved my hands at her, and shook my head in exasperation.

A week or two after that, I was looking out the window over my kitchen sink when John pulled into the driveway in his pink and white Packard that he had bought to match the house. He went around to the trunk of the car where I could see he had brought home a new power lawn mower. He started calling out for Jack and Nick, and then he saw me looking out the window and waved for me to come outside. "Oh no." I yelled out to him, "I know what you're up to. I'm not coming out so you can teach me how to start that damn thing. I have no intention of using it. I wouldn't care if the grass grew up over the windows."

Once in a while I would go over to the old estate property on the other side of the stone wall to pick flowers. One morning I was over there with Suki, when I heard some voices nearby. In a few minutes, two men walked past, so I stood up and said, "Good morning," and we made some idle chatter. They said that they worked for the developer who had bought the old estate, and were there because a lot of valuable shrubs had been dug up and stolen from the property. I assured them that I was only there picking lilacs and we just chatted for a few more minutes. I said, "Goodbye," and went back over the stone wall with Suki and went home.

I knew that Vic Cordy and one of the other neighbors, Tom Mahoney, had been over in the estate property the night before, and had dug up a couple of shrubs and taken them to transplant in their own yards. I had turned on the outside light in the backyard, which cast light out onto them, so they had dropped the shrubs and ran out of the light because they didn't want to be seen.

So, when I got back into the house, I picked up the phone and called next door to the Cordy's, and Annarae answered. I whispered into the phone, "Annarae, there's two men over in the estate."

Immediately picking up on my clandestine tone, she whispered back, "Really, who are they?"

"They're from the developer who bought the property," I continued, very cloak-and-dagger. Then I asked her, under my breath, "Why are we whispering?"

Suddenly, she hissed back, very excitedly, "Oh my God, they're walking through my back yard right now."

Well, nothing ever came of it, and Vic and Tom didn't go back there again. It was just funny that Annarae and I were furtively whispering over the phone like two fools, as if it was the crime of the century and the two men would have heard us outside and dragged us away in handcuffs.

~~~~

About two months after we moved into the Pink Palace, I heard there was going to be a meeting at Saint Paul's Episcopal Church, in the cul-de-sac around the corner. It was going to be a meeting to try to form a community organization to get all the new neighbors acquainted and involved with various neighborhood activities. I was a few minutes late in getting there, so when I walked into the church there were quite a few people already sitting in the pews and there was a man speaking to the group. He was asking for volunteers for something, but I didn't know what specifically he was talking about. I raised my hand because I wanted to know what it was he was talking about, but he took it that I was volunteering before I could even ask my question. "That's great," he said, "what's your name?"

"Fifi McFadden," I answered.

"Oh, John's wife," he responded. Most of the people attending knew John because they had all bought their houses from him.

"What did I just volunteer for?", I asked, a little confused by what had just happened.

"To be Chairman of the Halloween Party Committee.", he enlightened me.

Well, I was very excited about the idea of setting up the party, so when I got home I said to John, "Guess what, I volunteered to run the Halloween party."

But, par for the course with John, he just looked up at me and said dryly, "How come I'm not surprised?"

So I took on the job of planning and running the Halloween party. I rented the Armory in Ossining, and arranged for the food and liquor, and to have a piano on hand.

~~~

When Halloween night came along, Vic and Annarae Cordy were going to have a small cocktail party at their house next door, prior to the big neighborhood party at the armory. When John and I went over, Annarae answered the door dressed as a butler in a tuxedo. Vic was wearing a French maid's outfit and was walking around serving drinks. I forget what John had on, but I wore the silk Japanese kimono that he had brought back from Nagasaki, and I had apple blossoms in my hair.

After one cocktail we left because I had to get down to the armory. Annarae said they would be along in a little while because she and Vic had to tidy up from their party and pick up their babysitter. So off we went.

We had a very good crowd at the armory and everyone was in costume, eating and drinking. As we sat down, during a lull in the music, we couldn't help but notice two guys that had gone onto the floor and were passing a basketball around and shooting baskets. They were dressed in red basketball shorts and were really quite a distraction to all of the guests sitting and chatting at their tables.

Vic and Annarae hadn't arrived yet and we were just wondering what might be taking them so long, when the basketball players lost control of the ball and it came bouncing wildly into our table. As the two came over to retrieve the ball, I was about to start lacing into them when I looked up and realized that the two players were Vic and Annarae. They had changed their costumes and were throwing the ball around noisily, just to mess with us. They were just crazy, but so much fun.

I didn't volunteer for anything else that year, although I did become known as the "Pearl Mesta" of Torbank. She was a very famous party hostess who would host all the big shindigs in Washington, DC.

Impromptu house party - Summer, 1958.

~~~

We used to throw a big party at our house every New Year's Eve. One year, 1957, John wanted to build a bar for serving drinks downstairs in the playroom, and Vic Cordy and Bob Masters said they would come over and help him build it. So that New Year's Eve day, John took Philip and went down in the playroom and started cutting up some of the wood for the bar.

I was in the laundry room and suddenly I heard Philip screaming. When I ran into the playroom to see what was wrong, John, his face red and grimacing in pain, ran past me into the bathroom holding his hands together. I could see that there was a lot of blood and sawdust all over the white keyboard of the piano, and a ragged, dark red line across the ceiling above the area where John had been working, where blood had sprayed up from the blade of the power saw that he had been using. Poor Philip was crying hysterically, but I could see that there was nothing physically wrong with him, he was just frightened to death by what he had just witnessed.

I went into the bathroom with John and saw that blood was filling the sink. He gasped, "I think I cut my thumb off!", so I ran and got a clean towel and gave it to him and he wrapped his hand in it. Then I grabbed the phone, called Annarae Cordy, and asked her to come over and watch the kids as I had to run John down to Phelps Memorial Hospital. As I was on the phone, John came upstairs and leaned against the wall, looking very pale and shaky. He had the blood soaked towel wrapped around his right hand.

I got him into the car and took off. I was speeding though stop signs and red lights, praying that a cop would see me and give me a fast escort to the emergency room.

On the way to the hospital, John would lean forward with his head on the dashboard and weakly say, "I'm gonna pass out," and I'd reach over with my right arm and push him back in the seat. It took a good ten or fifteen minutes to get to the hospital. When we pulled into the parking lot he started to get out of the car, but I told him to stay there till I got a wheel chair.

When I ran into the emergency room, two nurses were sitting there casually crocheting and, as much as I tried, I couldn't get them to respond with the same amount of urgency that I was feeling, but one of them calmly got a wheel chair and brought John inside. After a few minutes I could hear them paging a doctor, and then they took John into the emergency room. About an hour later, he finally came out with his hand swathed in bandages. He told me that, while they were working on him, the doctor had been wisecracking with the nurses and joking about what kind of stitch he should use to suture up John's nearly severed thumb.

When we finally got home and went downstairs, I could see that all of the blood and sawdust was gone. Our neighbors had come over and cleaned up the entire mess and finished building the bar. The New Year's Eve party went on as planned, in spite of John's terribly injured hand. God forbid we ever miss a chance for a good party.

New Years Eve Party - 1957.

~~~

About forty or fifty people showed up that night for the festivities. All our neighbors came and lots of people from town that we knew. Bill Baer, who lived down the hill from us, came clad in only a big baby diaper, dressed as "Baby Time" for the New Year. I wanted to kill Harry Minnick, he had brought a rifle with him and started shooting it off out on the patio at the stroke of midnight.

New Years Eve Party - 1957.

At about 4:00 a.m. there were still about fifteen or twenty people dancing and drinking. I was up in the kitchen cleaning up a bit, when I heard knocking on the door and the door bell ring. I thought to myself, "Oh oh, that has to be the police." So I answered the door but it wasn't the police. It was several young couples who I didn't recognize. I said, "Yes, can I help you?"

One of them asked, "Is this the McFadden's?"

"Yes," I said, and again asked, "what can I do for you?"

But they all just looked at each other, barely acknowledging that I was there, and drunkenly giggled, "Okay, this is the place." Then they brushed right past me, took off their coats and went downstairs, and started dancing.

So I went downstairs and asked John, "Are they friends of yours?"

"No," he said, laughing, "I thought maybe you knew them."

It turned out that they were friends of Harry Minnick. He had called them at another party that they had been attending, and each tried to talk the other into coming to the party that they were at. Finally Harry had told them, "When your party's over, come over to McFadden's, and if the lights are still on, come on in." So they came, and stayed and danced and drank.

After a while I said that I was going to go to seven o'clock Mass at Saint Theresa's, in Briarcliff. Another neighbor, a guy named Paul, who was always the comedian of the group, said that he would like to come to Mass with me, and I said,"Okay." It was a cold, clear Sunday morning and we started down the hill at a pretty good clip. I was driving, but Paul rolled down his window, reached over and started blowing the horn and screaming, "Happy New Year," out the car window.

When we got to the Church, there were only about twenty people inside, and we sat down in a pew. In the quiet of the church I heard paper rustling, and when I looked over at Paul, he had a small brown paper bag that had a sandwich in it. I asked him, "Where did that come from?"

"It was on the pew," he slurred, and started eating it.

The Priest started saying Mass, and in the middle of the eulogy, Paul, much to my chagrin, started snoring very loudly. When Mass was finally over I woke him up and left. As we were driving home, he went on and on about how he, "…never enjoyed New Year's Eve as much as this. This was the greatest party ever."

When we got back to the house and went inside, John was in the kitchen making bacon and eggs, one handed, for everyone who was still there. The last of the guests finally stumbled out of the house at about eleven in the morning New Year's Day, but by that time all of the boys were up and running around. John went to bed and I had to get my second wind.

Jack, Nick, Philip and Brian.
Sledding - March, 1956.

229

We already had our Boxer, Suki, but one day John bought home a big Doberman pincer that turned out to be a nightmare. Its name was Von and it was too big, and far too wild, for me or any of the boys to walk. One afternoon I had to run down to the store, and I left Jack and Nick to keep an eye on Philip and Brian. I wasn't gone long, but when I got home, and was walking up to the front door, I could hear all the boys screaming inside. They were so scared of Von that they had locked themselves in one of the upstairs bathrooms to keep him away, and wouldn't come out till I came in and locked Von up, down in the utility room.

There was another time that John was sick in bed with a bad case of the flu. It was a miserable, gray day, and Von had to go out, but I told John that the boys and I weren't strong enough to walk him. This was before all of the houses in Torbank had been completed and there weren't many neighbors yet, so John said, "Oh just let him loose outside, he'll come back," so I did.

After a while, at around five o'clock, I thought, "Oh, I better go let Von in." When I looked outside, I saw him sitting across the street on Ricky Reilly's front porch, but when I called him, he just ran off. So I put on my coat and got in the car to go look for him.

The development was still being built and there were no lawns yet, just dirt yards, and it was raining out. As I drove around the block I would catch a glimpse of him every few minutes, running through people's back yards. Then I came to a house where there were a lot of cars parked outside. There was a very nicely dressed couple crossing the street to the house; he in a suit, she in a cocktail dress, so I slowed down so they could walk in front of me. People were walking over wooden planks that had been placed on the muddy front yard, up to the house, and I could see that there was a cocktail party going on inside. Then, to my horror, I saw the Doberman pincer, Von, walking past the window, inside where the party was going on. "Oh my God!!", I said out loud to myself, "How the hell did he get in there?" I wanted to run and hide, and deny that I had anything to do with that damn dog, but I parked the car, took the leash and went up to the front door.

I was mortified at how I looked; my hair was a mess, no make-up, and I was completely disheveled. I knocked on the door and when the man answered the door I asked sheepishly, "Do you have a big dog in here?"

He smiled, obviously amused at my situation, and said, "Oh yes, is he yours?"

"Yes, unfortunately he is.", I replied, and I went inside and got him, apologizing the whole time to all the party guests. Thank God he hadn't gone up on the tables and tried to eat their food.

Suki was starting to get a little older by then, and Von was always being nasty to her, which was another reason why I didn't like him, but after that little episode I gave John an ultimatum and I told him that either Von had to go or I would. I'm not so sure that the outcome would have been the same if Von could have cooked and taken care of four young boys, but John ended up giving that dog away to a friend too.

~~~

Over the years, I was always trying to talk John into taking some time off and going away for a weekend, but he never would because the weekends were always his busiest time with the real estate office. But shortly after Frank and Rita Critchley moved down to Florida, Rita invited me to come down and visit her. John wouldn't go, and asked me who would take care of the boys while he was at work. I told him that I would find somebody to look after them if I went to Florida.

Elizabeth was a young black woman who, at the time, I would have come once a week to clean the house. I thought she might be up for the job, so I asked her if she had ever taken care of young kids before. She said, "Oh yes," she had taken care of a four month old baby and two older children for several weeks, and she liked kids. So I asked her if she would be able to stay at the house for a week or ten days while I went away. I told her that she would have to get Jack and Nick off to school, bathe Philip and Brian, and feed them all their meals. She could sleep down in the den while she was there. So she said, "Okay," that she could handle it.

Then I called my mother and asked her if she would like to go to Florida with me, and she said, "Yes." She was always very adventurous, so we made a reservation and took the train from New York to Fort Lauderdale.

Nama Nell - Fort Lauderdale, Florida - 1957.

Before we left, I left instructions with Elizabeth about the boy's school bus schedules, what to feed the kids and certain chores and things that needed to be done around the house. I also spoke to Jack and Nick about making sure they carried out their chores of walking and feeding Suki, and feeding their pet parakeet that we had at the time.

When Mother and I returned from Florida a week later, John had some pretty amusing stories to tell me.

One night when he had gotten home from work, the boys were already in bed and Elizabeth was down in the den watching television. John went in to her and asked, "Elizabeth, I'm gonna fix myself something to drink, would you like something?"

"Oh yes," she said, "that would be nice"

As she followed him up the stairs to the kitchen, he continued, "I'm gonna have some scotch in mine, would you like some in yours?"

She clasped her hands together in delight. "Oh yes," she said emphatically, "that would be **VERY** nice,"accentuating the word,"VERY", and augmenting her enthusiasm with a little shake of her hips and shoulders, and a broad, toothy grin. John had gotten a real kick out of that.

Another morning, he came down into the kitchen before he went to work, and Elizabeth was loading the breakfast dishes into the dishwasher. John said, "Good morning," then inquired, "How's the bird doing, Elizabeth?".

She turned to him with a wide-eyed, puzzled look on her face, speechless for a moment, then nervously managed to mutter a one word question, "Bird?"

When he looked over in the corner, the cloth cover was still on the bird cage. He removed the cover and there was the poor parakeet, lying on the floor of the cage, feet straight up in the air, dead as a door nail. Jack and Nick had completely neglected it and Elizabeth didn't know to feed it. John told me later that, "The look on her face was priceless when she asked timidly, 'Bird?'"

Elizabeth did a great job while she was there. The boys all loved her and were always happy to see her. But she couldn't continue as our live in help, as she took care of her grandmother down in a big house in Ossining that she lived in with some of her aunts and uncles. Some years later I got a call from my mother saying she had read in the newspaper that Elizabeth had been shot by one of her uncles. I don't think she was killed, but I had lost contact with her and I don't know what the outcome was.

~~~

At one point John and I decided that I would go to work in his real estate office, and that fostered the idea that we would need to get a live-in maid. So one day my mother and I went down to an agency in New York City and filled out an application for a maid to come help with the housework, cooking, and taking care of the boys.

A few days later I got a call in John's office, from a woman who identified herself as "Marie." She said she was the maid that the agency had sent to come to work for us, and was down at the Tarrytown train station and needed to get a ride up to our house. I told her that I would come pick her up and asked how I would recognize her. She said she was wearing a blue jacket and black pants, "…and I'm big," she added. So I told John that I was leaving to pick up Marie and that she had said she "…was big."

Well, never being one to miss an opportunity for a good zinger, he looked up at me and asked facetiously, "Did you tell her that you're big too?"

So I picked Marie up at the station, and as for her saying that she, "…was big," well that was an understatement. She was easily two hundred and fifty pounds. We drove up to the house and, once inside, I introduced her to my four boys and Elizabeth, who was the other young black woman that had been working for us for a while as a babysitter and housekeeper. I told Marie that I had to drive Elizabeth home, and would be back in a few minutes. While I was gone though, John came home to meet the new housekeeper, and when he pulled into the driveway Jack came running out to him by his car and wisecracked, "Hey Dad, did you get a load of the load?"

But by that evening Marie had outdone herself. She had bathed Philip and Brian, and fed all the boys, set the table and cooked a beautiful candlelit dinner for John and me.

Everything was great until one night, a week or two later, when John and I had gone out to dinner and left the boys with Marie. After dinner we were on our way to visit some friends, and on the way up Route 9A we decided to swing past the house and check in on Marie and the boys. But when we pulled up in front of the house we couldn't

Brian, Jack, Philip and Nick - 1957.

234

believe our eyes. We could see the boys through the front bay window, and they were carrying on like a bunch of wild Indians. They would sprint up the stairs and along the balcony, then climb over the railing that overlooked the living room, jump down to the couch, about six feet below, and roll off onto the floor. Then repeat the whole thing again, screaming and whooping it up the whole time. And Marie was nowhere in sight.

When John and I walked through the front door, the boys all looked up in surprise. There mouths were wide open, but there was dead quiet. They all knew that they were in big trouble. In a low, menacing tone, John demanded, "Where's Marie?", and Jack pointed downstairs toward the den. I took all the boys upstairs and settled them down and got them to bed, while John went downstairs to deal with Marie.

He found her down in the den, half asleep in front of the TV. She hadn't even realized that we had come in the front door a few minutes earlier. He told her that we were both shocked and disappointed at the unruly behavior we had seen, and the fact that the boys weren't already in bed, and under no circumstances was she ever to let anything like that happen again.

Then, about a week later, when Marie had gone home for the weekend, I was giving Philip a bath, and was very upset to see the red imprint of a hand on his upper leg. I asked him, "Who did that to you?"

"Marie," he confessed, and he told me that she had hit him because he hadn't eaten all his lunch the day before. Well, that was the kiss of death for Marie. She would always leave to go home for the weekends, and when I drove her to the train the following weekend, I told her not to come back anymore.

~~~

One night the boys were all in bed, John was out, and I was sitting in the den watching TV. The bathroom window was open and there was a warm breeze coming up from the river. There were some newspapers stacked in the utility room and I could hear the papers rustling, but I figured it was just the breeze coming in the window that was rustling them. The kids used to have a bad habit of leaving the sliding glass doors at the back of the house open sometimes, so I went to check the back doors and found that, sure enough, one was partially open. I shut it and went up to bed.

The next day I was downstairs cleaning the den, and I pushed John's big leather chair aside so I could vacuum under it. Suddenly, this humongous gray rat darted out from under the chair and damn near gave me a heart attack. It scurried right along the molding of the wall and disappeared into the utility room, and I realized that it must have been the rat that I had heard rustling the papers the night before. I was petrified but I walked over, reached in and closed the utility room door to trap it inside.

I ran upstairs and called John and told him that I had just seen a big rat in the house and he should bring home a rat trap. He laughed at me and rationalized, "Oh Fifi, it's not a rat, it's probably just a big mouse," and he didn't bring anything home with him.

I had to do some laundry the next day, so I bravely convinced myself that it would be okay to go down into the utility room. I didn't see the rat at first, but after about ten minutes, suddenly the damn thing bolted right out from under the washing machine, almost tripping me as it skittered between my feet. It scampered across the floor by the oil burner, then jumped up onto the top of the foundation wall and disappeared into a small hole in the sheetrock that formed the wall with the garage. Again, nearly apoplectic with fear, I slammed the utility room door shut, ran upstairs and called John. I pleaded with him to bring home a rat trap, but again he laughed and pooh poohed me. That night I put Suki in the utility room and closed the door, hoping that she might kill it if it came out, but nothing happened. Maybe Suki was afraid of it, even if it did come out.

The following day was Sunday. The kids were out playing, John was at work and it was very quiet in the house. I was cooking a turkey breast for dinner, and had been downstairs, but I went back up to check on the turkey. I started to open the silverware drawer to get a fork, and I opened it quickly. But then my heart almost leaped out of my chest when I felt and heard something scratching at the back of the drawer. I must have caught the rat's leg or tail or something in the drawer. It had obviously come up through the walls and was in behind my kitchen cabinets.

I screamed and slammed the drawer shut, then ran headlong out of the house and across the street to Ricky and Marge Riley's house. I called John and threatened, "You'd better bring home a rat trap tonight because I'm not going back in that house till you catch the damn thing!" But he evidently thought that I was still just exaggerating things because he just continued to scoff and laugh at me.

Then, that night, we were sitting at the table eating dinner with the boys when suddenly I heard some noise. I waved my hands for them to be quiet and whispered, "Listen," and we could hear the rat running back and forth inside the cabinets behind the kitchen sink.

John and one of the boys went down to the utility room to see if they could get a glimpse of it, and that's when John finally saw the damn thing. He slowly came back upstairs with a look of shock on his face, and his tone had changed from derision to dismay as he grudgingly admitted, "Oh my God, it really is a rat."

So he went back downstairs and waited in the utility room.I didn't know what he planned to do if he saw it, but I had put the boys to bed and was sitting nervously in the living room. Then I heard a loud "THUD, THUD, THUD". A minute or two later, John came upstairs holding the dead rat by its tail. He had beaten it to death with a mop.

We later figured out that it must have come in the open sliding glass door, from the abandoned old house next door, when the construction of the new development had started over there.

~~~

The entire back wall of the playroom in the Pink Palace was comprised of two huge sliding glass doors that opened out to the backyard, and gave us a beautiful panoramic view of the Hudson River. One evening John and I were going over to the Cordy's house for a little gathering with some of the other neighbors, so we left Jack in charge of his three younger brothers, and went next door.

We had only been there for about half an hour when the Cordy's phone rang. It was Jack, and he said, "Mom, can you guys come home?"

"What happened Honey?", I asked, "Is everything all right?"

"Nick broke a window," he disclosed timidly.

It didn't dawn on me that it was anything other than one of the regular windows in the house, so I told Jack to keep the younger boys away from any broken glass, and I would be home in a few minutes. So John stayed at the Cordy's, and I went home to check on the boys, and clean up the broken glass.

When I got back to the house, all the boys were sitting at the top of the playroom stairs, and looked up at me with very grim expressions. I said, "Where's the broken window?", and Jack motioned downstairs, toward the playroom. So I walked downstairs to check what was broken, but I couldn't believe what I saw.

One entire panel of the huge sliding glass doors was completely smashed, and the pieces of shattered glass were everywhere on the playroom floor and the patio. I looked at Jack and Nick and screamed, "What happened!", but none of the boys would answer, they could only look up sheepishly at me because they knew they were in deep trouble. I called over to the Cordy's and told John, "You'd better come home and see what they did now," and when he got home we finally got Jack and Nick to fess up to what had happened.

It turns out that, after we had left, the boys had started playing a game that they called "Land of the Pharaohs", which they loosely based on the movie of the same name that they had seen on the old "Million Dollar Movie" about a million times. In their little reenactment of the film, Jack played the "Pharaoh", Nick was the "slave driver", and Philip and Brian were "slaves". Jack, the Pharaoh, had apparently sentenced the two slaves to be punished for some imaginary crime against the Egyptian gods, and ordered them to stand, facing up against the glass doors, with their hands over their heads lashed to an imaginary "whipping post", and Nick was pretending to whip them, using one of their wooden croquet mallets as a whip. Well, Nick must have gotten a little overzealous as he swung the croquet mallet, pretending to whip them, because, suddenly, the head of the mallet came off the handle, flew right over Brian's head, and smashed the sliding glass door into a million pieces.

They were very lucky that none of them got hurt or cut by the flying shards of glass, and, needless to say, they were forbidden from playing "Land of the Pharaohs" or using croquet mallets in the house ever again.

Jack, Nick, Phil and Brian with cousins Eileen and MaryAnn Budny, August, 1958.

~~~

Sometime during the mid to late fifties, John started to become disenchanted with his partner, Frank Critchley, and their business arrangement. They were still good friends personally but Frank's work ethics were less than satisfying, and becoming more and more questionable as time went along.

Frank, for some reason, fancied himself a bit of a ladies man, and more than once John had spotted his car at the home of clients at times that husbands would have been at work, or during hours that would have been inappropriate for purposes of business. He would also, often out of the blue, take off to Florida to go deep sea fishing or tarpon fishing, although in fairness, John would sometimes do the same thing as long as Frank would stay in town to cover the office. But Frank was

239

Fifi with Frank and Rita Critchley.

also lax about putting in time at the office, and very undisciplined when it came to work. John started feeling that he was doing the lion's share of the work and making the greater number of sales, while Frank seemed to be running around and relaxing while still taking his normal cut of the profits. John wished that Frank would put more time and effort into their real estate sales and spoke to him about it on several occasions, to no avail.

Then Frank's brother, Joe, lost his job, and Frank asked John if they could put him on in their office and let him draw a salary. John, the softy that he was, agreed.

At some point, Frank and Rita had taken several trips to Florida, and from then on he was always talking about how he wanted to move to Florida where he could fish all the time and enjoy the warm weather. So John finally decided that maybe it was time to buy out Frank from the partnership. They spoke about it for a while, and things remained

Frank Critchley - February, 1952.

240

amicable. It seemed that a buyout would give them both what they wanted. Frank could move to Florida and John could resume full control over his business. So they agreed that John would buy him out, and Frank would move on.

They sat down with their accountants and agreed on the terms of the buyout. Then John went to see Charlie Fryler, who was the manager of the bank in North Tarrytown, to arrange a loan so he could buy Frank out.

In the meantime, Uncle Johnny Foley and his cousin Tom Foley had heard that John was going to buy out his partner and had gone to Charlie Fryler to procure a loan. The two of them approached John one day in his office and told him that they would like to make the loan to him, and there was no need for him to go a bank or outside the family if he needed a loan.

So, after some cursory discussions, John agreed, and they drew up the terms of the loan. John bought out Frank, and he and Rita moved to Florida.

July 1, 1955

McFadden Takes Over Business

John J. McFadden of the real estate and insurance firm of Critchley and McFadden, has purchased the Chritchley interest, the Daily News learned today. The business will continue in its present location in the A. and P. business block, North Broadway, opposite Wildey Street.

Mr. McFadden started his business in 1946 upon his release from the Marines and in 1950 the partnership of Critchley and McFadden was formed. Shortly after entering business he persuaded the Tarrytown Trustees to rezone the A. and P. store area on Broadway for business. The partnership sold 555 single family new homes in the Tarrytown, Ossining and Briarcliff areas, 136 of which were built for the Bogdanoffs at Tarry Crest.

241

I don't remember when the first payment on the loan was due, but John was going to be short in making it. He had four or five pending real estate sales that were scheduled to close in the next ten days which would have brought in a big influx of cash, more than enough to satisfy the loan payment, so he called his Uncle Johnny and asked him if he and his cousin Tom could come to his office to talk. They came down, and John explained that he would have the five closings in the next ten days and asked for their patience and a ten day grace period on the payment. Uncle Johnny seemed amenable to extending the time, but Tom Foley was not. He scowled at John and blustered, "Are you telling me that you're not going to make your first payment?"

John had his accountant there with him to help review the money that the closings would bring in. He said, "The money will be there, I just need a little more time."

But with that, Tom Foley gruffly put on his hat and coat, then, turning abruptly on his heel, callously rebuffed John, "No!", and walked out of the office. Uncle Johnny went outside and tried to talk to his cousin, but Tom was set in his position and wouldn't budge.

At the time, Uncle Johnny Foley lived in the house in the cul-de-sac on Macy Road in Briarcliff. A night or two later John went there with his accountant, to speak to his Uncle Johnny and Tom Foley, to try a last ditch effort to work something out, but they still weren't interested.

After John had left our house to go meet them, I got in my car and went over there too. The boys were all asleep in their beds, but I was so out of control with anger that I left them alone in the house. I was shaking with anger, and livid that Uncle Johnny could do this to John and me.

When I left our house I was so angry and consumed with rage that I wanted to kill Uncle Johnny and his cousin Tom. I sat in the car outside Uncle Johnny's house, watching them through the big bay window and debated back and forth with myself whether or not to go in and commit mayhem. Thank God reason finally won out over rage. I often wonder to this day what I would have accomplished if I did storm into the house that night. What would have become of me? What would have become of my sons?

During the time that this was all going on, I had become pregnant again, with Patrick. At the time, we had two Packards, and John would drive the new one and I drove his two year old car. But we had to return both cars to the dealership because we couldn't afford to pay for them after Uncle Johnny and Tom Foley took John's business.

My cousin, Ricky Reilly, who lived across the street from us, worked in a car dealership and was able to get an old, used Dodge for us. John drove that down to Florida to see if he could get a job down there, because one of the stipulations of the agreement with Uncle Johnny and Tom Foley when the loan defaulted was that John couldn't operate within thirty five miles of Tarrytown.

So John drove down to Florida and stayed with Frank and Rita Critchley for several weeks. While he was there he found out that you had to be a resident of Florida for one year before you could get a real estate brokers license. Obviously that wouldn't work, so he came back up to Ossining.

On his trip back up, he drove non-stop from Fort Lauderdale to our house. I remember that when he pulled into the driveway and got out of the car, he was all hunched over. It took him a few minutes to straighten up all the way because he was so stiff from driving for so long. When he came inside he told me that all the way up from Florida he wasn't sure if he would have enough money to pay for the tolls at the New York City bridges. He went upstairs and fell into bed, and slept right through till the next day.

The following day, as if by fate, Duke King called. Duke had been a friend of John's during his college days at Villanova. He had become an attorney and had a successful law office in Wantagh, New York, out on Long Island.

When he called, I had answered the phone and, after some small talk, Duke asked to speak to John. When I told John that Duke was on the phone, he didn't want to talk to him at first, because he was feeling so dejected, but I finally persuaded him to get on the phone.

Duke had called to invite John to a golf outing out on Long Island that was a day or so away. John balked at first, but I convinced him that it would be good for him to get out and relax a little. On the day of the outing, Duke said to John, "Why don't you come down and work out of my office? I have some extra space where you can set up to work out of."

So John took him up on the offer and started commuting back and forth to Long Island every day, and working out of Duke's office in Wantagh.

~~~

Throughout this whole period, I was pregnant with Patrick, we had no money and the future looked bleak. There were nights during that fall and winter of 1958 when we had no heat in the house because we couldn't afford fuel oil. We would make a fire in the fireplace, and have the four boys sleep on the floor in front of the fireplace to keep warm. Some days John would take a five gallon can to the gas station and buy a few gallons of diesel fuel to heat the house during the coldest days.

I was pregnant and I was thirty-six years old. I constantly wondered why God would give me another baby at this time in my life, especially when we were going through such hard times. But I knew that there must be a reason for it all, and so I held onto two things, my faith, and the feeling that this baby would be a comfort to me in my old age.

~~~

One night after John got home from work on Long Island, I told him I wasn't feeling well. He said, "Well, maybe you should call the doctor." My OBGYN doctor at the time was a Danish woman named Dr. Nani Hanjie, who was married to a Chinese doctor, a gastroenterologist, named Dr. Fu Chu. Dr. Hanjie told me to come down to the hospital, so I called my cousin Ricky Reilly, and asked him to come over and watch the boys and John drove me to Phelps Memorial Hospital.

When I got up to the delivery room, the Doctor was having a hard time because Patrick was breach. She had another doctor and nurse come into the delivery room and they started pressing on my chest and stomach to help push the baby down and around. I think Patrick was born at around 11:00 o'clock at night on December 9th, and the next morning my chest and stomach were sore as hell from the doctor and nurse pushing him down into position.

When I brought Patrick home to the Pink Palace, I was carrying him in a small bassinet. We went inside and I put him down on the coffee table in the living room. Brian came in to see his new baby brother, and looked down at him in the bassinet. When he saw Patrick he was ecstatic, he threw his hands up to his face and knelt down next to him, staring at him in amazement.

Brian and Patrick - Mansfield Drive, Seaford - Spring, 1959.

~~~

It was a tough time for us. John was commuting to Long Island every day, and I was home keeping the day to day going with the four young boys in school and a newborn. The toughest part though, was trying to come to terms with the knowledge that we would soon have to leave our home and our roots in Westchester, and move to Long Island where we would try to start over.

Chapter Eight

THAT GODFORSAKEN ISLAND

About four months after Patrick was born, John found a house on Mansfield Drive, out in Seaford, Long Island, that we could rent. But we were told that we would only be able to stay there for two years, as the State of New York was taking that property to make way for the proposed Seaford/Oyster Bay Expressway that was going to be built.

So I asked my mother if she could take care of Patrick for two weeks while we moved and got settled. When I think about it now, my mother must have been in her seventies by then. It must have exhausted her to have to carry a heavy four month old baby boy up and down the stairs of her house every day.

As we were packing and making plans to move to Long Island, my sister Helen was worried sick about us and was telling all our friends that I was going to be moving. She would lament, "Oh, poor Fifi, she's going to be moving to that Godforsaken island. I'm sure something drastic is going to happen to them, it's

Brian, Jack, Philip, Nick and Patrick - June, 1959.

surrounded by water," as if she thought we would all be swept away by a great tidal wave.

And maybe she was right, for there were many times, especially in those early years on Long Island, that I felt like we had indeed been swept away and lost.

The day that we moved into the house, we had no money. We had no phone because our phone bill in Ossining had been so high and so delinquent that the phone company had cut off our service and wouldn't give us a phone.

Kevin Cox, Brian, MaryAnn, Nick, Aunt Hellie, Philip, Eileen and Jack.
November, 1959.

Vic Cordy and Ricky Reilly helped us load all of our belongings into a moving truck. John drove the truck down from Ossining to Seaford, and Jack and Nick rode with him. Philip, Brian and Suki rode in the car with me. Duke King had arranged to get some help to unload everything into the house once we got there. Peggy King, Duke's wife, had cooked a roast beef dinner and brought it over to the house so we could at least have something to eat.

The first night in the house, I noticed that Nick was running a very high fever. It was very chaotic, and, all in all, a pretty inauspicious start to life in our new surroundings.

247

On the first floor of the house were two bedrooms, a bathroom, dining room, living room and a small kitchen. The second floor had another bathroom at the top of the stairs, and a very large bedroom to the left of the stairs where all the boys slept like it was a bunkhouse. There was also a smaller bedroom to the right of the stairs. The basement of the house was finished and the boys used it as a playroom.

The house was on a corner piece of property at the intersection of Seaman's Neck Road and Mansfield Drive, and it had a small side yard and backyard. Across Seaman's Neck Road was a small shopping center with a "Hills" supermarket, a drug store and a candy store. In a way it was convenient for me because I could send Jack or Nick across the street for milk or bread if we needed it.

Brian, Patrick, Jack, Nick and Phil.
June, 1959.

I think that, shortly after we moved in, I had a nervous breakdown of sorts. John would go off to work every morning and I would stay home all day in my flannel night gown with no make-up. I would look at a table and think, "Oh, I should dust that table," then I would sit down in a chair, look at the table again and think, "Oh, I'll just do it tomorrow." John would get home in the evening, and I would still be in my flannel night gown, with no make-up. The kids would get fed, but the dust was still on the table. I think I went into a deep depression over having to leave my Pink Palace, my family and friends, and the community that I had known all my life. I stopped taking care of myself, and started putting on a lot of weight.

The boys met some other kids, that lived around the corner, by the last name of Cox. The oldest was a girl named Jan, who was about the same age as Jack. She always had fish tanks that she kept snakes and turtles in, but no fish. Then there was Thomas who we all called "Tad," he was about Nick's age. Then there was Paul who was the same age as Philip, then Kevin who was Brian's age. The youngest was Brendan, who was two or three years older than Patrick.

Fifi, Philip, Brian, Jack Henry, Nick and Jack - June, 1960.

The Long Island Railroad ran behind the house, only a bout a half a block away, and when we first moved in, all the boys would get very excited when they heard the train's whistle coming or going from Seaford station. They would all run outside to the backyard or to the upstairs' bedroom windows to see the trains going by. But after a few weeks, running out just to watch the trains go by started to become

249

"old hat". It didn't take too much longer before the boys and their friends started to get very daring with the trains, and would put pennies on the tracks. Then they would hide in the woods and wait for the next train to go buy at high speed, and run over their penny, flattening and stretching it into an oblong piece of copper. By doing this, the pennies had been rendered worthless, but the boys all thought it was really "cool".

~~~

One day during the summer of 1960, Jean Cox, the mother of all the Cox children, stopped by the house, looking for her kids. I was out in the yard and the two of us got talking. We were just making small talk, chatting about the usual, mundane stuff, like kids and groceries and what we were going to make for dinner that night. But then, out of the blue, she started a conversation that would change my life.

First she casually asked, "Fifi, do you have a college degree?"

"Yes," I confided, lazily.

Then she pried a little, "Have you ever taught?"

"No," I answered, listlessly.

Then she prodded, "Have you ever thought about 'subbing?'" meaning substitute teaching.

"No," I replied, still somewhat detached and disinterested.

Then she provoked, "Fifi, you're missing out on a gold mine."

Well, now she had my attention. "What do you mean?", I asked.

"Seaford Schools system is desperately looking for substitute teachers," she proclaimed, "and you'd be foolish not to go up and apply."

So,that August, just before school started, Jean came and all but dragged me up to the Seaford High School to register for substitute teaching. When we got there, I told the woman in charge of calling in the "subs" that I didn't have a phone. Jean intervened and said, "Don't worry, call my house and I'll send one of my kids over to contact her."

I had met two other women in the neighborhood, Adrian Krusch and Mary Anderson, who also had small children, and they said that they could watch Patrick for me on days that I was called in to teach.

I think that the first time they called me to "sub" was for the Seaford Avenue School. It started out sporadically, only a day or two a week, and scattered over all of the schools in Seaford, through all the grades; elementary through high school, covering any and all subjects. One time I went for an entire week to replace Mr. DeFeis, who ran the high school Drama Class, while he was on jury duty.

Any time that I was working at the high school and ended up teaching a class that Jack or Nick was in, they would try to act like they didn't know me. They were embarrassed to have their mother teaching in their school.

Eventually, substitute teaching developed into a full time teaching career in Bethpage, Long Island, which lasted for many years, but more about that later.

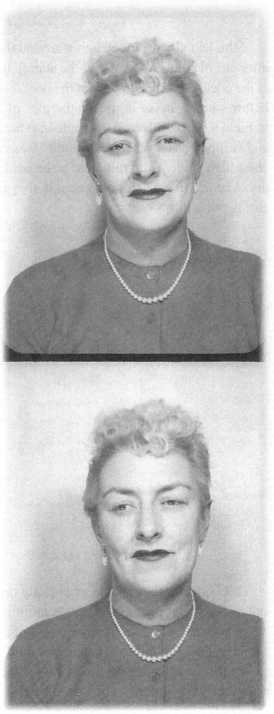

Fifi - Early sixties.

John had always loved being around the ocean and the beach, so, after our move to Long Island, he started to get into surf fishing down at the ocean beaches on the south shore. Lots of times he would get up before sunrise, make himself a thermos of hot coffee, and drive down to Field 9 at Jones Beach, to wade into the surf and fish for bluefish and stripped bass. When the weather was cold, he would put on his chest high waders and rain gear so he could wade into the surf and stay dry. And as the boys got old enough, they all started to get into surf casting with him.

John surf casting at Jones Beach - April, 1961.

Occasionally they would even camp out overnight on the beach and be fishing at daybreak the next morning. They would pitch a tent on the beach, and make a campfire out of driftwood that they would gather in the sand dunes. Then they would cook a supper of hot dogs and beans over the fire. In the morning, John would wash their frying pan in the surf, and then cook bacon and eggs over the fire for breakfast.

John with Philip and Patrick - Surf fishing at Jones Beach.
April, 1961.

I remember one time, I think it was Memorial Day weekend, when I had dropped John, Nick and Philip off at Field 9 with all their fishing and camping gear on a Saturday afternoon. The next day I drove down to the beach to meet them and see how they had survived their night on the beach. As I drove to the edge of the parking lot I could see where they had pitched their tent on the beach, so I blew the horn to let them know that I was there. John and the boys picked up their gear and started walking towards me, but as they got closer I couldn't believe my eyes. Their backs, shoulders and legs were a bright, bright red from sunburn.

We loaded everything into the car and went home. After the boys took a cool shower to wash the sand and salt off, I carefully started putting Noxzema on their sunburn, but they were both in a lot of pain. Nick's sunburn was bad, but Philip's was much worse. He actually had huge blisters on his shoulders and the tops of his feet. They went down in the playroom and sat, watching TV, but neither one of them had an appetite, and they both actually felt nauseous from the terrible sunburn covering their bodies. Their skin was so sensitive that I couldn't even put a sheet over them when they went to bed that night. At some point, Philip got up to go to the bathroom and collapsed in the hallway. They were so badly burned that it would be several days before either of them could go back to school.

John also used to take the boys fishing at the Jones Beach piers. They would go down there lots of evenings when the weather was nice, or early on weekend mornings. They would fish for hours and hours, and catch flounder, fluke and blowfish, and lots of spider crabs.

~~~

We knew when we moved into it, that the house on Mansfield Drive would only be available to rent for two years because the Seaford / Oyster Bay Expressway was going to be built right on the land that the house occupied. But John, through his real estate contacts, found out about another house, on Harding Avenue in Bellmore, that was available to rent. So, in the summer of 1961 we had to move again, and once more get the boys established in a different school district. Jack and Nick went to Mepham High School, and Philip and Brian went to the Martin Avenue Elementary School. Patrick was home with me.

On the days that I got called to substitute teach, I would leave Patrick with the next door neighbor, Nancy Gerbino. She was married to Bob Gerbino, who at the time was a physical education teacher in Seaford high school. She had two little girls that were around the same age as Patrick, so it worked out well. On some days, when I was called to work in the Seaford high school, I could even hitch a ride to work with Bob.

Patrick - April, 1961.

Jack and Nick would often walk all the way from Bellmore to Seaford, probably four or five miles, to go hang out with the Cox kids and some of their other Seaford friends. But after only a year, the owner of the house on Harding Avenue, who was in the Navy and decided to retire, needed the house back, so once more, in the summer of 1962, we had to move yet again.

For a while John and I considered moving our family back up to Westchester, to Tarrytown or Ossining, but by now the boys, especially Jack and Nick, had made lots friends on Long Island and didn't want to leave.

Philip, Brian, Jack and Nick - April, 1961.

So we looked around, weighed our options, and chose to return back to Seaford again, to a neighborhood where all the streets were named after something to do with horses. There were names like Saddle Path, Stirrup Lane, and Paddock Road, and we ended up moving into the house at 2109 Bit Path. After all, horses had always been an influence and presence in our lives, so it just made sense.

~~~

We had first actually gone with a real estate agent to look at the house next to number 2109, I think it was 2105 or 2107. The agent was showing us around that house and we had gone out into the back yard, when I happened to look to the right, toward 2109, and noticed that it had green-striped canvas awnings over the front windows and over the patio in the back yard. "Oh, that's nice," I commented, "the way those awnings are on that house."

The agent said, "Oh, that house is for sale also."

"Really," I perked up, "could I see it?"

John, never wanting to make any waves, looked at me and downplayed, "Oh Fifi, it's the same as this one."

"Fine," I chafed, "but I'd still like to see it."

So the agent took us into number 2109, and right away, the first thing I noticed was that there was a dishwasher in the kitchen, which the other house didn't have. Well, that was a big selling point for me, along with the awnings over the patio and all the front windows. It was the first house that we looked at when we came back to Seaford, and we decided that it was the one for us. Because we were still so strapped, we had to borrow money from my mother to make the down payment.

~~~

There was a big wooded area and a stream that ran behind the house that was the main selling point for the boys. They would spend their days out in the woods climbing trees, and building tree houses, or wading through the stream to catch turtles, frogs and eels. They would build secret underground forts, where they could plan their strategies during games of "War," or hide from other groups of kids, or any parents. It was a constant source of recreation and adventure for them and their friends.

~~~

On our new street, we had a whole new set of neighbors, and one of the first couples that John and I got to know was Tom and Maggie Clooney, who lived across the street from us. They had two kids, Kristin and Thomas, Jr., both of whom went to Catholic school at St. William the Abbott in Seaford. Kristin had a crush on Nick, and vice-versa.

I can remember Tom, always sitting on a lawn chair, out in their garage, on the bleakest of days. He would be smoking a cigar and drinking his martinis while he cooked a steak on the grill. I remember him as being kind of a sullen, humorless person, who seemed to have an unhappy view of the world.

His wife, Maggie, was a terrible alcoholic who would sit out on their front steps every afternoon, hoping to get one of the neighbors to come over and have a drink with her so she would have an excuse for being so pie-eyed by the time Tom got home every evening. Maggie would be so drunk every night that she would have trouble keeping her balance when she got up to go into the house. She would "goose step" all around as she walked, because I think she had lost all the feeling in her feet from all her years of excessive drinking.

I can remember that as I would be driving down the street to the house, on my way home from school in the afternoons, and see Maggie Clooney, sitting out on her front steps with a cocktail, I would try to come up with all kinds of excuses why I couldn't join her. But she was always very insistent, so sometimes I would go over and have a drink with her. Then Tom would come in, after his commute home from the city, and make a bunch of sarcastic remarks about her drinking. I don't think Maggie ever made dinner, which evoked more even more sarcastic remarks from Tom. Their son, Thomas, Jr., would do a lot of the cooking.

They had an above ground swimming pool in their back yard, and Nick, Philip and Brian would spend entire days swimming in their pool with Thomas Jr., Kristin, and some of their other friends during the summers.

~~~

Then there was Bill and Marge Miller, who also lived across the street from us, to the left of the Clooney's' house. Bill Miller was a retired New York City cop, and he and his wife, Marge, had two adopted children named Lorraine and Gary. Bill and Marge weren't very outgoing and in fact kind of prudish in some ways, and they were extremely protective of their two kids.

Their son, Gary, was a real character, and could do no wrong in their eyes, despite the fact that he had wrecked more cars than you could shake a stick at.

Lorraine attended Catholic school at Queen of the Rosary Academy in Amityville. She was a lovely girl, and she and Jack became good friends.

There was one day when Jack had gone across the street and was standing outside, talking to Lorraine. It was Patrick's birthday, December 9th, and he was probably six or seven years old, so it would have been in 1964 or 65. I had made a birthday cake for him so we could have a little party for him later that afternoon.

In those days, all my boys used to call Patrick "Fatso Fogarty," to tease him because he was kind of chunky when he was a little kid, and as Jack was talking to Lorraine across the street, I had come out onto to our

Jack and Lorraine Miller - QRA prom.
Spring, 1964.

258

front porch and started calling for Patrick to come in. Jack saw me come out on the porch, and thought he would invite Lorraine over to join us for birthday cake, so he turned to her and said, "Why don't you come over and have some birthday cake with us?"

"Okay," she said, "who's birthday is it?"

"Fatso Fogarty's," he chuckled.

"Really," said Lorraine, and with that she jumped up, started waving, and shouted across the street to me, "Happy birthday Mrs. McFadden."

Well, at that point, Jack just collapsed in laughter at Lorraine's faux pas. I stood there on the front porch wondering what it was that Jack was laughing so hysterically at, so I yelled across the street to them, "What's so funny?"

Jack yelled back, "I told Lorraine it was Fatso Fogarty's birthday today, and she thought I meant you."

Well, then I too collapsed in laughter. Poor Lorraine was so embarrassed that she wanted to crawl into a hole and disappear. But I didn't care, that little episode has provided us with lots of laughs over the years.

~~~

There was an interesting family that lived across the street and a few houses down to the left. Their name was Cody. The father, John Cody, was the President of the New York City teamsters union, but he was also reputed to have ties to the "mob." His wife, Mary, was a very friendly, quietly reserved lady. He was Irish, and she was Italian. Their oldest was a boy named Michael, and they had a daughter named Theresa.

While they were still in high school, around 1966, Michael Cody had formed a band with the kid that lived across the street from him, named Melvin Wax, and a drummer named Liberty DeVitto. There were lots of evenings during the summer when they would practice in the back yard of the Cody's house, and all the neighbors and kids from the block would gather in the back yard to listen to them play. They would play all the popular rock and roll tunes that were on the radio at the time, and they were very good. Liberty DeVitto would go on a few years later to become the drummer for the Billy Joel band.

~~~

Part of my daily routine was to walk our dog, Laddie, in the mornings, and I would often see John Cody out walking his two Doberman pincers. He was always very pleasant, and would tip his hat and say, "Good morning," to me.

Then one Saturday morning, when I was returning from grocery shopping at Waldbaums, I was driving past the Cody's house and I saw Mary sweeping broken glass out of John's Cadillac. I didn't think too much of it at the time but, later that evening, I heard some noise outside and went out on the front porch to see what it was. I could see a couple of red flashing lights down in front of the Cody's house, so I went inside and told my boys that there was, "…something going on over at the Cody's."

They all said, "Ma, come inside and mind your own business," but I walked down there anyway.

When I got to the corner, I met Herb and Rose Goudket, my next door neighbors, standing there, and there was a Nassau County Police tow truck there, towing John Cody's Cadillac away. The reason they were towing it was because all of the windows had been shot out of it the night before, while it was parked in their driveway. That had been the glass that I had seen Mary sweeping out of it earlier in the day.

~~~

A few years later, on the day that Michael Cody was getting married, Jack Gillen, our neighbor who lived across the street to the right of the Clooney's, was up doing some work on the roof of his house, and saw a line of yellow taxi cabs pull up in front of the Cody's house, and all the wedding guests got out. The men and women were all dressed to the nines, in tuxedos and furs, and everyone went into the house. Then, within a minute or two, two Nassau County Police cars showed up and parked on both sides of Natalie Boulevard, facing the Cody's house. The whole time that the guests were inside, the taxi drivers sat outside on the fenders of their cars, talking and smoking cigarettes, while the two police cars stayed posted out on Natalie

Boulevard, opposite the house. But after only about twenty minutes, when they realized that the police were parked outside, all the wedding quests started leaving. They must have thought that the police were photographing them, because all the men started pulling their coats up around their heads to hide their faces as they scurried back to the taxis and drove off. Then, after the last cab was gone, the two police cars left too.

~~~

Around 1963, John was working for a company that sold insurance policies to gas and service stations. John had the east coast sales region, and was given a beautiful motor home so that he could travel up and down the east coast to visit all the gas stations, to meet with the owners about their insurance needs.

The motor home was about thirty-five feet long. It had a small kitchenette that would convert into a double bed, a couch that also would fold out into a double bed, and two sets of bunk beds in the rear, so it could sleep a total of eight people. There was a small bathroom with a shower in the rear, and the kitchenette had a small stove, oven and refrigerator. It was all self-contained, and the lights, refrigerator and air conditioning could all run off a separate generator when you weren't driving.

John J. McFadden - 1961.

John would get up very early on Monday mornings and leave in the motor home, to go do business down in south Jersey, Pennsylvania and Maryland, and be gone most of the week. The camper would serve as his transportation, mobile office, restaurant and sleeping quarters while he was away on the road. During the summer, when they were off from school, the boys would all take turns going on trips with John, and sometimes he would even take our dachshund, Fritz.

~~~

One week, Jack and Nick went with their father on the road to south Jersey, and one evening they pulled the camper into a campsite for the night and had hooked up to the water and electric services. John was getting ready to cook some Cornish game hens for their dinner, when the boys asked him if they could go to see a movie at a drive-in theater that they had passed a little earlier on the road. So John told them to go to a pay phone and call the drive-in to see if they would allow the camper in. The manager of the drive-in told Jack that they could come in, but they would have to park in the rear.

So John turned off the stove, disconnected from the utility hook-ups, and off they drove to the drive-in, and when they got there, the manager came out to see the camper and show them where to park. John offered him a drink and he ended up staying and watching the movie with John and the boys, and even had some of the Cornish game hens with them.

~~~

When John would get home, on Thursdays or Fridays, I would stock up the camper's refrigerator with food, and all the boys would go to sleep in the bunks. Then John and I would get up before dawn and we'd all head out to Montauk Point for the weekend. The boys could sleep the whole time we were driving, and would wake up just about the time that we were reaching Montauk, all the way out on the east end of Long Island.

We would find an isolated area near a beach where we could park and camp for the weekend. The kids would play on the beach and in the ocean all day, it was great. I remember one Sunday afternoon when I had a turkey breast roasting in the oven, the boys were all playing in the surf, and John and I were contently watching them while we sat, relaxing in the captains chairs of the camper, sipping martinis in air conditioned comfort. Boy, talk about "gracious living".

~~~

These types of self-contained motor homes were pretty rare in those days, and just starting to become popular. I remember one of the first times that we took it out to Montauk, we made a stop at the Shinnicock Canal in Hampton Bays so that the boys could see how the boats would pass through the canal's locks, to go from the ocean on the south shore, to the Peconic Bay, between the north and south forks of Long Island. While we were there, several other families came over to look and admire the camper, so we let them come inside to see how the kitchenette, bathroom, bunks and everything was arranged.

Most of the times that we went out East with the camper we would stay at a place called Ditch Plains, just a couple of miles west of Montauk Point, because they were set up with camp sites for trailers, with water and electrical hook-ups. I think there was even a restaurant or bar there where John and I could go in to have a cocktail.

~~~

During one of our trips to the East end, there was a Sunday that one of the fishing boats from the Montauk fishing fleet must have capsized or something, because a lot of bluefish and stripped bass washed up on the beach. The boys had a field day collecting some of the fish as they washed up in the surf, and that night John filleted and cooked some of them for dinner.

While we were eating, Patrick suddenly started gasping for air and grabbing at his throat. He was choking on something, and when I looked down his throat I could see a big fish bone lodged there, but I couldn't reach it to get it out.

We quickly packed up the camper and started driving West on Montauk Highway, looking for the nearest hospital. Because it was late Sunday afternoon on a summer weekend, there was a lot of traffic headed back west from Montauk and the Hamptons, and thankfully we saw a cop directing traffic.

The cop gave us directions to an emergency clinic that was nearby and, when we got there, the doctor was able to reach into Patrick's throat with a big, long set of tweezers, and removed the fish bone.

John and Patrick - Jones Beach - August, 1967.

~~~

We had many memorable weekends in that camper, but I think the most memorable one of all was the time when we were leaving Ditch Plains and had to empty the camper's septic tank before we hit the road to head home.

There was a public sewage disposal area, not far from Ditch Plains, where we had to go to drain the septic tank. I remember driving up a big hill, and, when we got to the top, there was a huge rectangular septic basin that looked like an Olympic sized swimming pool, only bigger, filled to the top with greenish brown sludge. And it smelled to high heaven.

John pulled the camper up next to the edge of the basin and started to hook up the discharge hose to the camper's septic tank, and all the boys and our dog, Fritz, the dachshund, jumped out of the camper and ran around to the other side of the sewage basin and were playing in the sand dunes. It took about ten minutes for John to drain the septic tank and re-stow the discharge hose, and when he finished, he yelled across the sewage basin, to the boys on the other side, and told them it was time to leave.

All the boys came running around the sewage basin, back to the camper, but Fritz didn't. He stayed, sitting on the other side of this huge pool of raw sewage, looking around and not knowing what to do. When all the boys got back to the camper, they turned around and realized that Fritz hadn't come with them. Then, when they saw him still sitting on the other side, they all started calling him, whistling and clapping for him to come to them.

At that point Fritz jumped up but, to our revulsion, he didn't run around the edge of the septic pool, he jumped right into it and started to swim across to us. All of us started screaming and laughing at the sight of poor Fritz dog paddling through the raw sewage with just his head visible above the surface. As he was getting closer to our side, the boys realized that he would try to shake himself dry when he got out, and they started climbing trees to get away from him. John started yelling at me to get some towels.

Fritz climbed up out of the sewage, panting and wagging his tail, apparently exhilarated after his little swim, then John got him and wiped him down with a towel, but still none of the boys would go near him. Then John put his leash on him and tied him up in the shower stall in the rear of the camper. We drove a few miles till we found a gas station, where we hosed him off and washed him with shampoo.

~~~

In June of 1967 I was invited to a graduation party, in Queens, for a girl that had been doing her student teaching with me. Nick was going to be driving his girlfriend, Phyllis Smith, back into Lennox Hill

Nursing School in the city that day, so he dropped me off at the party in Queens, and continued on in with Phyllis. After he dropped her off at Lennox Hill, he came back to pick me up at the party. He picked me up at around 11:00PM, and I got in the car and immediately fell asleep as we headed East, out to long Island.

Fifi, Nick, Phyllis and John.

Nick had had a long day that day. He and Phyllis had been down at Jones Beach all day before they drove into the city with me, and I didn't realize how tired he was. We drove down the Wantagh Parkway, and then took the exit ramp to get onto Sunrise Highway. Nick remembers looking over his left shoulder towards Bellmore, to see if it was clear to merge onto Sunrise Highway, but then he must have closed his eyes for a split second. I don't remember exactly what woke me up, if it was the bump of the car going over the curb, or if Nick yelled, but I looked up and could see the leaves of the trees brushing against my window and the windshield. Nick was trying to steer the car back to the left, back onto the road. Then the right front fender of the car slammed into the corner of the stone bridge abutment, and my right leg went completely numb from the knee down.

266

Nick had only had the car for about a month, and at first he started bemoaning it's fate, "Oh my car, my car, it's wrecked." I must have hit my face on the dashboard, because my nose was bleeding, so I got some Kleenex out of my pocket book and held them to my nose.

I could see a public phone booth a little ways down Sunrise Highway, at the corner of Wantagh Avenue, so I said, "Nick, you've got to go to that phone and call home and tell them what's happened." And in my minds eye I can still see Nick running over the bridge towards Wantagh Avenue.

As Nick was running to the phone, a police car drove past, and then backed up when he saw our car, so Nick ran back to talk to the cop. Another police car arrived a minute or two later. One of the cops was outside talking to Nick, and the other cop opened the driver's side door and asked me, "Are you all right?"

I just said, "I think my leg is broken."

So he shined his flashlight down by my legs and I heard him mutter, "Oh my God," to himself.

A third cop came to the passenger side of the car and tried to open my door, but it wouldn't budge. He looked in at me and saw that besides the bloody nose, I had gotten a very bad cut on my right elbow, and a big flap of skin was hanging from my arm. I hadn't even noticed that until he pointed it out. He went back to his police car and came back with a first aid kit, and bandaged my arm.

Within a few minutes an ambulance arrived, and they had to get me out of the car and onto a stretcher. One of the cops got into the back seat to help lift me out. They had to cradle both of my legs so they could swing them over and get me out through the driver's door. The cop in the back said, "This is gonna hurt ma'am," then they swung my legs over and got me out onto the stretcher. My leg was still numb and I still didn't know the extent of my injury, but they got me into the ambulance. Nick was sitting next to me and fortunately, thank God, he only had a small bump on his head.

The accident had happened only about a mile from our house and someone passing by had recognized Nick's car and stopped at the house to tell the rest of the family what had happened. Then John and Jack came up to the scene of the accident.

I had been wearing my fur stole, and Jack was standing by my feet at the rear door of the ambulance, so I gave him my fur piece and my pocketbook and told him to take them home. Poor Nick kept taking my face in his hands and patting my cheeks, saying, "Don't close your eyes Mom! Don't close your eyes!"

John followed us to the emergency room at the Nassau County Medical Center and I can still remember the emergency room doctor holding the bottom of my right foot and saying, "I'm not getting a pulse." So he pulled down on my foot and felt again, then he said, "Okay, now I have a pulse." He had realized that the broken bones were somehow constricting the arteries in my leg. If they hadn't gotten a pulse, they would have had to amputate my leg.

This is kind of funny, not "Ha ha" funny, just odd, but one of the things I remember from that night was that, as they were wheeling me into the X-ray room, the paramedics were talking and joking about a man who had been brought in earlier in the night with pellets in his behind from a shotgun wound. I never did actually see that poor guy.

The next thing I remember was looking up at some X-rays of a broken leg. "Someone has a nasty broken leg," I said, not realizing that the x-rays that I was looking at were of my own leg. There was a big jagged break below the knee.

Then they rushed me into the operating room, where there was this tall man in scrubs, pushing his glasses up the bridge of this nose. His name was Doctor Nackman, and he was the surgeon who was going to try to save my leg.

He started moving the bottom half of my leg, which had me screaming in agony. There was a black man in green operating room scrubs, standing behind my head, putting up a stainless steel bar and hanging a screen over it so that I couldn't see what they were doing. I was screaming at them to leave my leg alone, "Don't touch my leg! Don't touch my leg!", I pleaded.

The black guy tried to calm me down, saying sedately, "Take it easy ma'am, it's all in your head."

But I glared angrily up at him and screamed, "I kid you not."

The next morning I woke up in a huge plaster cast, up to the middle of my thigh, with two steel pins going through it. One was high on my shin, and the other was just above the ankle. Doctor Nackman was leaning over the bed talking to me. He said, "Figure eighteen months." He was talking about how long I would need to be in the cast. My right arm had a bandage wrapped around it where they had stitched up the gash on my elbow.

Later that day, the black doctor, who had been behind me in the operating room, and two others, one who I called "The Plaster Man," took me, bed and all, down the hall. I asked, "Where are you taking me?"

"To the 'plaster room'," they answered, "we have to work on you."

The three of them took me into a room and started working on the cast on my leg. They started cutting the cast with a thing that looked like a pizza cutter. Boy did that hurt, as the vibrations from the "pizza cutter" aggravated my freshly broken bones.

I found out later, that, after they had put me in the original cast, they took some more X-rays and realized that the gap between the broken bones was too big to heal. So they removed a section of the cast, between the steel pins, pushed my leg up to close the gap between the bones, and re-plastered the cast together. Because of this, my right leg ended up being over a half an inch shorter than my left leg. It took months and months before the gap finally started to heal and knit together. To this day I have a lump on my shin where the gap had been, and the bones never really set in the right alignment.

I couldn't get out of the hospital bed for eight or nine days, but finally the doctor said that I could go home. He said that I should try walking with the aid of either crutches or a walker. So a little while later, Plaster Man came in to see me, and gave me the choice of either crutches or a walker. I chose a walker. He came back a few minutes later with a walker, and told me to, "Swing your legs over the side of the bed." Before I even tried, I had visions of being able to move around pretty easily with the walker. But little did I know. When I swung my legs over the side of the bed, I thought I was going to catapult right across the room. The weight of the cast almost flipped me right out of the bed. When I looked down, I could finally see the toes on my right foot for the first time since the accident. They were black.

I started to hop on my left foot, leaning on the walker with both arms. It was much harder than I had anticipated, and I didn't think I would make it to the door of my room. When I finally reached the door, Plaster Man told me to lean back against the door jam, while he took the walker from me and adjusted the height. By now I had broken out in a cold sweat and my right leg was throbbing. Fortunately, he told me to head back to the bed. So I hopped back to the bed, and when I reached it I literally threw myself, gasping, onto it, and Plaster Man had to lift both of my legs up onto the mattress.

~~~

The next day I was released from the hospital, and John came to pick me up. I remember that when we pulled up in front of the house, Patrick came running out to me in the car. He was all excited, shouting, "Mommy, Mommy, I got a gerbil."

While I had been in the hospital, John had gotten a hospital bed from the Seaford Lions Club and set it up in the dining room, under the window that looked out onto the back yard. He had also gotten a wheel chair and a commode. Everything was set up so that I didn't have too go up or down any stairs. For some reason, he had also gone to the pet shop and bought a gerbil for Patrick.

Thank God, Jack was home from college and was able to take over the running of the house. He did the laundry, he cooked, he vacuumed, he did everything.

Jack - Febuary, 1971.

That first night home from the hospital, John set himself up to sleep on the living room couch so he would be near to me if I needed anything. As we were all settling down to sleep, and the house was getting quiet, I suddenly heard something go, "Eeek, eeek, eeek."

"What the hell is that?", I asked to nobody in particular.

John replied, "Oh, it must be Patrick's gerbil," which was in a cardboard box down in the playroom. He went downstairs, and when he came back up he told me he had, "…put the gerbil out in the garage."

The next day, when Patrick came home from school, he ran right downstairs to check on his new pet. A minute later he came running back up and asked, "Mom, where's my gerbil?" I explained that his father had put the box out in the garage, and off he ran again. He came bursting back up a few minutes later all excited, and exclaimed at the top of his lungs, "It had babies." Then he ran back down to his new gerbil family.

I shook my head and thought to myself, "Great, that's just what we need, a bunch of baby rats."

But then he was back up to me again very quickly, with a disconcerted look on his face. "Where's the other one?" he asked solemnly.

"What other one, Honey?", I asked, weakly smiling through the pain in my leg.

He proceeded to tell me that, the day before, there had been two adult gerbils, but now there was, "…only one big one and a bunch of babies."

Well, I wasn't smiling anymore. "What the hell do you mean? Does this mean we have a gerbil running around loose in the house? Give me my walker, I'll go down and kill the damn thing right now."

Anyway, Patrick and Jack started looking for the missing gerbil by putting out food for it. Jack finally found it behind his old, antique pump organ down in the playroom. So I told them to put the box with all the gerbils in it out in the backyard, and put a screen over it so they couldn't get out. From my hospital bed I could see the box out on the patio, under the dining room window.

At the time, we had a cat that the kids had named "Crazy Cat," because its front legs were shorter than its back legs. John said the cat looked deformed, like it was always walking "downhill." Anyway, Crazy Cat would sit on the screen, on top of the box, and stare down at the gerbils. I never saw the screen off the box, so I don't know how, but they all eventually disappeared.

~~~

I had broken my leg right near the end of the school year, and one day, shortly after I got home from the hospital, several of the administration from Bethpage high school; George McElroy, Vinnie Parlotta and John Mazur, came to the house to visit me. They told me about who had covered my classes and given my final exams in the last two weeks of school. They never once intimated that I wouldn't have my job back once my leg healed, even though they knew it was going to be a long process before I would be even be able to walk again. The whole conversation was based around when I would be returning to work.

After they left and went back to school, Vinnie called to tell me that he had arranged it so that all my classes the following year would be in one classroom, next to the elevator, on the second floor. He had even made arrangements with the teacher in the adjacent classroom, to assist me in the event of a fire drill or something.

~~~

A week or two after I got home from the hospital, two of my co-workers from Bethpage called to say they were on the way over to visit me. I asked Jack to put Laddie, our Shetland sheepdog, down in the playroom, because he would always bark at anyone at the door, and wouldn't let them in. He was harmless, but the women would have been intimidated by him. After they arrived, the three of us where sitting in the living room, chatting. I was in the wheelchair with my leg extended straight out in front of me, and Jack was sitting in the room with us, reading the newspaper. A little while later Brian came home, and Laddie started barking down in the playroom when he heard Brian come in through the front door.

I finally said to Brian, "Oh, go let Laddie come up here, he should be okay by now," so Brian let the dog up into the living room with us and started petting him.

Brian and Laddie - Spring, 1969.

Then Brian boasted to the two women, "I've been teaching Laddie how to do some tricks, would you like to see them?" He motioned with his hand and said, "Roll over," and Laddie rolled over. Then he motioned in the opposite direction, and Laddie rolled over the other way. The two women "ooohed" and "ahhhed" at Laddie's display of tricks, then suddenly, Laddie, still very excited because of the two strangers in the house, squatted in the middle of the living room and

273

did a big load of dog poop, right there on the rug. Well, Brian collapsed on the floor, laughing. The two women were appalled and didn't know what to do or say. I was mortified with embarrassment.

Then, with meticulous comic timing, Jack glanced up over the top of his newspaper and very matter of factly asked, "That's great Brian, what does he do for an encore?" Needless to say, that brought the house down, and we all roared with laughter. My two friends left soon after, with a story that they couldn't wait to tell the rest of my co-workers at school.

~~~~

That turned out to be a rough month because, only a few weeks after the car accident that broke my leg, Patrick broke his wrist in gym at school. Doctor Nackman also set his wrist and put a cast on it.

About eight weeks after the car accident, John took Patrick and me to Doctor Nackman's office for our respective injuries. While we were sitting in the waiting room, another patient looked over at the two of us in our casts and commented, "Geez, that must have been some accident."

"No," I chuckled, "it was actually two separate accidents."

That day, the doctor changed Patrick's cast and took the two steel pins out of my leg. I can remember that I was lying flat on the examination table, and the nurse was holding my hand. I could hear him ask the nurse for some tools. Then he used some kind of saw to cut off both of the steel pins close to the cast, on the inside of my leg. As he was cutting, I could feel the pins kind of moving and vibrating in my leg. Then I heard him ask the nurse for the pliers. I felt like I was a project in Shop Class. He grabbed on to the pins with the pliers and, one at a time, pulled them out of my leg. I could hear each one make a sucking noise as it was pulled out through the flesh and bone of my leg, and I was screaming the whole time. When it was over, I was lying exhausted on the table and asked weakly, "Why didn't you give me something to knock me out, or at least warn me?"

"Oh come on Honey," the nurse said condescendingly, "that didn't hurt so much. It's like taking a skewer out of a roast chicken."

"Yeah sure," I snapped back, "but the chicken is dead."

When school started the following September, John would drive me to work in the mornings, and an aide would come out to the car with a wheelchair. I'd hop out of the car on one leg and get into the chair, and they would tuck my attaché case next to me, between my hip and the side of the wheelchair. Then the aide would push me into the building, to my classroom. I would use an overhead projector for some of my lessons, and all the students were very cooperative when I came back to school.

Fifi in leg cast - June, 1968.

Sometimes, some of my students would push me around in my wheelchair to get from place to place. They would get a kick out of bringing me, in my wheelchair, to the top of the stairs, then asking me if I wanted to, "…go downstairs."

Later that year, as my leg healed and I could start to put some weight on it, I would sometimes walk down the hall, leaning on the wheelchair and pushing it in front of me. I had a canvas boot on, over my cast, which would make a "swooshing" noise as I dragged my bad leg along. The kids would hear the "swoosh, swoosh, swoosh", coming down the hall and remark, "Oh oh, here comes Mrs. McFadden."

~~~

I was able to finish that entire school year with the cast on. During the thirteen months that I had it on, Doctor Nackman changed it six times. Every time he changed it, they would wash my leg and rub it down with alcohol. It would feel so good. Finally, thirteen months to the day after the accident, he took the cast off and very casually said, "Okay Fifi, you can leave."

Well, I hadn't been expecting that. I thought he would just change the cast again, so I wasn't quite ready for this. "Go ahead," he insisted, "you can walk on it."

At first I was afraid that my leg would just collapse under me. I still couldn't bend my knee, and I was afraid to put weight on it, so I had John bring me out to the car in the wheelchair.

That night I was sitting in the living room, in the wheelchair, when Nick came in. He looked at my leg and exclaimed, "Is that skin I see?", he was so relieved to see that I was finally out of the cast. Then he and Jack got on either side of me and helped me up the stairs to my bedroom. When I got up the next morning I still didn't trust my leg, so I limped cautiously down the hall, sat down at the top of the stairs, and went down them, one at a time, on my fanny. One of the boys kept an eye on me as I went down, until I got to the bottom.

For the next thirty years, until I got my hip replaced, I walked with a severe limp because my right leg was over a half an inch shorter than my left. When I had the hip replacement in 1998, the doctors were able to adjust the length of my right leg, and even it out, to eliminate my limp.

~~~

At some point, during the late sixties, my mother's health was beginning to fail and it was becoming difficult for her to live alone in the big house on Union Avenue. Finally, one day Mary tried to call her but she didn't answer the phone, so Larry and Jimmy went over to the house to check on her. When they got inside they found Mother on the floor of her bedroom. She had fallen and was unable to get up, and had somehow ended up almost completely under the bed. So Mary and Larry brought her down to live with them in their house on Rosehill Avenue.

Mary and Mother - January, 1971.

But after a while, as her health continued to deteriorate, Mary and Larry decided that she needed a greater level of care than what they were able to provide, and, after looking at their options, they decided to bring her to a nursing home. However, her stay there was very short-lived. She called Mary the next day, in tears, crying that she didn't want to stay there and was very unhappy. So Mary went and picked her up and brought back to their house that same day.

Nama Egan - Spring, 1968.

Then, in early January of 1971, she suffered a stroke and fell again at Mary and Larry's house. This time she also broke her hip in the fall, so there was a minor debate over the cause. Did she fall and break her hip, causing the stroke, or did the stroke cause her to fall, breaking her hip?

But what did any of that matter? All I knew was that I wasn't able to comfort her, and I felt helpless and guilty about that. I just remember driving up to Tarrytown to see her in the hospital, but her eyes were closed. I tried to talk to her, but I couldn't tell if she could hear me, she was so unresponsive. She never opened her eyes again, and passed away three days later on January 11th, 1971.

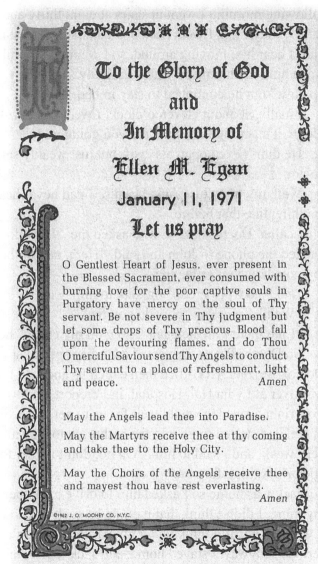

To the Glory of God
and
In Memory of

Ellen M. Egan

January 11, 1971

Let us pray

O Gentlest Heart of Jesus, ever present in the Blessed Sacrament, ever consumed with burning love for the poor captive souls in Purgatory have mercy on the soul of Thy servant. Be not severe in Thy judgment but let some drops of Thy precious Blood fall upon the devouring flames, and do Thou O merciful Saviour send Thy Angels to conduct Thy servant to a place of refreshment, light and peace. Amen

May the Angels lead thee into Paradise.

May the Martyrs receive thee at thy coming and take thee to the Holy City.

May the Choirs of the Angels receive thee and mayest thou have rest everlasting. Amen

©1962 J. O. MOONEY CO., N.Y.C.

In the early fall of 1969 there was a week or so when John hadn't been feeling well and was very tired all the time. One evening he asked me to wake him up by eight thirty the next day. So, the following morning I went upstairs at eight thirty and woke him up. He said, "Okay," and I went back downstairs. Over the next hour or so I didn't hear him moving around, so I went up several more times to wake him. Each time he would groggily say, "Okay, okay, I'm getting up now," but he continued to stay in bed.

Finally, at about eleven o'clock, I went back upstairs and nagged, "John, it's getting late, what are you going to do?"

He didn't even open his eyes, but just weakly said, "Call the doctor."

Well, my heart just sank, because I had never heard him say anything like that before.

I called Doctor Pazow, who asked me, "How does he feel?", so I handed the phone to John and said, "Here, talk to the doctor, he wants to know how you're feeling.

"No," he whispered, "you talk to him."

"Well," I pressed, "how do you feel?"

"Like there's an elephant sitting on my chest," he murmured.

So Doctor Pazow contacted a cardiac specialist by the name of Doctor Weizner. His office then called us and said that Doctor Weizner was over at Lydia Hall Hospital, in Freeport, and we should bring John over right away. He would wait for us to get there. So John got up out of bed and started to go into the bathroom to take a shower. But he was very weak, and I said to him, "Oh no, don't bother to shower, the doctor's waiting for you."

Jack was home so I asked him to drive his father to the hospital. In my mind, I didn't think that it could be such a serious problem. Maybe it was just wishful thinking on my part, that I didn't want it to be serious. Anyway, I stayed home, and Jack took John to the hospital.

Finally, at about four o'clock in the afternoon, Jack called me from the hospital and reported, "Mom, I had to admit Dad."

I was surprised by this, and asked, "Why," but Jack wasn't sure.

"What time are the visiting hours?", I inquired, figuring that I would go over to the hospital as soon as I could.

Jack said, "I don't know Mom. I don't think there are visiting hours where they have him."

"What do you mean?", I asked.

"They have him in 'I' something.", he explained vaguely.

"You mean ICU?" I prompted nervously, already dreading his answer.

"Yeah," he confirmed, "I think so."

"Oh, Jack Honey," I said, abandoning any trace of composure, "that's the Intensive Care Unit." And that's when I realized that the situation was indeed very serious.

I called Doctor Pazow again, and he told me that he had spoken to Doctor Weizner, and that John was in very grave condition. So I called Doctor Weizner and spoke to him. He quickly briefed me on the status of John's condition and then told me that he would meet me outside the Intensive Care Unit at ten minutes to seven that night. So when I met him in the hallway later on, Doctor Weizner told me, "John's going to have a heart attack. I don't know when, but it's going to happen. When he came in this afternoon, his heart rate was over two hundred. He may not know you when you go in to see him," he added, "we have him heavily sedated."

When I went into his room, John's eyes were closed, and he was hooked up to a lot of machines. The heart monitor would go up to one-eighty, then down to seventy-five, and then back up. It was all over the place. I tried to talk to him, but he didn't respond.

The next day, when I was going over to the hospital, I called the doctor and asked him if it would be all right if I brought Patrick over to see his father. Patrick was only ten years old at the time, so the doctor left it up to my discretion as to whether or not Pat would be okay to see his father in that condition. I decided to take him.

John ended up staying in Lydia Hall hospital for about a month, and during that time he had two cardiac arrests. During one of them, one of the nurses told me that she had to jump right up on the bed to do CPR on him until they got him back. After about three weeks in ICU, he was moved to a regular room.

John hated being in the hospital and wanted desperately to go home, so finally Doctor Weizner said he could be released. They had gotten him stabilized with medication, and the doctor gave him strict instructions that he was not to drink or smoke.

The next day, when I went to pick him up and bring him home from the hospital, I was dreading what the cost would be. Because John had been self-employed, and money was always so tight, he didn't have any health insurance. I had medical insurance through my job at school, but I had never had to use it, and didn't know what it would or wouldn't cover. I brought Patrick with me that day, and I joked with him that we might have to leave him as collateral to get his father out of the hospital.

When I went to the front desk, to get the release papers, the woman took out a big file folder containing John's records. She told me that John had set a hospital record for the number of EKGs that they had done on him, and I thought to myself, "Oh my God, this is going to be like the war debt." I asked, "How much do we owe?", and braced myself for the answer.

She flipped through some of the papers, then looked up at me and said, "A dollar fifty, for phone calls from his room."

I couldn't believe it, but I thought to myself, "Thank God for the medical insurance."

So we brought him home that day. Philip and Patrick had come with me to get him, and it was Phil's eighteenth birthday, October 17, 1969. After we got him home, John sat on the couch in the living room just watching some TV and taking it easy. Then after a while I suggested that he go upstairs to bed, and I would make dinner, bring it upstairs and eat with him. So we all went up and ate dinner on TV trays, in the bedroom with John. After dinner and a couple of TV shows, we all settled in to our beds and went to sleep.

Jack, Patrick, Nick, Brian and Philip. - September 27, 1969.

Then, at about four o'clock in the morning, John reached over, touched my arm, and said that he had to go to the bathroom. He got up and went into the bathroom, and closed the door. After a few minutes, I heard the toilet flush. Then the bathroom door opened, and I can remember seeing his silhouette standing in the bathroom doorway. As I looked at him, he started to lean to one side, and I realized that he was falling. I screamed and went right over the foot of the bed to try to catch him, but I was too late. He passed out, and collapsed on the bedroom floor, hitting his head against the doorjamb on the way down.

He was lying on the floor, face up with his eyes open, but unresponsive. Nick was away on his honeymoon with Phyllis, but Jack, Phil, Brian and Patrick all came running into our bedroom. I yelled at them not to touch their father. I thought he was dead.

I ran over and grabbed the phone on the night table, and called 911. I told the operator that, "My husband is a cardiac patient and just came home from the hospital today, and he's collapsed on the bedroom floor."

"Okay," she instructed, "don't hang up," then she asked me our name and address and told me to, "Hang on." A few seconds later, she came back on the line and said that the police and ambulance were on the way.

We had two dogs at the time, Laddie and Mugs, and I knew that Laddie wouldn't let the police into the house when they arrived, so I ran downstairs to put the dogs down in the playroom. As I tried to grab them, Laddie, right on queue, made a big poop in the hallway, right at the top of the playroom stairs. That was how he reacted anytime there was any excitement in the house. So there I was, with a bunch of paper towels in my hands, cleaning up Laddie's mess when the police officers arrived. I let them in and sent them up to the bedroom.

Then I thought to myself, "I have to call Doctor Weizner, and tell him what's happened." So I picked up the phone in the kitchen to call him, and when I put it to my ear I heard the 911 operator.

"I told you not to hang up," she scolded, "now stay on the line with me." Then she grilled, "Who's your doctor?",

I told her, "Doctor Weizner," and gave her the doctor's phone number.

Again she warned, "Now don't hang up," and she put me on hold as she went to contact the doctor. Finally she came back on the line and said, "Your doctor says to take your husband to the emergency room immediately." The police were already up with John, so I thanked her, then hung up and ran back upstairs.

John had come to, and was sitting up on the floor. He was confused and upset, and he had a bump on his head from where he had hit the door jamb as he fell. Then the paramedics arrived and brought up a stretcher so they could take him out to an ambulance. When John saw the stretcher he became very upset and started to weep, and I could hear the defeat in his voice as he sighed hoarsely, "I don't want to go back to the hospital."

I tried to comfort him, saying, "John honey, you have to go, but it's okay, we'll be with you." So the paramedics took him out and put him in the ambulance. Philip and I got in and rode with him, back to Lydia Hall hospital, and Jack followed in the car.

I can't remember exactly what happened after we got to the hospital, but they put John back in the ICU for observation, He ended up staying in the hospital for about ten days that time, between ICU and a regular room. The doctor explained that he hadn't had another heart attack, it was just that when he stood up in the bathroom, his blood pressure dropped, which caused him to pass out. But it caused quite a scare for all of us, especially John.

~~~

After that, John had to take it very easy. Then, the following June, he and I took Patrick out to his sister Dolores's summer house out on Lake Erie in Madison, Ohio. It was John's fiftieth birthday, and Dolores's brother in law, Father John Mulligan's birthday too, so Dolores had a little party for the two of them.

John's father had died of a heart attack at the tender age of forty-nine, and for all of his life John had always said that he too would die at forty-nine, because his father had. I don't know why he felt that way, he just had this very fatalistic attitude about it. So much so that it almost became a self fulfilling prophecy. That day out at the lake house I looked at John, smiled and wished him a "Happy fiftieth birthday," and added, "My God, you made it in spite of yourself."

John with his sister Dolores and her husband Gene Mulligan at their house in Madison, Ohio.

~~~

Over the next seven years, John was in and out of hospitals on a regular basis because of his heart problems. His sister Dottie and her husband, Bill Bassett, were familiar with a good cardiologist at Phelps Memorial hospital, in North Tarrytown, by the name of Doctor Finucan, so John started seeing him and spent a lot of time up at Phelps when he wasn't feeling well. Also, Doctor Finucan sent John up to New Haven Hospital in Connecticut to have some testing done, to see if he would be a candidate for open heart surgery.

In those days, open heart surgery, valve replacement and those kinds of things were just in their infancy, not nearly as commonplace as they are today. Doctor Finucan spoke to us about a heart surgeon in New York City who was having a lot of success with open heart surgeries. He said to John, "I don't know how you would feel about it, but he's black."

"That doesn't matter to me." John bristled, "I don't care if he has polka dots, as long as he's a good surgeon."

We were told that John would have to stay at Phelps, following the testing in New Haven, until the heart surgery could be scheduled and performed by the doctor in New York City.

Then, the following week, I took the train from Seaford to Grand Central, then up to Tarrytown. I was going to visit John at Phelps, and then stay over at my sister Mary's. Before I left the house I spoke to him on the phone, and he told me that his cousin, Vera Foley, and her husband, Bobby Dorn, were there visiting him, and he said that he was, "…feeling pretty good." It took a few hours for me to get up there by train, but when I finally walked into his room Vera and Bobby were gone, and I could tell that John wasn't feeling very well.

He was starting to sweat profusely, so I went out into the hall and got the head nurse, who was a woman that had gone to school with my sisters, Helen and Mary, named Marie Cancro. She brought in some clean towels and started mopping the sweat from John's head and chest. Then they took him back down to ICU again.

When I finally saw Marie again, a few hours later, she said, "I hoped you didn't realize it when we were up here, but John was having another heart attack."

"I kind of thought so," I confided, "just by the way he was sweating so heavily."

~~~

That heart attack proved to be a big problem. Because it caused additional damage to John's heart, the doctors decided that he was no longer a good candidate for the open heart surgery that they had been considering, and they would only be able to treat his condition with drugs. He tried to continue to work but found that he no longer had any stamina. During the stretches that he did work, in between stays in the hospital, it wasn't uncommon that he would be too tired and weak, and often could work only one or two days a week.

Despite Doctor Weizner telling him that he had to give up smoking and drinking, he never really did, not completely. The doctor would ask him, "How are you doing with the cigarettes John?" and he'd admit, "Oh, I have one here and there," but it was more than just "here and there."

He had lost a lot of weight, and that weakened him too, but there were many days, when he had been too weak to go to work, that he would come down from the bedroom at maybe two o'clock in the afternoon and fix himself some bacon and eggs and home fried potatoes, all things that he shouldn't have been eating. Then he'd leave the kitchen a mess and go back up to bed. There were many days that I left for school thinking that John would also be leaving soon to go to work, but I'd get home in the afternoon, and as I turned the car onto Bit Path, I'd see John's car, still parked in front of the house, and I'd realize, "Oh sugar. He's not feeling good again."

Some days, if he was feeling better, he would take Patrick and drive down to the Jones Beach fishing piers, to go fishing. He loved that. He didn't even care if he caught a fish or not, he just loved being by the water.

~~~

During those years when John was sick, I was attending evening classes to complete my graduate work at Hofstra University. I would make him dinner when I got home from school at night, but there were lots of nights that he just didn't feel like eating. He was on a lot of medication, so he kept a pad and pencil next to his bed where he tried to keep track of all of the pills that he had to take every day. And every night was a vigil. I would wake up, in the wee hours, and listen, in the quiet of the dark, to make sure that he was still breathing.

~~~

I remember one night when John, Patrick and I had been down in the living room watching TV, and John was sitting in his leather recliner. I think it was in late 1974 or 1975. Patrick was about sixteen years old, and was the only one of the boys still living at home at the time.

John - August 2, 1972.

I had dozed off on the couch, but I woke up to hear Patrick anxiously trying to rouse his father, "Dad? Dad?"

John had passed out while sitting in his chair. Patrick had started to say something to him then realized that his father wasn't responding to him. I told Patrick to go upstairs and get a cold, wet facecloth, and we put that on his forehead. Then I got a some brandy, and made John sip a little of it.

He came to, but was all confused, and asked, "What happened? What's going on?" I told him that he had passed out again and that I was going to call Doctor Weizner. That got him very upset, as he knew that the doctor would probably put him back in the hospital. When I insisted on calling the doctor he got very angry and growled, "Well, that's it, it's finally out in the open. You and Patrick just want to get rid of me."

When Patrick heard his father say that, he got so upset that he bellowed, "Jesus Christ," swearing so loud that I thought the whole neighborhood would hear him, then he turned and smashed his fist through the glass of the front storm door, yanked it open, almost ripping it off it's hinges, and stormed off into the night.

I didn't know where he was going, so, after I made sure that John was stable, I got in the car and went out to look for him, but I couldn't find him and went back to the house. About a half an hour later, Patrick called me from a pay phone and said he was downtown in Seaford. I asked him if he had cut his hand and he said, "No, I'm okay," and said that he would be home soon. He came back in a little while later, and never said a word about the "incident." We all just acted like nothing had happened.

John, Nick, Brian, Philip, Patrick and Fifi - Brian and Debbie's wedding - 1974.

John never wanted any attention brought to himself or his condition. He was always very afraid that the doctor would put him back in the hospital, and he just hated hospitals with a passion.

~~~

I was teaching summer school in the summer of 1976, and one afternoon when I got home, Patrick was outside in the street throwing a football around with his friend, John Gillen, one of the neighbors' kids. I went into the house and put down my pocket book and attaché case on the dining room table. Then I called upstairs to John, but he didn't answer me. I thought that maybe he was sleeping so I quietly walked upstairs and into our bedroom. John was lying in bed, his head turned away from me, facing the window. I called out his name again, softly, because I didn't want to startle him, but he didn't respond. As I walked around the foot of the bed I said, "John. John," a little louder, but still he didn't stir. As I got around to the other side of the bed, I could see that his right arm was extended out off the bed, and his eyes were closed. I called out his name, louder this time, but he still didn't respond. At that point I realized that something was wrong and grabbed him by the shoulders and shook him, but his body was limp and his head just rolled from side to side, and he fell back onto the pillow.

So I ran downstairs and out the front door. I was running to go across the street to get Jack Gillen, who was a Captain in the New York City Fire Department, as I thought that maybe he could help. As I ran across the street, Patrick saw me and realized that something was amiss. He yelled, "What's wrong Mom?"

"Daddy's dead!", I screamed.

"He can't be," he shouted back at me, "I just talked to him a few minutes ago."

I got Jack Gillen, and as we were running out of his house he yelled to his wife, Mary, to call the Fire Department for an ambulance. As we ran back across the street he grabbed his son, John, and Patrick and told them to come with us. When we got back into the house he told me, "Fifi, stay down here and watch for the ambulance." Then he and his son ran up to John in the bedroom, and Patrick stayed downstairs with me.

I was standing at the foot of the stairs and I could hear the sirens of the ambulance as it approached our street, and a minute or two later the firemen arrived with the rescue unit. Mary Gillen must have also called the Rectory at Saint Williams Church because, a few minutes later, Father Levy showed up at the house and went upstairs. Young John Gillen came back down and was sitting on the couch with Patrick. I could hear the firemen upstairs, yapping at Father Levy, saying, "Father, you can't get around here. Climb over the bed if you have to." Apparently, Father Levy was trying to get around the firemen to get closer to John.

The next thing I remember was the firemen carrying John out to the rescue truck, on a stretcher. Jack Gillen had come down with them and was sitting on the couch with Patrick and his son John. We were all very upset. I can remember standing at the foot of the stairs with Father Levy, who was very perturbed that the firemen hadn't let him get closer to John, to administer Last Rites, and I was consoling him. After a few minutes Jack Gillen turned to me and said, "Come on Fifi, I'll drive you to the hospital." The rescue unit had taken John to the Nassau County Medical Center, so that's where we went.

Everything after that is kind of a blur, but I remember seeing John lying on a gurney in the hospital. He was yawning and I was thinking, "Oh, that's a good sign. Maybe he'll be all right." But then one of the nurses told me that it wasn't a yawn, it was just some kind of involuntary reflex action. He was in a coma.

~~~

They did a tracheotomy on John's throat, and kept him on a respirator, and for the next few weeks I would go to school every morning to teach and then go to the hospital every afternoon. After that I would go home and make dinner for Patrick and myself, then go back to the hospital till visiting hours were over.

After a few weeks of this routine, I went to my homeroom at school one morning and became very short of breath. Some of the kids were coming in and asking if I was okay, and I said, "Oh, I just need a minute," but I still couldn't catch my breath.

I must have looked pretty bad, because one of the boys said, "I don't care what you say, I'm going to get the nurse."

A few minutes later, George McElroy and Vinnie Parlotta came into my room with the school nurse and a teacher's aide. They had the teacher's aide take over my class, and they took me down to the nurse's office in a wheelchair. Then they called my doctor, and Frank Leahy, the assistant principle drove me over to his office. As the doctor was examining me, he asked, "What have you been doing?", so I told him about all the running around I had been doing between home, school and the hospital. He said, "You have to stop pushing yourself, and cut back a little. Don't be trying to go twice a day to the hospital." He said that my problem was, "…most likely an anxiety attack, but you could have a partially collapsed lung." Anyway, I recovered.

~~~

Even though John was in a coma, his heart would fibrillate sometimes, which would cause his whole body to move slightly, in rhythm with the irregular heartbeat. I remember that I could always hear the "WHOOSH, WHOOSH, WHOOSH" of the respirator when I would get off the elevator near his room. Then one day, as I got off the elevator, I didn't hear the "WHOOSH, WHOOSH, WHOOSH", and I thought to myself, "Oh my God, he must have died. Maybe they tried to call me at school, to tell me, but I had left already." Well, it turned out that they had temporarily turned off the respirator, and were reducing it every day in an attempt to wean John off it and get him breathing completely on his own. I just wish one of the doctors would have told me that before then.

One evening I went in to see him, and I could see that his tracheotomy tube needed to be cleaned, so I went out to the nurse's station and told them. The nurse there said, "Okay, we'll send somebody in to clean it."

When I went back to the room, I was standing in the doorway, looking at John, and I heard a voice ask softly, "Mrs. McFadden?"

I turned to see a young man standing behind me, in a white lab coat. I said, "Yes."

He said, "You don't recognize me, do you?"

"No," I apologized, "I'm sorry, I don't."

I couldn't remember his name, but he identified himself as a former student of mine from Bethpage. He asked, "Is that your husband?", and I nodded. He continued, "I recognized the name, but I was hoping it wasn't your husband." Then he said, "I'm so sorry." He had been sent to clean John's tracheotomy.

~~~

Eventually it got to the point where John was breathing on his own. There would be days when I would walk into his room and feel encouraged because his color was good. We would all hold on to the hope that maybe by some miracle, John might wake up from his coma. But it was a false hope. For every day that he looked like he might be coming around, there were two or three days that his pallor was gray, and life had all but left him.

Then one day I got a call from NEWSDAY asking some questions about John's condition. They were doing a series of articles on coma patients nationwide, and the ethics of removing coma patients from respirators, and had somehow heard about John. They wanted to interview me for their article, but I said, "No," John was a very private and very proud man. He always took pride in his appearance and would not have wanted to be seen or talked about in the condition that he was in, and I wasn't going to let that happen.

~~~

Then came Friday, November 12th. It was about five o'clock in the morning and I was just waking up to start getting ready for school when the phone rang. It was a doctor from the Nassau County Medical Center, and he said, in a very collected tone of voice, "Mrs. McFadden, I'm calling to tell you that your husband passed away about fifteen minutes ago."

I just sighed heavily, and said, "Oh. Okay. Thank you."

But before I could hang up he groped, "You're not surprised?", most likely perplexed that my demeanor was as collected as his own in the face of such bad news.

I thought for a moment, and then slowly replied, "No. In fact I've been praying for this. My husband was a very proud man, and this was not the way he would have wanted to be remembered."

294

I went up to Patrick's room and gently woke him up to tell him. Then I called the rest of the boys to break the news of their father's passing. None of them were surprised, and to some extent there was a general feeling of relief. Not so much for themselves, but for their father, that he had finally been released from the teasing clutches of purgatory that had held him for ninety-two long days and nights.

~~~

Jack was working at Baylor University at the time and had told me that he would be driving home for the Thanksgiving break. I called his apartment in Waco, but got no answer. So, on a hunch, I called Marjorie Lawrence's house in Hot Springs, Arkansas, thinking that maybe Jack had stopped there on his way up to New York. Her husband, Doctor King, answered the phone, and I said, "Doctor King, this is Mrs. McFadden, Jack's mother. I was wondering if you had heard from Jack, because he mentioned that he might try to stop to see you on his way home for Thanksgiving."

He said, "Mrs. McFadden, Jack is sitting here in my living room with us right now."

So Jack got on the phone and I told him the bad news. He immediately left Hot Springs, and drove straight through to New York.

~~~

The next day was Saturday, and Patrick was supposed to play in a championship football play-off game up at Seaford High School. Patrick of course was very down and reluctant to play, but I told him that he had to play in the game, the team was counting on him, and his father would have wanted him to play. So Patrick went up to the school, and as the team was getting ready to take the field the public address announcer introduced them. With that, the football team came bursting though a big green and white paper banner that read, "SEAFORD VIKINGS," and Patrick was the last player onto the field. He wore number 76 on his football jersey, and as he ran onto the field the loudspeakers announced, "And in the 'SPIRIT OF 76' (1976 being that year), number 76, Patrick McFadden." Everyone in the stands stood up and cheered as he ran onto the field. Most of them were aware that he had just lost his father, only the day before.

I was watching all of this, standing on the sideline, wearing my green "Seaford Super Fan" jacket, tears streaming down my face from the emotion of the day and everything else leading up to it. I felt someone put their arm around my shoulder. It was Vinnie Parlotto, my dear friend from Bethpage High School.

I don't remember the final score, but after the game we had to go back to the house and get ready to drive up to Westchester the next morning, as we had made arrangements to have John waked at Dwyer's Funeral Home, in Tarrytown. The same funeral home where so many of our family members had been waked, for so many years before.

Patrick - MVP of Seaford vs Carey playoff game - Thanksgiving Day, November 25, 1976 at Bethpage.

~~~

Following the wake on Sunday and Monday at Dwyer's, a funeral Mass was held for John on Tuesday, November 16, at the Church Of The Magdalene in Pocantico Hills, right across the street from the house that he had grown up in. From there, the hearse took him to "Gate of Heaven Cemetery" in Hawthorne, where he was laid to rest alongside his mother and father, and some of his other Foley aunts and uncles in the Foley family burial plot, which had been purchased by John's grandmother, Honora Foley.

296

Obituaries

John J. McFadden Jr.

John J. McFadden Jr., a former resident of Tarrytown and Ossining and a former real estate broken in the area, died this morning in Nassau County Medical Center after a long illness.

He was born in Tarrytown June 29, 1920, son of John and Laura Foley McPadden, was educated in local schools and was graduated from Villanova (Pa.) University. He was a captain in the Second Division, U.S. Marines, in World War II. He returned to Tarrytown to become a real estate broker, operating under his own name and later under the firm name of Chritchley & McFadden from 1947 to 1958. He lived in Ossining for a time but for the past 17ears he resided in Seaford, L. I.

He was a former president of the Hudson River Valley Real Estate Board.

Surviving are his wife, the former Kathryn Rgan; five sons; John J. II of Waco, Tes. Nicholas E. of Mount Sinai, L.I., Philip J. of West Islip, & I; Brian M. of Islip; and Patrick Jr. of the home address; two sisters, Mrs. Eugene (Dolores) Mulligan of Cleveland, Ohio; Mrs. William (Dorothy) Bassett of Macy Road, Briarcliff, and two grandchildren.

In the ensuing years since his death I have come to understand that, as much as what had plagued John were his physical problems, a lot of his demons were spiritual and emotional in nature. I think that he was, fundamentally, a very sad man. But mostly I think that life had dealt him a series of setbacks that had combined over time to have a crushing effect on his soul, that he just couldn't ever recover from. I think that they started with the sudden, unexpected loss of his father, followed closely by the terrible things that he had experienced during the war. Then came the loss of his business; made all the more painful by his feelings of betrayal at the hands of a trusted family member, which culminated in having to leave behind his home in Westchester, seemingly exiled to that wretched island that Helen had fretted about years before.

But it was our home now, and had been for some time. It was the place where our sons had grown up and were now planting their own roots, starting their own careers and families. So we would mourn our loss, and shake off our grief, and life would go on. And like it or not, Godforsaken or not,we would make the best of it, out here on Long Island.

Family photo - Labor Day, 1980.

298

Chapter Nine

BETHPAGE

Back in the early sixties, it soon got to the point where I was substitute teaching in the Seaford Schools almost every day. Then one day the secretary called from the school district to see if I was available for the day, and as we were talking she said to me, "You must be very good at what you do."

"Why do you say that?", I asked.

"Because," she informed me, "the principals of the schools are all asking for you by name now."

That made me start to think that maybe I should try to teach full-time so that I could get all the benefits of a full-time job.

So, just before Thanksgiving in 1963, I contacted a company that was like an employment agency for teachers. In those days there was a shortage of teachers, and the agency quickly set up a couple of interviews for me. The first one was with the principal of the Amityville high school.

When I arrived there at about noon time, the bell was ringing for a change of classes. As I was walking down the hall to the administration office, the hallways were filled with kids that seemed very loud and unruly, rough and out of control. I wasn't sure if I would be able to cope with the situation that I saw there. I went into the office and introduced myself to his secretary and said that I had an appointment with the principal. She said that he had been called away to an emergency meeting regarding a serious disciplinary problem with one of the students. Then she asked me if I could wait for him to return, or come back in about an hour. But I wasn't too thrilled with what I had seen there so I told her I couldn't, as I had another appointment that I had to go to that afternoon.

So I left Amityville and went up to my next appointment which was at Bethpage High School. When I got there, Lydia McNamee, the principal's secretary, took me in to meet Frank Sabatella, the high school principal. After he and I chatted for a few minutes, he took me over to meet Vinnie Parlotta, the assistant principal. In his office I also met with Bill Testerman, the head of the English department. After talking with them for about a half hour, Vinnie took me to meet the superintendent of schools, Charles Bryan. Each one of them had a few questions which I answered, and then I left.

Then, right around that Thanksgiving, I got an unexpected phone call from Lydia McNamee, asking me if I, "…could come in to observe Mrs. Heisenbuttle."

"What for?" I asked.

"Don't you know?", she bubbled, "You got the job."

"Really, I did?", I questioned, afraid to believe my own ears.

"Yes," she confirmed, adding, "you had the job before you left the building that day you were here."

Probationary appointment to teach English at Bethpage high school.
December 2, 1963.

~~~

Mrs. Heisenbuttle was an eleventh grade English teacher who was going to be taking maternity leave soon. They wanted me to come in and observe her for a few days, and then take over her class when she left to have her baby. The first days that I was there with her was more like a baby shower. The kids were bringing in presents for her and her baby every day.

Before going on leave, Mrs. Heisenbuttle told me that she had been giving vocabulary tests to the kids every week. They were given lists of about fifteen words on Mondays, and would be given a test on Friday, that would include the spelling, definition and use of the word in the context of a sentence.

At first, the kids all had an attitude. They looked at me like I knew nothing, and they knew it all. So one day we were reviewing the vocabulary list and one of the words was "antipodes." When I said it, the kids all burst out laughing. I looked at them and asked, "What's wrong?"

"That's not the way you pronounce it," giggled one of the girls. They thought that the word was pronounced "ant - ee - podes".

So I told her to come up and look it up in the dictionary, and offered, "You know, I learn something new every day, and if that's the way you pronounce it, I'll be the first to admit it."

So she looked it up in the dictionary, and when she found it, and looked at the diacritical markings that indicate how a word is pronounced, she looked up at me sheepishly and admitted, "Geez, Mrs. McFadden, you're right."

Well, I never had another problem with that class again after that. The rest of that year went well, and the kid's attitudes improved.

~~~

The next year, 1964, Vinnie Parlotta asked me if I would be the Class Advisor for the incoming freshman class, and I said, "Yes." Every year each class would have a fundraiser, and my first year as the freshman class advisor I spoke to a guy who had a candle business that had candles with holiday scenes on them. I originally told him that we would take one hundred cases of the candles, but he was thinking that five hundred would be more appropriate for the number of students in the class. At first I balked, but he persisted, "Trust me on this," and I said, "Okay."

I had to find a place to store all the cases, so I got the upstairs storage room to store all the candles and distribute them to the kids as they were sold. Well, the first day, the kids cleaned me out, they had sold so many. It ended up being the best fundraiser that the school had ever had.

I was the Freshman Class advisor until 1977, and then I became the Senior Class advisor, along with Bob Sarli, until I retired in 1990.

Fifi and Bob Sarli with Senior Class Officers - Class of 1990.

One of the things that Bob and I would do would be to oversee the Senior Proms. During the proms, he and I would sit near the front door and observe the kids as they came in. If a kid looked like they had been drinking or something, Bob and I would just look at each other and nod, and know that we had to keep an eye on that kid for the rest of the night. We had other chaperones too. George McElroy and his wife Lynn, Vinnie Parlotta and his wife Anne, and some of the other teachers would help keep an eye on the bathrooms and everything else that was going on.

Over the years I also chaperoned a lot of class trips to different places. Guido Agostini asked me to help out on many of the trips that his social studies class took. We went to Ronald Reagan's inauguration in Washington D.C. and several trips to Europe.

Fifi and John - Senior prom chaperones.
Bethpage High School. - May 12, 1972.

As in high school and college, I got involved with a lot of activities during my years teaching at Bethpage. I used to organize and run the yearly Christmas party. This included all the details from the menu and the table cloths, to the music and the bar. I used to run some of the retirement parties and end of year parties too. Sometimes we would put on faculty plays, where the faculty members would get up on stage and perform. I remember singing a song with John Lundy, a terrific Irish singer. We would often be the brunt of different skits and make fun of each other. The kids would always get a big kick out of that.

Bethpage Faculty Variety Show - March 13, 1976.

We became like a big family in Bethpage high school. Every morning we'd have coffee together in the faculty cafeteria. We'd tell jokes and laugh, and catch up on each others families. When the bell would ring for "home room" to meet, we'd all go out to our rooms to start our day. At the end of the day, many of us would gather again in the faculty lounge, to chat, tell jokes and catch up on each others day before we went home to our families. It was a very close knit group.

Christmas Party at Bethpage Country Club - December 16, 1988.

~~~

After I had been teaching at Bethpage for three years, a problem came up that we had to deal with. When I had graduated from college in 1943 you only needed thirty credits of post graduate work to qualify for a teaching certification. But I never did the post graduate work because It had never dawned on me that I might someday become a teacher. Then, one day during the school year in 1966, I was in an English Department meeting when George McElroy beckoned me out into the hallway. He asked, "Are you taking any courses?"

"No," I said, "why?"

"Because you're coming up for tenure next week," he advised, "and I have to be able to tell the Board of Education that you're taking the courses you need to get your permanent teaching certification."

George and my friends at Bethpage knew that I couldn't afford to take the courses that I needed, but they also knew that there was a program at St. John's University where I could enroll in a course for free if I had a St. John's student doing their student teaching with me at Bethpage. So George had the English Department make arrangements to get a student teacher from St. John's, and got me enrolled in the post graduate courses that I needed. The student teacher that I got was a very hard working young girl who would come teach my classes, under my supervision, and sometimes some of her professors from St. John's would come to observe.

~~~

The first course that I had to take at St. John's University was called "Nineteenth Century American Literature". It was given on Saturday mornings, so I would have to get up early and catch the 7:00 a.m. train from Seaford to Jamaica, and then I'd have to walk up the hill to the building where the course was being given.

The professor, whose name escapes me, gave us the worst course I had ever taken. He stood up at a podium, looking down at us, a class of about twenty older students like myself. For the first assignment, he handed out a list of names of American writers and journalists, all from the nineteenth century. Names I had never heard of. We had to pick a name from the list and write a minimum of ten pages on that person, and then give a speech about them, prior to handing in the report. This report would count for one half of our final grade.

The second half of our grade was going to be based on questions about all of the other reports that the rest of the class had handed in, where if you hadn't listened carefully to the other student's reports, you wouldn't be able to answer the questions.

I don't even remember the name of the writer that I did my report on. He was so obscure that when I went to find information on him at the Seaford Library, they had to send away to Albany to get the only copy of a book about him. It was so old, and falling apart, that I was afraid to open it or turn the pages.

We all thought that we had failed, but I think someone at St. John's must have talked to the professor and got him to grade us on a curve. I think I got a "C". Anyway, I passed.

The following spring, my student teacher graduated from St. John's and invited me to her graduation party at her home in Queens, near the Throgs Neck Bridge. It was Sunday, June 11, 1967. That was the day that my leg got broken in the terrible accident in Nick's car

Because of my recovery from the broken leg, it took longer then we expected for me to complete all the courses that I needed to get my permanent teaching certification, so George McElroy had me get a letter from Doctor Nackman, to send to the New York State Board of Education, to get an extension of the time that I could work without my permanent certification. George also told the Board that I was a valuable asset to the school and that my absence would have a negative impact on the English department if I was not allowed to continue to teach.

Fifi and Vinnie Parlato in the main office the day the
1978 year book was dedicated to her.

~~~

Over the years at Bethpage, I chaperoned several trips to Europe. I had always wanted to travel, but John had no desire to do so. I don't know if it had anything to do with all of the traveling that he had to do during the War or if he was just afraid to leave his business alone, as weekends were always the busiest time for him, but the bottom line was that we rarely, if ever, went anywhere beyond a few hours drive from home.

Anyway, a few years later, after John had passed away, I got a couple of wonderful opportunities to do some real traveling, and decided to take advantage of them.

Bethpage Senior Prom - June, 1980.

In 1980, John DeGuardi, the head of the Art Department, came to me and asked if I would like to be one of the chaperones for a trip that he was planning for his art students, to Italy and Sicily, and I jumped at the chance.

The trip was scheduled for the Easter school recess. We tried to take mostly seniors, as it would be their last chance to go, and we tried to hand pick the best kids, who we felt deserved the most to go.

Although these trips were organized by the teachers, for the student body participation, Bethpage School District did not want to be held legally responsible for any of the trips to Europe. So we would have our meetings to organize and schedule the trips at the Bethpage Public Library. We would talk to the students and their parents to let them know what the kids should or shouldn't bring with them, and about what they could expect to see or do on the trip.

Parents were told that if any of the students caused a serious problem while in Italy, they would be taken to the nearest airport and sent back home. John told all of the girls that were scheduled to go, and their parents, that under no circumstances were they to make any eye contact with, or smile at, any Italian men. He warned that Italian men would immediately drop whatever they were doing and follow the girls if they even so much as glanced in their direction. And during the trip we found this to be very true.

John DeGuardi's wife had said that I was the only one that she trusted going on the trip. I didn't know if I should take that as a compliment or not.

~~~

We left on the Wednesday night before Easter, but we were late in taking off because of some terrible thunderstorms that swept past the airport. This was going to be my first big airplane flight and it wasn't starting out very well. I was sitting in a window seat and after the plane took off I finally got the nerve to look out the window. All I could see was the black ocean below. I started to get nervous and think, "Oh my God, what if we crash, there's nothing down there." Anyway, I finally, mercifully, fell asleep.

A few hours later the stewardess came by and pulled down the window shade. I asked why she had done that and she explained that, although it was dark out, we would soon be flying into the sun and she didn't want it to wake us up too early. I fell back asleep, and when I finally woke up, I raised the shade to look out. The view took my breath away. The sun was reflecting off the snow covered peaks of the Alps, sparkling below us. It was really quite a spectacular sight to see.

~~~

After landing, we met our tour guide and were taken to our bus. We weren't the only school that was on the tour, there was a school from Virginia and another from upstate New York. Each school would have maybe twenty or twenty-five students, and three or four chaperones which were teachers, not parents.

We headed towards our hotel which was on the outskirts of Rome. Traffic was heavy as we drove, and I noticed, as we were sitting at a traffic light, some of the girls laughing in the back of the bus. When I turned and looked, I saw several of the girls looking out the window of the bus, and waving. Then I looked out my window, towards the back of the bus, and saw a car next to us with several young Italian men in it. They were gesturing to the girls on the bus to write down a phone number. This went on at several more red lights as we drove through traffic.

After a while we turned into the parking lot of our hotel, and I noticed that the car full of young men had followed us into the lot, parked, and its occupants were getting out. We walked into the hotel lobby, and the young men followed us, so John DeGuardi went to the hotel manager and said, "These young men have followed our group here to the hotel, but they're not part of our tour. Would you please ask them to leave?" The manager agreed, and ushered the young men out of the hotel.

We all went up to our assigned rooms; my roommate was a woman named Pat Kennedy. John DeGuardi and John Wyskowski, the other male chaperone, also shared a room. All the rooms had a little balcony outside, overlooking the parking lot. Again, I heard a lot of laughter coming from the room next to ours, so I went out on my balcony and looked over to my right and found two of our girls out on their balcony, waving and talking to the group of young men who had followed us to the hotel. I told the girls to get back in their room and not cause any problems. But John had been quite right, the Italian men turned out to be just as bold and determined as he had warned us about.

~~~

The next day we went to The Vatican where we saw Saint Peter's Square, the Sistine Chapel, the Pieta, and the Pope's garden. We also saw the Spanish Steps, and the Trevi Fountain, where I threw some pennies in for good luck. It was very impressive to see all of the beautiful architecture and history of Rome.

From Rome we headed south, and stopped at a place where they were making beautiful cameos out of seashells, and then we continued on to the Isle of Capri, where the water of the Mediterranean was a deep, deep blue. When we got there we had to get on a launch to go out to see the Blue Grotto.

There were maybe seventy-five to a hundred people on the launch as we headed out to the island. After a while, they stopped and dropped the anchor, then the Captain explained that they would put a rope ladder over the side of the launch, and we would have to climb down into small wooden rowboats waiting about ten feet below. He explained that the rowboats would take us over to the Blue Grotto, and when we got there we would have to lie down flat, in the bottom of the rowboat, so it could pass through the small opening in the face of the rock cliff, into the grotto.

As the Captain was moving people toward the rope ladder, to climb down into the rowboats, he kept pointing and shouting, "Go, go, go!", to keep everybody moving. But the more he shouted and pointed, the more I kept backing away from him. I was thinking, "I'm not going down that damn ladder. I'll probably fall into the Mediterranean, and I can't swim."

Two of the young girls from Bethpage were next to me, and they didn't want to go down the ladder either. But finally I said to myself, "Oh well, I might as well go. I may never get back here to have a chance to do this again." So I spoke to the two girls, and we decided to go for it, and with white knuckles and grim faces we climbed down the ladder and were the last ones into the rowboat.

The oarsman started rowing toward the island, but as we got closer he had to hold up a little as there were about six other boats waiting to enter the grotto in front of us. Finally he started rowing again, but as we got closer still, he had to wait, and time the rise and fall of the waves for our approach to the face of the cliff, as the swells would constrict the height of the opening as they rose.

At the top of the mouth of the opening into the Blue Grotto there was a heavy iron chain that was attached to the stone, which then passed through to the inside, along the ceiling of the stone passageway. The oarsman rowed us over to the opening, in time with the waves, then we all lied flat in the rowboat and he grabbed the chain over our head and pulled us, hand-over-hand, inside the Blue Grotto.

It was huge inside, and you could see other tunnels going off from the main chamber. There were no lights on inside but the whole ceiling was a pale blue from the light coming through the opening and reflecting off the water. There were maybe five or six other boats inside, but room for many more.

Inside the Blue Grotto of Capri.

After looking around for a while, we reversed the process. The oarsman pulled us back outside by the chain, and we returned to the launch. We had been the last rowboat, and as we returned, everybody on the launch was clapping, whistling, and cheering that we had all braved the rope ladder and the rowboat ride, and gotten to see the famous Blue Grotto of Capri.

~~~

Once we were all back on board, the launch sailed around to another inlet at the Isle of Capri, where we got off the boat and went on the Funicular, which is kind of a cable car, that took us up the side of a vertical rock face, above the tree line. On the way up we were passing beautiful houses that had magnificent views. When we got above the tree line, everyone let out a gasp at the stunning view of the

Mediterranean and the island below us, and we could see Jackie Onassis' chalet off in the distance. We had lunch at a little café at the top, then went down and got back to the launch.

~~~

That night, we were going to let the kids go to a disco down the street from the hotel. We were all going to accompany the kids, but my roommate, Pat, wasn't feeling well and didn't go. John DeGuardi had put a call in to his wife, and was waiting for her to call back, so John Wyskowski, the other male chaperone, and I ended up being the only chaperones to go to the disco. At one point, John returned to the hotel with most of the kids, but I ended up staying at the disco with three very attractive girls from Bethpage. I had planned to get them back to the hotel by eleven o'clock, so I finally told them that we had to leave.

The streets and sidewalks were very narrow as we were walking back to the hotel. Then a car full of young Italian men pulled up next to us, and they started talking to the girls in Italian. I could tell they were talking about me because, interspersed with their words, I heard them say "Mama" several times. I figured that they were trying to tell the girls to, "...ditch the old lady...," and run off with them, but I finally managed to get the three girls back to the hotel, with their virtue still intact, and admonished, "Now go to your rooms, and stay there."

~~~

There was one girl in particular that we thought needed more attention paid to than most of the others because she continued to flirt with some of the Italian boys that we saw. Our kids had also started to become friendly with some of the kids from the other schools, and she flirted with those boys also. So when I got back to the hotel, John Deguardi was sitting in the lobby where he had finally gotten the call back from his wife, Ann, and I asked how the young lady, the one who we had been concerned about, was that night, because she hadn't gone to the disco with the rest of us. He said that she had spent some time during the evening talking to some of the boys from the school from Virginia, but now she was in the hotel bar, talking to another young man.

As I walked into the bar, she was sitting with a young man whom I didn't recognize from any of the other schools, and she had a drink in front of her. So I went to the bartender and asked him how many drinks she had had. He said he had served her "…two while she has been sitting there."

"That's it," I ordered, "cut her off!"

The bartender was getting ready to close for the night, so I went back out and sat down with John in the lobby. A few minutes later she came tramping out of the bar, sat down between John and me, and proceeded to throw a tantrum. She went on and on about how, "This trip was a birthday present from my parents for my eighteenth birthday" and how she, "…would have had a better time if I stayed home and hung out in the park with my friends," presumably to drink or do drugs with them. We "…had ruined the trip for her!", she accused.

John and I just sat there and listened, not saying a word. After about twenty minutes of her ranting at the two of us, she finally started to slow down. John looked at her and very quietly asked, "Are you finished?" She went on a little more, with lots of attitude, until finally John had had enough. "Okay," he growled, cutting her off, "I think it's time we all got some sleep."

Begrudgingly, the petulant girl went off to her room for the night, as did John and I, to our respective rooms.

~~~

I think it was the next day that we headed down to Sicily, where we visited the village of Taormina. We told the tour guide that some of us wanted to go to Mass on Easter Sunday, but she said that the tour was scheduled to go somewhere else on Easter Sunday morning. However, after John DeGuardi, Pat and I, and even some of the students complained that we wanted to go to Mass, she relented and said that she would drop off those who wanted to go to Mass at the cathedral, while the rest of the tour went on as scheduled, and return for us later.

The cathedral that she took us to was not to be believed. It was huge, taking up the equivalent of about two New York City blocks.

The piazza in front of it was paved with huge marble stones of alternating tan and cream colors. There were pigeons flying around everywhere and it was a magnificent sunny day. The church bells were ringing brightly as the people were filing into church.

Inside the church, the floor tiles were black and white, and everything was grandly massive. Set back into the walls were catafalques, where Bishops and Cardinals that had died over the years were buried in coffins that had life sized stone likenesses of them carved on top of their lids.

Someone gasped, "Oh look!", and when we turned around there had to be forty or more altar boys, in red and white gowns, carrying candles in a procession. Behind them were Priests, Monsignors and Bishops, all carrying bibles. At the end of the procession was the Cardinal, who followed into the church, to the altar. It was the most beautiful Easter service and we were all so glad that we had decided to attend Mass that day. The Church and the Mass were all very impressive.

~~~

For a while I actually entertained the idea of becoming a travel agent. That was in 1981, when one day I noticed an ad in the newspaper that read, "LEARN HOW TO BE A TRAVEL AGENT", so I called up and enrolled in the course. I forget where it was, but it was given by a man who owned a travel agency on the north shore of Long Island, and I soon realized that what he really was trying to do was to sell franchises. What I learned in that course I could have put on the tip of my little finger.

But one day, a few months later, I got a call from a woman who owned a different travel agency in Bethpage. She had somehow heard that I was a travel agent, and wanted to talk to me about being an outside agent for her. Actually, she was hoping that she could get some of the Bethpage teachers to book their vacations and trips with her, through me, and I told her I'd be happy to book any trips that I could.

Then one day she called me at home and asked me if I would like to be included in a "...trip for travel agents?" She explained that it was going to be a promotional trip, just for travel agents, to learn more

315

about the destinations that they would be booking other peoples trips to. It was going to be an eight day trip to Ireland, and included all airfare, hotels, meals and everything, and would only cost me three hundred dollars. It all sounded great until she told me that it was going to be in March. I told her that as much as I would love to go, it was during the school year, and I wouldn't be able to get the time off, so I would have to pass.

When I got off of the phone, Patrick asked me who I had been talking to, so I explained the call, and the trip that I was passing on. When he heard all that the trip included, and how cheap the cost was he said to me, "Mom, you're crazy. You should go."

So I kept thinking about it, then one day Mary McQuillen said to me, "Isn't your mother's house still standing in Ireland? Why don't you tell the school that you have to go there on family business?" So I went and spoke to George McElroy, and explained the situation to him. He in turn spoke to the Board of Education and got me the clearance to take the time off, and before you knew it I was on my way to Ireland.

~~~

That trip consisted of a group of fun, interesting people who were all travel agents. What I didn't realize, was that this trip would be taking us up through Northern Ireland, where, at the time, there was still a war going on between the British and Irish Protestants who controlled the North, and the Irish Catholics who were being persecuted there.

Our flight left New York on March 26, 1981, and when we first landed in Ireland we went to a little cottage where we had breakfast. They served us Irish coffee, with whiskey in it, at seven o'clock in the morning. After breakfast our tour bus headed North, and we had to pass through several checkpoints along the way. We were stopped at one where there were British soldiers with machine guns. They questioned Tom O'Shea, the tour manager, but never actually asked for our passports. A little past that checkpoint, we had to drive up a hill where there was a big letter "H," made out of large stones, painted white, on the side of the hill. The "H" stood for "H-block," which was

316

a nearby prison where the British were holding Irish Catholic political prisoners. The prisoners were all in the middle of a hunger strike to protest against the British rule in the North, and were starving themselves to death.

A little further along we passed a beautiful old castle that looked like it had been deserted. A lot of the buildings were old, and every night we stayed in hotels that were old, but very beautiful.

My friend, Mary McQuillen, had an aunt who owned a house in a village called Cushendall, and Mary used to travel back and forth very frequently to visit with her there. She would stay at the house, sometimes even if it was just for a long weekend. Mary's brother P.J., short for Patrick Joseph, had married an Irish girl, and lived in Northern Ireland, near Belfast.

The next day, the tour bus pulled up in front of an inn where we were going to stop and have lunch. When I saw the name of the inn, I recognized it from stories that Mary had told me, and realized that it was right next door to Mary's aunt's house.

We had arrived at the inn a little ahead of schedule and the staff weren't quite ready for us, so they asked us to wait in the bar area while they finished preparing our lunch. We were having Irish coffee in the bar, when two young men walked in and sat down at a table. I walked over to them and said, "Excuse me. I was wondering if you could tell me if that is the McQuillen house next door?"

But they just looked at me with wary eyes.

"I work with Mary McQuillen, and we're close friends," I continued, "does her aunt own that house?"

They kept looking at me very suspiciously, so I talked a little more about Mary, and mentioned her brothers, P.J., Hugh, and John.

I asked one more time if the house next door was Mary's aunt's, and I think they must have finally gotten sick of my asking because, very abruptly, one of them squinted at me and spoke, but all he had to say was a very terse, "T'would be," then they turned their backs to me.

Because of the war with the British, all of the Irish in the North were very guarded when talking to strangers. Finally our lunch was ready, so I thanked the two young men, and went back with my group to eat.

After lunch I had Grace, the woman who was my roommate, take a picture of me with my hand on the doorknob of Mary's aunt's place, as if I was walking into the house.

As we boarded the bus to leave Cushendall there was a parade going on in protest of the British. People walked along next to the bus as we drove out of the village, many of them carrying signs that said things like "REMEMBER H-BLOCK."

~~~

Another one of our stops along the way was at a place called The Giant's Causeway. This was an area that was thought to have been an ancient bridge across the Sea of the Hebrides, to Scotland. There were huge octagonal stones that, according to legend, had been placed there by a giant, by the name of Finn McCool, to the edge of the water.

Later, as we were driving to our hotel, we could see where buildings had been burned or blown up in the conflict between the British and the Irish Catholics. Everywhere were signs or graffiti that referenced "H" block or lamented, "REMEMBER H-BLOCK."

~~~

Prior to my leaving for this trip, Mary had told me that her brother, P.J., lived in the North, near Belfast. His birthday was coming up, and she asked me to deliver some presents to him while I was there. P.J. and his wife had a new baby that Mary had never seen so she sent some men's underwear for P.J. and some Mickey Mouse toys for the baby. It seems that things like that were very hard to get in Northern Ireland in those days.

When we got to Belfast, our hotel was another old building that was very beautiful except for the fact that it was surrounded by barbed wire, with search lights scanning the barbed wire fence all night long. There was a message at the front desk for me from P.J., asking me to call him, so I phoned him and we agreed to meet in the hotel bar after dinner.

At around eight o'clock, P.J. and his wife, Brona, met me at the bar and I gave them the presents that Mary had sent, then we sat and talked about the things that I had seen so far on the trip. They had left their son, Rory, with Brona's mother, and I was disappointed that I wasn't going to get to see the little boy. Brona asked P.J. if he thought the hotel would mind if he went and got the baby and brought him back so I could see him. So P.J. and I went out to the front desk and asked the female clerk if he could go get the baby, and bring him back. The girl looked coldly back and forth between P.J. and me, never smiling or anything, and then finally said curtly, "Yes, I guess it would be all right."

I went out with him, and we had to walk past a guardhouse where there were two British soldiers with machine guns. We had to explain to them that the hotel had given us permission to go get the baby. They said, "Okay," so P.J. left and I went back inside to wait with Brona.

About twenty minutes later, P.J. returned, so Brona and I went out to the car. Rory was asleep in the back seat, so I told P.J. that I would climb into the back so that he could take a couple of pictures of me with their son, and I could give them to Mary. When we were all done I said goodbye to P.J. and Brona, then walked back past the guardhouse and thanked the soldiers.

As I walked past them, I realized that they had never taken their eyes off of us. That's how tense it was over there in those days in Northern Ireland. They were probably suspicious that we might try to bring a bomb into the hotel, disguised as a baby.

~~~~

The next day, the tour headed down to the southern part of Ireland, where one of our stops was at a religious shrine known as Our Lady of Knock. There was a church there that I went into, and as I was walking up to the altar to say a prayer I noticed a small casket, off in a side aisle, under a window. Then, as I was leaving the church, I had to walk past the casket again, and I noticed that it had a brass plaque with a girls name engraved on it.

When I got back on the bus, I asked the tour guide if there was a body in the casket. "No," she said, "it's probably still being waked at the home, lying on a bed, and will be brought over in the back of a station wagon tomorrow morning for the funeral mass."

It was disturbing to me because it was a child's coffin and the girl must have been very young. I didn't realize it till later, but I never saw any funeral parlors in that part of Ireland. I guess people would just wake their loved ones in their homes before carrying them off to the cemetery.

~~~

I had noticed that our itinerary was going to take us down to Limerick the next day, so I went to the tour guide and asked, "If we're going to be in Limerick tomorrow, do you think we could stop by my mother's home, it's in Abbeyfeale, Limerick." She said she would see what she could do.

That afternoon we went to Bunratty Castle, in Limerick. To go into the castle you had to walk across a moat. We ate dinner with no knives or forks, you ate with just your hands, like it was medieval times, or the dark ages. There were minstrels walking around, singing and playing medieval music. After dinner at the castle we went next door to "Dirty Nellie's," a well known bar in Limerick. Our tour guide came over to me and said, "Be down for your breakfast at seven thirty tomorrow morning, and a taxi driver by the name of Matt Maloney will take you to your mother's house. You can join the group later at the airport, for your flight back to the United States."

Sure enough, Matt Maloney, the taxi driver, and a "…fine broth of a lad," was there the next morning waiting for me. When we got to Abbeyfeale we had to stop in the little village, where Matt went into the police station to ask for directions to my mother's house. We proceeded along a narrow gravel road for a short distance, and then

MAINISTIR NA FÉILE
ABBEYFEALE

Fifi in Abbeyfeale, Limerick.
March, 1981.

turned off the road into a meadow. Matt had to get out and open a gate, drive through, then get out again to shut the gate behind us. We drove through three meadows, and at each one he would have to open and close the gates so that the cows or sheep couldn't wander between fields.

Finally we came to two houses. The first one we came to was a fairly modern house that looked like your typical two story suburban house that you might see here in New York. A young man was there, who turned out to be a distant cousin of mine. His name was Dennis Horgan and he lived there with his mother, Julia, who was eighty-three years old. He was a riot. He only spoke if we asked him something, and then only in one syllable answers.

About ten feet from that house was a tiny, two room cottage, with a metal roof. There was electricity, supplied by a wire coming from a wooden pole by the road, but there was no plumbing or bathrooms, and it still had dirt floors. This was the house that my mother had grown up in.

Fifi at her mother's home in Abbeyfeale, Limerick - March, 1981.

My mother had been the ninth of twelve children that had been raised in that little house. Her nephew, my cousin Edmund Horgan, had been still living in the cottage but was visiting the United States at the time I was there, so I couldn't get in. I could only look inside through a little window.

I walked the two or three hundred feet from the house down the slope of the meadow to the edge of the Feale River. It wasn't very wide, only about forty or fifty feet, but it was bubbling with cold, clear water and I could remember my mother telling me and my sisters stories of how, when she was little, she and her siblings would come home after school, take off their shoes and socks, and wade into the river. Then they would catch trout for my grandmother to cook for dinner.

Fifi standing in the meadow in front of her mothers' house in Abbeyfeale. The Feale River is in the backround - March, 1981.

The older children would get one new pair of shoes per year, and the younger kids got the hand-me-downs from the older kids. Any shoes Mother ever got were always pretty worn out by the time they got to her, never new shoes.

It was very emotional for me when I saw how small the house was and imagined my mother, as a child, living in there with such a large family. It was probably very difficult living conditions, and although I still am amazed that Mother could muster the courage, it helped explain why she would leave home at such a young age and come, all alone, to seek a better life in the United States.

~~~

Soon Matt called to me that it was time to go to the airport and join the rest of the tour group to return home to the states. Later, as we were flying over Long Island, on approach into J.F.K. airport, we were all singing "New York, New York." It had been wonderful to visit Ireland, and emotionally moving to walk around and actually touch and look inside the house that my mother had grown up in, but I had to admit, it felt good to be home.

I never really did work for that travel agency after that, but I was glad I had gone on that trip with that group. I had taken a lot of pictures in Ireland, and, after they were developed, I brought them into school for Mary McQuillen to see. I told her that I had seen her brother and his wife and their new baby, and had gone to Cushendall, and when I showed her the pictures, and she came to the one of me with my hand on the doorknob of her aunt's house, she got all choked up and started to cry.

~~~

In 1983 we took the kids on a trip that combined time in Ireland and England, and this time Mary McQuillen came with me as one of the chaperones. After we landed, got to our hotel and checked into our rooms, I went into the bathroom, where there was a bathtub under a window. It felt chilly in the bathroom, and I noticed that the window over the tub was open a little, about an inch and a half. Anyway, I finished in the bathroom and went back out into the main room, and then Mary went into the bathroom.

Bethpage tour group to Ireland.
Killarney, Ireland. - Sunday, March 27, 1983.

Within a minute or two I heard a voice calling out, "Fifi, Fifi." It was Mary, calling out to me from the bathroom.

I said, "Yes."

"Can you come in here for a minute?", she asked.

"What do you want Mary?", I questioned.

"Just come in for a minute," she appealed.

So, detecting some anxiety in her voice, I opened the bathroom door, and when I looked up and saw her I started laughing so hard that it brought tears to my eyes.

Mary too had noticed the open window above the tub and had decided to shut it. She had taken off her shoes, stepped into the tub, grabbed the top of the open window, then stepped up on the edge of the tub, pushed the window up shut, and now had nothing to hold onto to get down. She had herself standing tip-toe, up on the narrow lip of the tub, with her body plastered against the window, her face turned to one side and her cheek pressed up against the glass, trying not to fall backwards into the tub.

"Stop laughing at me," she yelled, but then she started laughing too. I had to reach across the tub and put my hands up against her back, so she could safely step down into the tub. Then the two of us just stood there in the middle of the bathroom laughing like a couple of old fools.

"What if I hadn't been here?", I chided, "You'd have been stuck up against that window all day!"

Fifi on ferry - crossing the Irish Sea from Ireland to Wales - March, 1983.

~~~

One year I was teaching Greek mythology to the class and there was a boy who sat in the front row, to the right of my desk. It was a good lesson and the kids were all really into it, when, out of the corner of my eye, I noticed this boy discreetly pushing his books to the edge of his desk. He nudged the books over till finally they fell on the floor with a loud BOOM, which broke the attention of the class. He did the same thing a couple more times over the next several days, and each time he did it I would say, "Anthony, what are you doing?", but he would always play dumb and act innocent, like it had been an accident. Other times he would raise his hand in the middle of a lesson like he had some urgent question, but when I would acknowledge him he would always have some inane question or remark which was just designed to distract the class and draw attention to himself.

Finally I said, "That's it Anthony, go sit in the desk at the back of the room, and if this happens again you're in big trouble." But he continued to act out the same way in class almost every day.

Then one day he started cutting up and I said to him, "Oh Anthony, you're such extravert. Furthermore, you're an obnoxious extravert."

325

He got this very quizzical look on his face, and I could see that he didn't understand what I had just called him. He said, "I don't know what you mean by that."

So I told him to come up and get the dictionary and look up the words. He didn't know how to spell "obnoxious" so I had to spell it for him. He leafed through the dictionary, and then I could see him moving his finger along the page as he read the definition. Then he looked smugly up at me and said, "Oh Mrs. McFadden, I'm not an 'adj.'"

He, of course, was referring to the abbreviation for "adjective" following the main entry in the dictionary which indicates whether a word is a verb, adverb, adjective, noun or pronoun, and hadn't even gotten to the definition of "obnoxious." I laughed, but I was also appalled, that here he was in the ninth grade and all the teachers he'd had

Bethpage yearbook photo.

prior to that had never taught him how to use a dictionary correctly.

~~~

Another time, back in the early eighties, there was a student by the name of Tom Kilkenny who I had a problem with. He was a kid who was chronically late for class or would cut class completely. I had sent out mid-term notices to the parents of all the seniors who were in danger of not graduating, and I had called and spoken to Tom's parents, several times during the year, about his grades and his behavior, but he never improved.

On the day of the final exam, part of the test that I gave was an essay, and the entire exam was to be completed and handed in before the students left the room. When the bell rang, and the kids left, I collected all the test papers, but Tom had not left his papers for me. So I went down to my department head, Ed Cryer, and explained to him that Tom Kilkenny had not handed in his final exam papers. Then I called Tom's house and spoke to his mother. I explained to her that Tom had not handed in his exam, and that, coupled with his poor grades for the year, meant that he would fail English and thus not graduate with the rest of his class in June.

The next morning, as I was walking to my classroom, Mr. Kilkenny, Tom's father, was waiting for me with Tom. He was holding a manila envelope and he told me that Tom had been up until late in the night, working on the essay, and asked me to take his test papers, which were in the envelope.

I shook my head and said firmly, "I can't take them now."

"Why not?", he demanded belligerently.

"Anyone could have written this essay," I rebuked, "and besides, he didn't hand it in in the allotted time like all the other students had to."

They continued to walk along next to me till I got to my class. I said, "You'll have to excuse me now, I have to go into my homeroom."

"Do you have a free period when I can come back and talk to you?" asked Mr. Kilkenny, a bit more conciliatory now.

"Yes," I replied, "I have fifth period free."

"Would it be all right if I came back then?" he asked.

"All right, but," I reiterated, "it's not going to change anything."

I called George McElroy, the principal, and Ed Cryer, the head of the English department, and told them that the Tom and his father would be coming back at fifth period and they both said they would be available if I needed them. When fifth period came around both Mr. and Mrs. Kilkenny showed up with Tom, so I took them into the conference room and we all sat down at the table. Tom sat down next to me, and kept pushing the manila envelope over to me, and I kept pushing it back to him. Finally his father blustered, "Tom, she's obviously not going to look at it!", as if I was just being unfair to him.

But I refused to be intimidated by them, and they finally got up and stormed out.

When I got home that evening I was upset about the episode, and I told my son Patrick what had gone on that day with the Kilkennys. I think he must have called his brothers and filled them all in on the situation too.

The next morning, Patrick said he needed to borrow my car, so he drove me up to school and carried my attaché case inside for me. When we walked into the building, Mrs. Kilkenny and Tom were already there and waiting for me in the office. Patrick gave Tom a good looking over, then put my attaché case down, kissed me goodbye, and left.

Mrs. Kilkenny asked if she could speak to me and I said, "Yes," and again took her and Tom into the conference room. This time, George McElroy and Ed Cryer joined us.

Mrs. Kilkenny tried to make a case that I, "…was ruining her son's life if I kept him from graduating with the rest of his class."

I replied that, "It would be unfair to the rest of the class if he was given special privileges that they hadn't gotten. The rest of his classmates had completed the exam according to the school's rules, and Tom didn't. Not to mention all the other lateness and cut classes that Tom missed during the year."

Finally, George McElroy intervened and told Mrs. Kilkenny that we all had classes and other school business to attend to, and that the discussion was over and the issue closed. When we stepped out into the hallway, Tom started to argue with George and even began yelling obscenities at George and me. As Tom was carrying on with his verbal tirade, I happened to look between him and George, and there, just a little down the hall, was my son Nick. He was leaning against the wall and had been quietly keeping an eye on the situation the whole time. George finally said, "That's it Tom, I'm going to ask you to leave the building immediately." Both Tom and his mother continued their verbal assault as they left.

George, Nick and I walked back to the office and were talking about the situation, but within a few minutes Mr. Kilkenny was calling on the phone and was looking for George. He said he was on his way up to the school and wanted to talk to him. So George hung up the phone and said to me, "Fifi, go get lost in the building, I'll handle this from here on." So I went off, up to the library where I continued grading papers, and Nick went back to work.

About an hour or so later, one of the secretaries came up to get me, and told me the latest development. "Boy, you really missed all the excitement.", she gossiped.

It seems that Mr. Kilkenny had come up to the school and brought Tom back with him. They were both sitting outside George's office when George went out and said, "Come in Mr. Kilkenny." Tom started to get up with his father, but George confronted him, "Oh no Tom, not you."

"Why not?", barked his father.

"Because," George contended, "Tom was very abusive to Mrs. McFadden and me earlier, and I had to ask him to leave the building. If you want to speak to me, fine, but I won't allow Tom in my office."

"Well," Mr. Kilkenny sputtered, "if Tom can't come in, then I'm not coming in either."

"Fine, have it your way!" said George, shaking his head in unabashed amusement, and started to show them the door.

At that point, both father and son started yelling and cursing at George. It got so bad that one of the secretaries thought that they might come to blows, so she picked up the phone and called the police. As she was on the phone, it seemed that things were starting to calm down, so she said, "Wait, I think it's okay now." But before she could hang up it got heated again, and she told the police, "Wait, I think you better come." Finally, with the threat of the police on the way, Tom and his father departed the school grounds.

When I came back down from the library and went in to see George, he filled me in on what I had missed, and while I was there he got another call. This one was from an attorney who said he represented the Kilkenny family. He told George that they were going to bring a lawsuit against me and the school district for not allowing Tom to graduate. He demanded that I turn over my grade book and attendance records to him. George finally hung up with the lawyer and told me, "Don't worry about a thing Fifi. They'er just trying to bully us. I'll let the school district's attorney handle this from here out."

Over the next week or so, till graduation, George assigned a couple of teacher's aides to keep an eye on my car in the parking lot, just in case Tom tried to vandalize it or follow me to my car. On Graduation Day he had several of the school security guards walk me out to the football field for the ceremonies. During the ceremony Tom drove through the school parking lot, blowing his car horn and just trying to be disruptive, but nothing else came of it. Tom ended up having to go to summer school so that he could finally graduate, several months after the rest of his classmates, in August.

Bob Sarli. Fifi and George McElroy - June, 1985.

~~~

There was another year that I was in a room by myself, running off copies of the Final Exam that I was going to give my classes. A boy, a known trouble maker who was in danger of not graduating because of his poor grades in English, came into the room and shut the door behind him. As he approached me he grinned arrogantly and said, "How much will it take for you to pass me?"

Well, I couldn't believe my ears, and barked sharply, "What did you just say to me?"

He repeated his question , but his grin now had a nervous twitch to it, and he had lost much of the insolence in his voice.

So I looked him right in the eye and read him the riot act, "You've got a hell of a nerve. Where do you get the unmitigated gall to think that you can come in here and speak to me like that? You get out of this room right now, and if you're lucky, I'll pretend I never heard you say that."

He couldn't return my gaze, and just turned and walked out of the room.

~~~

Then there was the time that I was teaching a lesson on how to find the subject, verb, and compliment of a sentence. The sentence that I was using as an example was:

"My pet peeve is having to go to bed at 9:00 o'clock at night."

I showed the class how to dissect the sentence, then asked, "Does everyone understand what we just did? I'll go over it as many times as we need, but there's going to be a test next week and I don't want anyone saying that they didn't understand."

They all nodded their heads that they understood, except for one boy who still looked a little confused. I said to him, "Tommy, Are you okay?"

"Yeah, I understand," he replied, "but there's just one thing I want to know. What kind of an animal is a 'peeve'?"

Well, this time I almost fell out of my chair laughing, but then I caught myself and apologized to him. I said, "Forgive me Tommy, but sometimes we forget that we use different words and terms in different generations, and I should realize that maybe not everyone knows all the words in the English language." Then I explained to him what a "pet peeve" was.

I think some of the other kids were also quite happy that I gave that definition to the class.

I was told a story by another teacher who had given an assignment to his class to hand in a report about World Wars I and II. On the day that the assignment was due, one boy came up to him and said that he had gone to the school library, the Bethpage Public library and even the East Meadow public library. He said he had been able to find a lot of information about World War I. Then he said, "I was even able to find all kinds of stuff about World War Eleven, but I couldn't find anything about World War Two."

The teacher could only shake his head in disbelief, not only that the young man could mistake the Roman numeral II, for meaning the number eleven, but that he could be so incredibly ignorant of one the most significant events in the history of the human race.

In 1984 Mary McQuillen and I chaperoned another school trip to Greece and Turkey, and there was a female student, named Toni, who was going on the trip, who had family over there. She asked Mary and me if we were interested in buying any leather or fur coats and jackets, or jewelry, as she had relatives in Greece who were in those businesses. Of course we both said, "Sure! We'd love to!", I mean, who doesn't like furs and jewelry.

Anyway, we landed in Athens and had to take a shuttle from the airplane, out on the tarmac, over to the terminal. At first I couldn't locate Mary, but when I finally I found her she ran up to me and breathlessly blurted out, "Fifi, I'm in big trouble."

Now, I was always somewhat uncomfortable every time we traveled to a new country on one of these school trips. I wasn't used to the strange languages and surroundings, and I guess, just like my sister Helen, I was prone to worry about almost everything.

I immediately had visions flashing through my mind, of Mary having unknowingly done something foolish to break the strict Greek laws, or had some kind of contraband in her luggage that she had not declared to customs, and they had found it. I was imagining all kinds of terrible scenarios, and each one had the potential to land us in some dark, damp, Greek prison. So I grabbed her by the shoulders, looked at her suspiciously and demanded, "What do you mean? We just got here. How could you have gotten into trouble already?"

She looked back at me, starry eyed, and sighed dreamily, "We just landed five minutes ago, and I've already fallen in love three times."

She thought the Greek men were just the most beautiful creatures she had ever seen.

Fifi with Mary McQuillen Rielly - 1986.

~~~

We got to the hotel without incident, and got all the kids squared away in their rooms, and something to eat. Then a woman, who was Toni's cousin, met us at the hotel, and she, Toni, and Jerri, another Bethpage girl, took Mary and me in her car to go shopping. We were whipping through all these dark streets in Athens, and finally came to a store that was all lit up. It was the fur and jewelry store that Toni's relatives ran. When we went in, there were two men waiting for us who started showing us fur coats. Mary was trying on beautiful, hand made leather jackets, and I was looking at mink coats. The coat that I liked was a very luxurious mink, but it needed a lot of altering to fit me. The jacket that Mary wanted also needed altering, but we were going to be leaving the next day for a four day cruise of the Greek Islands, and didn't think it would work out. They told us not to worry, they would do all the alterations, and have the two coats waiting for us at the hotel when we returned from the cruise. Mary's jacket was a hundred and fifty dollars and I think the mink was about eight hundred dollars, which was a steal, but they wanted us to pay in advance. Even though they were terrific prices, I didn't like the idea of paying up front, so I decided not to buy the mink, but Mary, Toni and Jerri all bought leather jackets.

It was getting late so we dropped Toni and Jerri off at the hotel, and Mary, Toni's cousin and I went off to the jewelry store. The entrance was an iron gate where we had to get buzzed in, and then we went up a couple of floors on an elevator that opened up to an area that was more like a plush living room than a jewelry store. There were beautifully upholstered couches and chairs to sit on, and a couple of men and women were there who knew Toni's cousin. They asked, "What would you like to see?",

"Diamonds and emeralds.", I told them, as if I thought I was the Queen of Sheba or something.

They brought out a couple of exquisite rings for me to look at, but I didn't buy anything because they were all more than what I wanted to spend. I guess we didn't like furs and jewelry as much as we thought we did, because nobody else bought anything either. We left the store, and one of the women who new Toni's cousin came with us.

I remember walking with Mary, behind Toni's cousin and the other woman, across a big piazza that was very dimly lit. It was about twelve thirty at night and we didn't know where our hotel was. I looked at Mary and muttered, "We must be out of our minds. We're in a country where we can't speak a word of Greek, we don't understand a word of Greek, and we have no idea where our hotel is." That's when we began to get scared.

Anyway, we finally got to the car and they started driving us back to the hotel. We asked them if they knew of a place where we could get something to eat, so they dropped us off at a place that was kind of like a luncheonette. When we went inside we quickly realized that that it was filled with nothing but Greek men, drinking coffee. We were the only two women in the place. We couldn't read the menu, so we just pointed to an ad on the wall for "Coke", and said, "We'll take that."

We had some Greek dish to eat but I don't know what it was. We didn't even know how to count the money to pay for it. Finally, thank God, we found our way back to the hotel and went to bed.

~~~

It was either Good Friday or Easter Sunday in Athens, when Toni and Jerri came and told me that they were going to go to midnight Mass. I saw through them right away, and knew that they really just wanted to go out that night to try to meet some of the handsome Greek men. I said, "Oh that's great. I've never been to a Mass at a Greek cathedral. I'll go with you." Well, they weren't happy about that at all.

So that night Toni, Jerri and I left the hotel and walked to the cathedral. As we entered, each person was given a long, thin, unlit candle to hold. The cathedral was packed, but we were able to go in and get a seat in one of the pews. It was dark inside as we waited for the Mass to begin, but at about a quarter to twelve it was brightened by a line of Priests and altar boys who emerged from behind the altar carrying lit candles. They formed a procession down all the aisles of the church, where they turned and lit the candles of everyone sitting on the end of the pews. Then in turn, those people turned and lit the candle of the person sitting next to them, until everyone in the church was holding a burning candle. Then the Cardinal walked out the front doors of the church, with the procession following, to the front steps. Outside, fireworks started going off from the roof, and lit up the sky above the church for about five minutes. When the fireworks were finished, they all came back inside, and the Cardinal said Mass.

Much to their chagrin, I never let Toni and Jerri out of my sight that night, and I made them return to the hotel right after the Mass was over.

~~~

While we were in Athens we also went to the Parthenon, where I walked up the ruins of the stone steps to the base of the huge columns that support the roof. On the island of Crete we saw the Palace of Knossos, where there was a tremendous ceremonial tub that had mosaic tile depictions of all the Greek gods and goddesses all around it.

335

In front of the Parthenon - Greece - April 20, 1984.

Fifi clowning with Roman ruins in Ephesus, Turkey - April, 1984.

While we were driving around in the tour bus, we could see where a lot of townspeople had butchered sheep as part of their preparations for their Easter Sunday feasts, and had them hanging outside their homes to drain their blood.

~~~~

The next morning we got to our cruise ship, the "Oceanus," and I remember stopping at the island of Mykonos, where we saw a lot of beautiful windmills.

Disembarking at Island of Mykynos.
Our ship, The "Oceanus", in the backround.
Greece - April 16, 1984.

One evening on the ship, Toni came to me and said, "I just called home on the ship to shore radio."
"What did you do that for?", I asked.
She said, "I was homesick and just wanted to talk to my parents," and explained that she had gotten permission from the Captain to make the call.

Later that same night, Mary went to the ship's disco with the kids. I was with some of the other teachers who had gone on the trip, in the ship's theater where we were watching a group of the local Greek men perform a presentation of some of their ancestral folk dances, dressed in traditional Greek costumes. A little while later Mary came into the theater and urged, "Can you come with me, back to the disco?"

"What's the matter?", I asked.

"I'm having a problem with Toni," she said, so off we went to the disco.

When we got there I asked, "So, what's the problem?"

Mary, noticeably agitated, pointed to an older man, probably in his forties, dressed in the cruise line's dress uniform. He was obviously some kind of officer on the ship. "That guy has been making eyes at Toni, and flirting with her all night," she fumed, "and she's been flirting back."

So I watched the situation for a few minutes, then I called Toni over to me and warned, "Stop flirting with that dirty old man over there or guess who's going to be making the next call on the ship to shore radio to your parents."

Reluctantly she obeyed and went back to her table, but I continued to give the third degree to the lecherous old wolf in the uniform. Eventually he got the hint, and slinked out of the disco.

~~~

The next night was the "Captain's Dinner Dance", hosted by the ship's Captain and his staff. Unfortunately, Mary wasn't feeling very well and decided to stay in our cabin. I went off to the dinner and left Mary down

Dinner on board Oceanus - Greece - April, 1984.

338

in our stateroom, which was on the last level, down in the bottom of the ship.

Later that night, when I came back to our cabin and opened the door, I found Mary all curled up against the wall in her berth. "Oh thank God you're here,"she whimpered, obviously shaken.

"What's wrong?", I asked.

"Can't you see the scratch marks on the inside of the door?" she sniffled.

Apparently, after I had left her earlier that evening, she had taken a nap and started to feel better, so she decided that she would go up to join the festivities. But when she went to leave the cabin, she wasn't able to open the cabin door from the inside. She had called upstairs to the party and asked, "Do you see a white haired lady in a purple dress?", but there were so many people that they couldn't find me. She thought, "Fifi will be back soon," but it turned out to be hours. Then, as she lay there in her bunk, she started to worry about what would happen if the ship started to sink and she couldn't get out of the cabin. That's when she started to hyperventilate.

Mary was fine, just nervous and shaken up. We never did figure out why she couldn't open the cabin door, but we had a lot of laughs over that silly incident, at her expense, for many years after.

That story took a weird turn a few years later, when the cruise ship that we were on, The Oceanus, actually did sink off the coast of South Africa in 1991.

Travel Company Defends Captain Of Downed Ship

REUTER

Johannesburg, South Africa — The travel company that chartered the Greek liner Oceanos yesterday defended the ship's captain, saying he was justified in leaving the sinking vessel while about 170 people were still on board.

Many passengers and entertainment staffers accused Capt. Yiannis Avranas and senior officers of fleeing the ship on the first helicopter, abandoning them while the ship sank.

Avranas said he left to supervise rescue operations from shore and the owners of the Greek-registered ship, Epirotiki Lines, backed his decision.

Lorraine Betts, British cruise director for TFC Tours and one of the last to leave the 7,554-ton ship before it sank Sunday, rejected criticism of the captain.

"I would sail with him again," she told a news conference called by TFC. "What he said he was going to do sounded good to me."

Betts, who helped coordinate the dramatic air and sea rescue from the bridge, said Avranas had told her he was going to another ship to get it to heave to alongside the Oceanos to calm the sea so that lifeboats could be launched.

Passengers and newspapers praised the South African Defense Force for the rescue operation, which saved all 571 people on board after the Oceanos sprang a leak in a howling gale Saturday night.

Most passengers and crew took to lifeboats and were picked up by ships responding to distress calls. A team of 14 helicopters winched about 170 people from the heaving, sharply listing deck and ferried them to shore.

Beeld newspaper said in an editorial the country was proud of the navy and air force, whose task was complicated because "the Greek captain and his crew apparently left the ship and its passengers in the lurch."

Retired South African ship captain C.J. Harris said that on the face of it Avranas was wrong to leave. "It's always been the tradition that the captain is responsible for the lives of everyone on board," he said.

NEWSDAY, WEDNESDAY, AUGUST 7, 1991

Article about our cruise ship to Greece that later sank in 1991.

In 1985 we organized a trip to Germany, Austria and Switzerland. This time, some of the students' parents came along, as well as my two friends Jean Cox and Gladys Schilt. Gladys' husband had been in combat in the Black Forest during Word War II, and she wanted to visit the area.

Gladys Schilt, Gene Cox and Fifi at Mountain Lake.
Poconos, Pa. - October 9, 1989.

We were scheduled to arrive at our hotel on Good Friday, and Jean Cox, being a devout Catholic, was adamant that we only eat fish on Good Friday. When we got to the hotel, late as usual, the manager was very proud to inform us that his staff would be serving us fresh fish for dinner, but when we went down to the hotel restaurant for dinner that evening, Jean took one look at her plate and decided, "I think I'll go back to my room, and get ready for bed." The fish that they were serving was the whole fish. Head, fins, eyeballs and all, so Jean had lost her appetite. I was able to eat a little of the body, but not much.

One night, while in Munich, we went down to a "Hofbräuhaus", which is the German word for Beer Hall. The manager of the hotel had told us to take the subway, and when we got there it was very crowded as there was a soccer tournament going on nearby. We were amazed at how the waitresses could carry three or four pitchers of beer in each hand. Everyone was seated at these big long tables, drinking German beer and singing German songs. It was a real party atmosphere.

When we finally left, we got back on the subway but we didn't know which way to go to get back to our hotel. Jean Cox said, "Oh, I'll ask somebody," so she walked over to a German couple that was standing on the platform and asked about our hotel, but the couple didn't understand English, or just didn't know where the hotel was. They just shrugged and shook their heads. Then Gladys, despite being very shy by nature, tried to ask another woman, but got the same result.

Then I saw this nice looking, well dressed young man and approached him and asked if he could tell us how to get back to our hotel. "Oh, of course," he said in perfect English, "I'm going that way myself. Follow me, and I can show you." So we got on the subway, and he sat with us.

As we were riding along I asked him, "How long were you in the United States?" I assumed he had spent time there because he spoke English so well.

"I've never been there," he confided, "the schools that I attended here in Germany all taught English as a second language." So we chatted a little more till we got to our stop, then thanked him and went on our way.

A day or two later we got to our hotel near the Black Forest, and that night a group of us attended an Easter Eve Mass at an old church that was all black marble inside. The pillars and the altar were beautiful, polished black marble. At the end of the Mass, everyone was given a lighted candle, and then we walked outside to a small cemetery next to the church, and placed the candles in front of all the timeworn headstones.

While we were at the Black Forest I went into a shop and bought cute little cuckoo clocks, and shipped them home to give to my sons.

~~~

From Germany we travelled to Switzerland, and at one place we crossed a river by walking across a beautiful covered bridge. It had exquisite scenes of the lush Swiss countryside, hand-painted on the wooden walls and ceiling.

Another day, we took a cable car gondola, kind of like the "Funicular" in Capri, Italy, up into the Alps. There were big glass windows all around, and I was standing near the front of the car. As it neared the top, it looked like we were going to crash right into a wall of ice. We got so close to it that I ducked my head down and pushed my hands against the back of some man in front of me, to brace for what I was sure would be the impact of us hitting the icy face of the mountain. But the gondola suddenly rose up over the vertical face and we all got safely to the top.

When we got out of the gondola, we sat down at a little restaurant at the top of the mountain. There were people skiing all around us, but it was so sunny and warm that many of them were skiing dressed only in T-shirts and short pants. We sat and enjoyed the view of the Alps for a while, then took the gondola back down to the bottom.

~~~

In 1987 we went on a trip to Portugal, Spain and Morocco. Jean Cox came with me on that trip also.

I remember going to the "Kasbah" in Morocco. It's kind of like an outdoor market place, and as we approached the area you could smell all kinds of different, strange aromas of the many exotic foods that were cooking. Some of the teachers and kids bought rugs that they shipped home. Others bought leather coats and jackets. I didn't think it was that impressive, and I got the feeling that our guide was in cahoots with some of the shop keepers and street vendors. He probably got a commission on anything that the people from the tour bought.

Fifi with a camel in Tangiers - April 10, 1990.

I remember that while we were taking the ferry from Spain, over to Morocco, we sailed passed the Rock of Gibraltar, and I kept thinking to myself, "I wonder if there are any submarines under us." For the life of me, I don't know what got me started thinking about submarines that day. Maybe I was subconsciously reminded of something that I had heard or read years before, about German U-boats patrolling the Straights of Gibraltar during the War.

~~~

I think it was in Morocco that, one night, a group of us were sitting out on the balcony of our hotel, drinking wine. We had been advised by the tour guide not to leave the hotel as it was an area where criminals would prey on tourists. There were lots of little side alleys and doorways where muggers could hide, then grab you and whisk you away.

It was a beautiful, clear, moonlit night, with lots of stars out. On the other side of the road, across from the hotel, there was a meadow where sheep were grazing. Suddenly, during a lull in the conversation, we realized that we could hear a flute playing softly, coming from the meadow across the street. It was the shepherd, playing music to his sheep, and it cast quite a magical spell over the night.

343

~~~

When I first started teaching at Bethpage, one of the first things that I told my students was that I would be in my room every day after classes were complete, and that if any of them needed extra help or wanted to talk about something, I would be there every afternoon. I was always kind of amazed at the number of kids who would come see me after classes. They would talk about anything and everything. Problems at home, problems with other students, even problems with boyfriends and girlfriends, not just school work.

There was one girl that used to come see me from time to time, who had a stuttering problem. But whenever she came in I noticed that her stuttering dissipated, the longer we talked, till by the time we finished she wouldn't be stuttering at all. A few times I offered her a ride home, and realized that as we got closer to her house the stuttering returned and became more pronounced. I knew then that there must be a problem at her home.

We never really got into it, although I wished she would have talked to me about it because it disturbed me. But at least she was able to relax and speak her mind when she came to see me after school.

~~~

Sometime during the 1980s, I got a message in my mailbox asking me to call a "Mrs. McKenna". I asked the secretary if she knew what it was about.

She asked, "Did you ever have a student named Eileen McKenna?"

At first I couldn't recall, but then I remembered that Eileen McKenna had been a student of mine back in the mid 1960s. She had come from a very dysfunctional family, and I remembered her as having a bit of a chip on her shoulder.

The note was from Eileen's mother. It said that Eileen had recently called her and inquired if her mother knew if I was still teaching in Bethpage. So I called Mrs. McKenna and she told me that Eileen was married and living in California with her husband and two children, and she gave me Eileen's phone number.

344

When I called Eileen she said she was very happy to hear from me, and said that she was attending college out in California. She also said that she was taking a public speaking course, and would have to make a speech, in two weeks, about someone who had made an impact on her life. Then she told me that she was going to make her speech about me.

May 9, 1988

Dear Mrs. McFadden,

First, let me apologize for taking so long to write. We always have two months in which my son (2 yr old) gets extremely ill, so needless much of my attention is toward him. This year, unfortunatly, I got sick myself. Anyway, once again I'm sorry.

When I started this speech class, our first assignment was a tribute speech. After thinking of someone who has been a positive influence and someone I think of in a very special way, the choice was easy. It was you. I knew most people would be doing their mothers or grandparents and I wanted to be different. Besides my mother knows how special & loved she is. But after all these years, I still think of you and only pray that my kids are fortunate enough to have someone like you during their school years.

I wish I could send you a copy of the speech, but I spoke from memories and the great fondness I still have of you. The teacher was quite pleased as some of his remarks were, from the heart, very unique and spoke with great admiration. I only got a B, because since it was my first speech, he didn't want me to get over confident. All I can say is I'm thrilled. This course is almost over. I find it very difficult standing in front of 28 strangers talking on different topics.

There's a chance I'll be coming back to N.Y. this summer. When I know for sure, I'll write so we can make arrangements to see each other. I know

will definitely [3] be back for
our 20th class reunion next year.
My God, where have the years
gone!

I'll close by telling you
once again that you have always been a special lady and
more important one hell of a
teacher.

Love,
Eileen McKenna
Fitzpatrick

P.S. Did you expect me to
marry anyone but an
Irishman and from
New York. I must be crazy)

I was overwhelmed when she told me this. I couldn't even speak, I was so touched. It seems that years before, while she was in high school, I had unknowingly helped her to cope with a family tragedy. She told me that the things that we had talked about during that time had helped her deal with many of the other hardships that life had brought to her over the years. She still calls me several times a year to tell me that she has been thinking about me, and will always end her phone calls by making a point to say, "I love you."

~~~

Over the years I have been contacted by several other young men and women who made it a point to tell me that I had been a lasting and positive influence in their lives. I don't know what I did or said in most cases, but it is one of the most rewarding aspects of my teaching career. It has made me realize, that as a teacher, charged with these impressionable young hearts and minds, you never really know what aspect of a lesson, a book or a poem you are trying to teach will get through to a person. Or perhaps it's more about how you convey not only the lesson of the day, but the lessons of life to a student, that will strike a chord, and leave an impression that can last a lifetime.

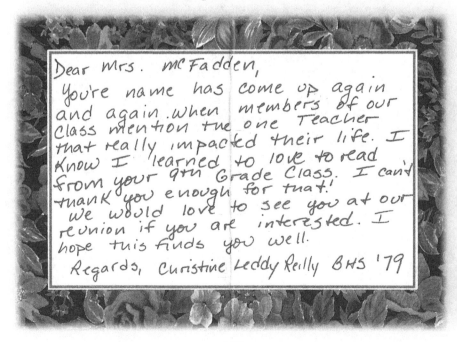

Dear Mrs. McFadden,
You're name has come up again and again. when members of our class mention the one Teacher that really impacted their life. I know I learned to love to read from your 9th Grade Class. I can't thank you enough for that!
We would love to see you at our reunion if you are interested. I hope this finds you well.
Regards, Christine Leddy Reilly BHS '79

Chapter Ten

CROOKED DISCIPLES

Being the mother of five boys meant that there was never a dull moment for me. I was the only female in the household, except for a couple of the dogs that we owned over the years, and John and the boys kept me hopping. Between teaching school and keeping up with the boys, there was rarely ever any free time. Cooking, cleaning, grading papers, preparing lesson plans, running the kids all over town; I don't know how I kept up. But I suppose I was typical of most working moms with kids in those days. I used to ask Jean Cox, "Is the broom in tight?", because we use to say that the only way to sweep the floor while simultaneously cleaning, cooking, making beds, doing laundry, making lunches and caring for the kids, was to stick a broom up your behind so you could sweep the floors while you were running around the house doing other things. It may have been a little crude, but it was our own little private joke, and became our standard greeting whenever we would see each other or talk on the phone. She would horse around and rib, "Fifi, is the broom in tight?", and I would play right along with a snappy come-back, something like, "It's so far in, it's starting to give me a headache!"

~~~~

I always referred to my five boys as my "crooked disciples," which was a phrase that I had heard my sister Mary use all the time. I have no idea where she got it from, but I liked it, and it fit. They were mischievous, but never malicious, and as much as they were good boys, they were boys nonetheless. And even if they didn't look for it, it seemed like trouble always had a way of finding them.

There were lots of bumps and bruises and stitches. They fell out of trees and off their bikes. They got hit with rocks and baseballs. They got stuck with fishhooks, rusty nails and broken glass. And they would brawl with each other over all kinds of things, but God help an outsider who picked a fight with one of them. They were like the

349

Cartwright boys on the old "Bonanza" TV show, if you wanted to fight one, you had to fight them all.

~~~

Back in the early fifties, when we were living in the garrison colonial in Tarry Crest, Jack and Nick were always finding ways to get into trouble. One charming little antic that they employed was that they would climb out their bedroom window, onto the roof of the attached garage, whenever John and I would leave them alone with a baby sitter.

I remember one time when Nick was about five or six years old, he did something that got me angry at him. I was down in the living room and I called to him. He came to the top of the stairs, and stopped, because he knew he was in trouble. I said, "Come down here to me."

He just looked at me, set his jaw defiantly and sassed, "No."

Now I was doing a slow burn. I glared angrily at him and warned, "Don't you make me come up those stairs after you. Come down here right now."

But he just dug his heels in deeper and vowed, "No," again.

So I took off up the stairs, two at a time, and he turned and ran into his room, to the far side of the bed. As I would run around the bed to try to grab him, he would roll across the mattress to the other side of the bed, out of my reach. We repeated this little dance a couple of times, and I was

Nick McFadden

getting angrier by the minute. Finally, he rolled across the bed, by the window, but instead of trying to run around it again, I just pushed the entire bed toward him and squeezed him up against the wall so he couldn't get away. With that he turned to try to open the window behind him, so he could try to climb out onto the roof of the garage, but I had him trapped. Then I reached across the bed, grabbed him and pulled him over to me and snarled, "Now, the next time I tell you to come down to me, you come down to me!" He was unhappy about being caught, but he survived to fight another day. And there would be lots of other days.

~~~

When the boys were young, and we were still living up on Ganung Drive in Ossining, I used to give them their hair cuts. During the summer I liked to keep their hair short, so I would cut their hair, almost like a buzz-cut, with an electric clippers. I used an attachment that would snap onto the head of the clippers, so I could cut their hair to a set length without too much trouble, but as I was running the clippers up the back of Nick's head, the attachment popped off, and in the blink of an eye the clippers cut his hair right down to the scalp, leaving a patch of bare skin on the back of his head. Jack and I started to giggle, and Nicked asked, "What happened, what's so funny?"

Jack, Nick, Phil and Brian - February, 1954.

351

I felt foolish for having messed up his haircut, so I told him to put a big bandage over the patch of bare scalp, and tell people that he had fallen out of a tree and hit his head, until his hair grew back in.

Nick had always been very particular about his hair so, needless to say, he would never let me cut his hair again after that.

~~~

When Brian was about a year and a half or two years old he had a funny habit of sucking the index finger of his left hand, and playing with his earlobe with his right hand. Sometimes if he was sitting on my lap, or I was holding him, he would reach up and play with my earlobe while he was sucking his finger.

Well, one Sunday we were at the Transfiguration Church, I think for Nick's First Communion, and we had gotten there late, so all of the pews were filled up. I was standing in one of the side aisles, holding Brian and listening to the Mass. My sister Helen was seated in one of the pews, and when she saw me, she motioned for me to give Brian to her so I wouldn't have to stand through the whole Mass holding him. So I did.

After they had been sitting there for a few minutes, Helen looked over at Brian and noticed that he was sucking his finger. She was aware of his habit of playing with his ear, or my ear, with his other hand, but he wasn't doing either. When she turned to look a little closer, she saw that Brian had reached up with his right hand and was playing with the earlobe of the man who was sitting next to them. The man was a total stranger, and was trying to discreetly pull away from Brian's grip, but Brian held on. Helen of course was mortified and apologized to the man, but I just laughed when she told me about it.

~~~

Another time, I was up in the kitchen and the boys were all down in the playroom, watching television. Earlier that day I had bought Nick a B-B gun at Woolworth's, and he was downstairs with his brothers, watching TV, but he kept shooting off the B-B gun in the playroom. It didn't have any B-Bs in it, but it still made noise, and the other boys kept asking him to stop shooting it because they were trying to watch a show. I kept hearing them complaining, "Nick, cut it out! Nick, stop it!", but he kept shooting his B-B gun.

So finally I went to the top of the stairs and yelled down to him, "Nick, you knock it off and stop shooting that gun right now, your brothers are trying to watch TV," but as usual, Nick had to push the limits, and shot it off a couple more times. Each time he did it I would yell down to him to stop. Finally, he shot it again, but I had reached the end of my rope. I yelled down to him, "Nick, if you shoot that thing one more time, I'm going to come down there and smash it."

Well, wouldn't you know, Nick decided to push his luck and shot it again. So I got up from the kitchen table, marched downstairs to the playroom, and took the B-B gun away from him.

He protested, "Okay, okay Mom, I'll put it away," but he had pushed me too far. I took the B-B gun out onto the back patio and, holding it by the barrel, swung it over my head and smashed it on the concrete patio till it was broken into pieces. He didn't believe I would do it, but I wanted them all to know that when I said something, I meant it, and, by God, they'd better listen.

~~~~

One day when Brian was about three or four years old, he went running out the front door, tripped and fell face down on the sidewalk. He was crying when I got out to him, and when I looked, I could see that he had cracked one of his top, front teeth. So I took him down to the dentist's office to see what he could do with it, but the dentist said not to worry about it because it was only a baby tooth, and eventually it would be replaced by his permanent tooth.

So we went back home, but over the next few days Brian was having trouble eating. Anything that was above or below room temperature would make him wince in pain, and he kept grabbing at his mouth with his hands, and crying. So finally I called the dentist back and told him what was going on, and he said to bring Brian in to his office again.

John took Brian to the dentist's office that afternoon and the dentist pulled the broken tooth for him. He must have given him something to sedate him, because, when they got back home, John had to pick Brian up in his arms and carry him in from the car, he was so knocked out.

For the next few months, till his new tooth grew in, I was worried that his teeth would all get crooked because when he sucked his finger, it fit perfectly into the gap between his teeth, and I thought it might push the rest of his teeth out of line.

Brian, Jack, Philip and Nick - 1957.

~~~

I remember a day during the first year that we lived on Long Island that something happened that scared me half to death. Patrick was only about six or eight months old at the time, and he was in his playpen, upstairs with his four older brothers. I think a couple of the Cox kids were over, and they were upstairs playing with my boys in their room. We had gotten a "Charlie McCarthy" puppet for Jack and Nick, and they were playing with it up in their room while I was down in the kitchen washing dishes in the sink.

"Charlie McCarthy" was a ventriloquist's dummy that was used by the famous ventriloquist, Edgar Bergen, in his comedy routines that we use to see on TV all the time. The puppet was about the size of a small child, and Edgar Bergen would have it sitting on his lap, to play the part his wisecracking partner, during his act.

Anyway, I was standing at the kitchen sink, which was right under a window looking out onto the backyard. I could hear the boys playing in the upstairs bedroom, right over my head, when suddenly I heard them all scream, and was horrified as I saw "Patrick" fall past the kitchen window, into the backyard. Then all the boys came running down the stairs screaming, "Oh my God, Patrick! Patrick!", and ran past me out to the back yard.

Patrick - 7 months old - June, 1959.

I panicked, thinking, "Oh my God. They must have been playing with Patrick near the open upstairs window, and somehow he had fallen out." My heart sank into the pit of my stomach, and I screamed as I ran out the back door expecting to find the worst. And when I got out there, and saw what had happened, I had to contain myself from killing the rest of the boys.

There, lying on the ground, wasn't Patrick at all, but the "Charlie McCarthy" puppet dressed up in some of Patrick's baby clothes. I was almost apoplectic with fear and worry, but when I looked down and realized it was the puppet, I gasped and looked around angrily at all the boys. They were all standing in a circle around the puppet, with their hands covering their mouths, until I looked down at them. Then they all started laughing hysterically at what they all thought was the greatest prank they had ever pulled off.

Apparently, while they had been upstairs playing with the puppet, one of them came up with the brainstorm that it would be funny to dress the dummy up in some of Patrick's baby clothes and throw it out the window, knowing full well that it would fall past the window where I was standing in the kitchen, and scare the hell out of me. Well, their plan worked to a "T," and they damn near gave me a heart attack. It's a miracle that I ever survived the five of them, and I'm sure it was episodes like that that contributed to my hair turning completely white so prematurely.

Jack, Nick, Philip, Brian and Patrick.
Brian's Kindergarden graduation - June, 1959.

~~~

Another little escapade that the boys and their friends had as part of their repertoire, during the winter when the plows had left large piles of snow along the sides of the street, was to get an old flannel shirt and a pair of old bluejeans, sew the shirt to the pants and stuff the whole thing with crumpled up newspapers, creating a near life-sized dummy.

Then they would lurk behind the plowed up piles of snow and wait for an unsuspecting neighbor to drive by, and, at just the right moment, they would throw the teenage-boy-sized dummy into the path of the car and let out a blood curdling scream.

L to R - Top - Jack and Nick.
Bottom - Phil, Pat, John Anderson, and Brian.
April, 1960.

The poor motorist would nearly go off the road thinking that they had just run over one of the neighborhood kids. They would stomp on their brakes and jump, grief stricken, out of their car expecting to find the broken body of some kid who had, just moments before, been out innocently cavorting in the snow.

But their grief would quickly turn to anger when they realized that the crumpled body under the wheels of their car was only a paper-stuffed, scarecrow-like mannequin. Then they would look around, fists clenched, for the culprits that had scared them so, but there was no one to be found. The boys had all quickly retreated to the concealment of the tunnels that they had dug under the snow. And there they would stay, giggling under their breath, until the angry motorist, grumbling obscenities, got back in their car and drove away.

Then they would recover their dummy, make any necessary repairs to it, and wait; stealthily behind the snow drifts, deviously anticipating the next unsuspecting driver to turn down our street.

~~~

During the winter of 1960 - 61 there was a severe snow storm, and we could tell by the way that the snow was coming down that there wouldn't be any school the next day. That evening there was a lot of snow on the ground and the boys all wanted to go out and play in it. They had been out in the front yard for a while, shoveling the walk, building snow forts and having snowball fights, when suddenly the front door flew open and in came all the boys, yelling for John and me, and helping Brian into the house. Brian was holding his hand to his forehead and there was a lot of blood streaming down his face.

Apparently, during their snowball fight, Nick had picked up

Nick and Philip - Winter, 1961 - 62.

the snow shovel and started scooping up shovels full of snow to throw at Brian and Philip. Unfortunately for Brian, as he was bending down to pick up some snow for a snowball, Nick was coming up with the snow shovel, and caught him in the forehead with the edge of it, opening up a big gash about two inches above his right eye.

I just sat there, stunned by the sight of all the blood, but John grabbed Brian and rushed him into the kitchen to try to wash the cut and get a better look at it.

I went to the kitchen door and shakily asked John, "Is it bad?"

He looked at me, his eyes wide, and while nodding his head "Yes," calmly said, "No, it's not too bad."

I asked, "Will it need stitches?"

Again, John emphatically nodded the affirmative, and held up five fingers, indicating five stitches, but very nonchalantly said, "No, I don't think so." He was trying to keep Brian from getting more upset than he already was.

The snow was so deep that we knew we wouldn't be able to drive Brian to the hospital emergency room, so I called my friend Jean Cox, who's father, Tom McCann, was a doctor in Seaford, and asked if her father would look at the gash on Brian's forehead. She called me back a few minutes later and said that her father could see him, so we got Brian into the car and drove the several blocks to Doctor McCann's house, up near the high school.

When we got there I stayed in the living room, talking with Mrs. McCann, and John went with Brian and Doctor McCann, to his small office downstairs. A few minutes later, as we were chatting, I noticed Mrs. McCann's eyes darting back and forth at something behind me. When I turned to look, there was John, coming slowly up the stairs, holding the railing. His face was ashen. He couldn't stand the sight of blood, so he looked at me and said, "Maybe you should go down with him."

So I went downstairs to try to help. Doctor McCann didn't have any anesthetic on hand, so I had to hold Brian's hands down while the doctor stitched him up. I think it took three stitches to close that nasty cut, but you would have thought it would have taken a lot more, judging by all the blood.

There was an expression that Grandma Laura, John's mother, liked to use whenever John and his sisters would come in and ask what was for dinner, when they were kids. She would tell them that she was serving, "Hot tongue, cold shoulder."

The term "hot tongue" comes from when you would yell at someone with sharp, critical words, and if you totally ignored them that meant that you were giving them the "cold shoulder." Anyway, I must have picked up that phrase from Mrs. McFadden when we were living with her in Pocantico for a couple of years after the War, because I would always tease my boys, and tell them that they were getting "hot tongue, cold shoulder," whenever they would ask what I was making for supper.

Well, one evening, shortly after we had moved into the house on Bit Path, Patrick, who was about four years old at the time, was playing outside in the yard. I asked Brian to call Patrick in for dinner, and Brian went out and

Philip, MaryAnn, Brian, Eileen, Nick and Patrick - December, 1966.

called him but Pat didn't come in. So I went to the door and yelled out to Pat, "Come on in Honey, it's time for dinner."

He yelled back, "What are we having?"

Well, I didn't want the whole neighborhood to know that we could only afford things like potato pancakes or baloney sandwiches and potato chips, so I replied, "Hot tongue, cold shoulder," whereupon Patrick immediately threw himself on the ground and started throwing a tantrum.

He was kicking his feet and pounding his fists into the grass and bawled, "Oh I hate that, I really hate that, and we have it every night!"

~~~

Behind our house at 2109 Bit Path, was a big wooded area with a stream running through it that stretched from Sunrise Highway all the way down to Merrick Road in Seaford, and when Brian and Philip were in junior high school, they and a couple of their friends used to go trapping for muskrats in the stream.

I remember one early winter morning when I heard them go down into the playroom, put on their winter clothes and hip boots, and go tromping out the back door to wade down the stream and check their traps. It was snowing and bitter cold outside.

A few hours later the two of them came bursting back in through the playroom door, all excited and yelling up to me, "Mom, come on down! Quick! You gotta see what we caught!"

So I went down through the playroom and looked out the back door, but I couldn't believe my eyes. There, standing on the patio, were Brian and Philip with a big raccoon, hanging, upside down by it's four feet, from a broomstick that they held between them. They were holding it the way you would see African tribesmen carrying a dead lion after the great white hunter had shot it on a safari in some copy of National Geographic. And to them, you would have thought that they had indeed brought home a trophy lion, they were so proud of their catch. The two of them were grinning from ear to ear.

It was very cold, so I told them to come inside, take off their wet clothes and tell me how they had caught it. But before they came into the house they hung it from the frame of the awning over the porch. That way they could look out the kitchen window to see their big catch as they told me about how their morning had begun, and how they had captured and killed the poor thing. They were both talking over each other with excitement.

The news spread quickly around the neighborhood, and before you knew it, I had lots of Brian and Philip's friends, and friends of friends, filing into our back yard to see what the two fearless hunters had come home with. The whole backyard was full of young boys, "Oooh"ing and "Aaah"ing, as Brian and Philip recounted their tale of danger, heroism and hunting prowess involved in overcoming that ferocious "racky".

Philip displaying the dead racoon.

I don't know where they learned to do it, but the next day Philip, Brian and their friend Tommy Umland went out in the backyard and skinned the raccoon, stretched the hide out on a piece of plywood, and hung it on the garage wall to dry. Apparently Tommy had watched enough episodes of "Sergeant Preston of the Yukon" to consider himself an expert fur trapper and skinner. That mangy looking raccoon skin, along with a couple of decrepit muskrat pelts, adorned the wall of my garage for the next forty years, until I sold my house.

There was another day when I came home from work and found Mrs. Turner, the housekeeper that I had hired to watch Patrick, very upset.

It seems that Brian and Philip, who were home during their mornings because school was in split-session, had set some of their muskrat traps out on the lawn in the backyard, to try to catch some squirrels that they had seen out there. They had broken up pieces of bread and spread them around the traps as bait, then they came back in the house and were watching their traps from the kitchen window, waiting for some poor, unsuspecting squirrel to take the bait.

Mrs. Turner was an older woman, probably in her later sixties, who was the wife of the Minister of the Episcopal Church in Seaford. She was from England and spoke with a heavy British accent. I had hired her to babysit Patrick, who was in kindergarten at the time, while I was at work. Typically, I would leave early for work, and then Mrs. Turner would arrive before John left for his office. She would make sure that Patrick had some breakfast before school, and would make sure he took his lunch with him. While he was at school, she would do some light housework and cleaning, and fold the laundry for me. After Patrick got home she would make sure that he changed into his play clothes and had a snack. She would stay with him until Jack or Nick or I got home in the afternoons, and for all this she charged me twenty-five dollars a week. She was a bargain, and I was lucky to have her.

None of the boys could stand her, because if ever they were home, sick or something, she would change the TV channel so she could watch her "shows", all the soap operas that she loved, no matter what they happened to be watching. Jack had a nickname for her, he called her "Stomach" Turner, because she always got him so agitated.

In any event, Brian and Phil were watching their traps from the kitchen window while Mrs. Turner was washing some dishes in the kitchen sink. She asked the two boys what they were looking at, but they just giggled suspiciously. So she walked over to the window to see for herself.

What she saw horrified her. There, out on the grass, were two or three squirrels, nervously walking around and in between the five or six traps that the boys had set, eating the pieces of bread. Right away she realized that the squirrels were in terrible danger. She shrieked in her high, British accent, "Oh you horrible boys!", and ran down the stairs to the playroom, and out the back door.

Philip and Brian thought that she would just try to save the squirrels by shooing them off, and started laughing, but she had other things in mind. She ran out onto the lawn, scaring the squirrels away, and then started trying to pick up the set traps. But she didn't know what she was getting herself into. When Brian and Philip saw her start to grab at the traps, they yelled from the kitchen window, to try to warn her, but it was too late. As she grabbed them, she triggered them, and a couple of them snapped on to her fingers. By the time the boys got outside to her, she had one or two traps clamped onto each hand. She was screaming in pain and trying to get the traps off her hands, while still trying to pick up the un-sprung ones. As she tried to remove them from her fingers, she was stretching and ripping the fingers off the rubber gloves that she had been wearing while dishwashing. The whole time she was screaming at the boys in her high pitched British accent, over and over again, "Oh, you horrible boys, you horrible, horrible boys."

Brian and Philip were hysterical, laughing at the whole scene, but managed to compose themselves long enough to remove the steel traps from her poor, bruised fingers.

I think it was lucky for the two of them that she was such a good, God fearing, Christian woman, or she might have killed them both, and I'm not sure I would have blamed her.

Philip and Brian - Easter, 1960.

There was a time when Brian was on the Seaford High School lacrosse team, and one Saturday morning before the season started he was going to go out with his friend, Albie Smith, and they were going to go to the school field and practice throwing a lacrosse ball around with some of their other teammates. John saw Brian getting ready to go and said to him, "Brian, I don't want you guys running around with lacrosse sticks, without the proper equipment on, somebody's gonna get hurt."

Well, a few minutes later, John left to go to work, and no sooner had his car turned around the corner, Brian breezed down the stairs with his lacrosse stick and went off to meet Albie.

It wasn't very long after he left, maybe a half an hour or so later, I heard him come back in the house and call upstairs to me, "Ma!"

So I came to the top of the stairs and asked, "What's up?"

He was holding his hand over his mouth as he reluctantly had to confess, "Mom, Albie hit me in the mouth with his lacrosse stick, and broke my teeth."

"Oh my God," I scolded, "didn't your father tell you not to practice without your helmet?"

Well, he didn't want to hear that, and just blew me off.

Anyway, I drove him down to the dentist's office and we went inside. The dentist took Brian in to take some X-rays, then a little while later came out to me in the waiting room. He said, "Mrs. McFadden, I'm sorry to tell you this, but not only are your son's teeth broken, his upper jaw is broken too, and we have to wire his teeth and his jaw closed."

I can't remember how long Brian's jaws were wired together, but through the whole thing he couldn't talk or eat. He could only eat soup or a milk shake through a straw. I won't repeat what his father had to say to him that night when he got home from work and saw Brian with his jaws all wired shut, but Brian could only mumble unintelligibly, through the wire and his broken, clenched teeth, to try to defend himself.

Sometime during the summer of 1969, Philip came home one day and announced to John and me that he was going to go to "Woodstock" with a couple of his friends. John and I had no idea what "Woodstock" was, and when I tried to get any answers from Philip about it, it seemed like he didn't know any more about it than we did, only that it had been billed as, "Three days of peace, love and music."

Philip, Patrick and Brian - March, 1970.

Philip had just graduated from high school and was only seventeen years old. I knew two of the boys that were going with him, but that was it. They left Seaford on a Thursday to drive upstate in his friend's car, and that day I kept hearing news reports on the radio about the traffic problems in upstate New York, due the crowds of young people converging on Woodstock. The reports said that police and emergency services couldn't get close to the area, and that people were getting sick from all the drugs that they were taking. I had no way of getting in touch with Philip, and he had no way of calling us. It was a nightmare, and it was all we heard on the news reports that whole weekend.

I kept getting more and more frightened and worried as the weekend went on. I hadn't heard from him in a couple of days, and he never told us when he would be home.

I remember that it was a beautiful, sparkling, Sunday afternoon, and I was in the house doing some dusting at around two o'clock. Suddenly the front door opened, and there was Phil. I ran over and put my arms around him and gave him a kiss, but I couldn't even talk, I was so relieved that he was home, safe and sound.

As meaningful as it had been for Phil to have been there to be part of something that turned out to be a historic event, and he had had a great time, it had been a long, sleepless weekend for me. Neither of us will ever forget Woodstock, but for completely different reasons.

~~~

Back in the fall of 1970, Brian was playing on the Seaford High School varsity football team. I would always try to get to all of the boys sporting events, and one Saturday afternoon I went up to see Brian playing in a football game.

At some point during the game, Brian broke his eyeglasses and had to come off the field. He was kneeling on the sideline, with his back to me, trying to repair his glasses so he could get back into the game. At first I couldn't tell what he was doing, but then I realized that he was trying to fix his broken glasses. It seemed like he wasn't having much luck, so I decided to see what I could do to help, and give him my glasses to use. We both had nearly the same prescription lenses, so I knew mine would work for him, and the only difference between his glasses and mine was that his had plain black frames, and mine had pale blue harlequin style frames with rhinestones around the edges. I thought they were quite "chic."

So I walked down from the grandstands, to the fence along the sidelines, and had my glasses in my hand, holding them out over the fence, to give to him. He still had his back to me, so I called out his name a couple of times, "Brian, Brian," trying to discreetly get his attention, but he still wouldn't turn around.

One of the other players, who was standing next to Brian, heard me calling, and tapped him on the shoulder, pointed over towards me and told him, "Hey Brian, some lady's calling you"

Brian, his voice dripping with disdain, whispered hoarsely, "I know. I'm trying to ignore her. Maybe she'll get the message and go away."

He had seen me out of the corner of his eye, and was mortified at the fact that his mother was standing there, trying to get him, the big tough football player, to wear what he considered to be her garishly flamboyant eyeglasses, and just wanted me to disappear before any more of his teammates noticed. He would rather have died than acknowledge that I was there, and what I was trying to do. He continued to ignore me, never even turning around to tell me to go away, say, "Hi Mom," or anything. I thought he was just being

Brian - Seaford High School football photo.

stubborn, so finally I just gave up and went back to the grandstands and watched the rest of the game.

368

One day when Patrick was in the ninth grade, he came home after school and surprised me by saying that he had decided that he was going to try out for the school ice hockey team, and said to me, "Mom, I'm gonna have my first hockey practice tomorrow, can you drive me to the rink?"

I asked, "What time is practice?"

"Five o'clock," he replied.

I shook my head and said, "Oh, honey, that's going to be a problem. Daddy's going to have the car tomorrow, and he may not be home in time from work."

Patrick looked up at me with a woeful expression on his face and implored, "No Mom, not in the afternoon, I mean five o'clock in the morning."

Well, that was an even bigger surprise, "Five o'clock in the morning?" I bellyached.

Anyway, I told him I would get up early and drive him to the hockey rink,

Fifi and Patrick - Christmas, 1973.

and I warned, "You'd better get up at four o'clock if you've got to be on the ice by five."

So that night, Patrick put all his hockey equipment down in the living room and slept on the couch so he could get right up and leave early in the morning. My little grandson, Michael, stayed over that night and slept in my bed with me, and he was all over the place. I had all I could do to keep from falling out of bed, and I had to sleep with one hand on the floor. I barely slept, and finally I just got up at 4:00 a.m. and went downstairs to wake up Patrick.

He got up and put on all of his hockey gear, in the house. When we left, it was pouring rain outside, and when I opened the front door Patrick looked around and observed sleepily, "Geez, it's dark out."

I just shook my head and said, "Of course it's dark out, its four o'clock in the morning. It's still the middle of the night."

We started driving towards Bellmore, to the Newbridge Road rink. It was teaming rain, and there wasn't another car on the road. As we turned onto Newbridge Road, I saw a kid walking on the side of the road with a hockey bag and sticks, and he was hitchhiking. I thought to myself, "This poor kid's soaking wet. Where are his parents?", so I pulled over and let him in. When we pulled up in front of the rink, I couldn't believe my eyes. The place was lit up like Times Square, and I could see all the white helmets of the young boys inside, skating around the rink.

I dropped off Patrick and the other boy, and headed home, thinking that I would have about an hour's rest before I had to go back to pick him up. I had just laid down on the living room couch, at about five thirty, when the phone rang. I picked it up and heard Pat say, "Hi Mom, It's me."

"Of course it's you," I razzed, "who else would be calling here at this hour?"

But, oblivious to my attempt at sarcasm, he just said, "I'm ready to come home now Mom," so I got back in the car and went back to the rink to pick him up.

As I was driving down Merrick Road, I saw another kid, riding a bicycle with his hockey bag and stick, heading home from the rink. I picked up Patrick and took him home. He changed out of his sweaty hockey equipment, and I gave him some breakfast. Then he went upstairs and went back to bed. By then, Michael was waking up and wanted some breakfast. And that was my introduction to hockey.

Patrick and a couple of his friends; John Posterino, Bobby Mancini, and Frank Vittucci, among others, all played on the Seaford high school hockey team, and every weekend all the other players parents and I would be at the ice rink, watching the boys play hockey.

Patrick and Bobby Mancini - Seaford High School Hockey team - 1975.

Then, about a year after they had started playing for the high school team, I think probably 1974, Patrick and a bunch of his teammates rented the ice at a place called "Racquet and Rink," in Farmingdale, Long Island, for a practice one Friday night. Patrick's three older brothers, Brian, Nick and Philip heard about it, and, even though none of them had ever played hockey before, they decided to go up to the rink with some of their other friends, who were also in their early and mid twenties, and skate with the younger boys.

Well, it was the funniest thing you ever saw. The older boys didn't have any real hockey equipment, so they borrowed and scraped together a mish-mash of various other athletic gear. They wore a mixed bag of poorly fitting, rusty figure skates, miscellaneous baseball

Patrick - Captain of the Seaford High School hockey team - 1976.

and football pads, lacrosse helmets and leather work gloves, and they had a cooler full of beer on the bench. They were all holding on to the side of the rink to keep from falling down. They couldn't skate, they couldn't stop, they couldn't pass or shoot, but they had a riot doing it. A few weeks later they did it again, and then again a few weeks after that, and little by little they started to improve. The next thing I knew, they were all starting to buy hockey skates and all the other pads and equipment, and were renting the ice, religiously, every Friday night.

Patrick, Nick, Phil and Brian at Raquet & Rink - March 1977.

After about a year of all of them playing pick-up hockey on Friday nights, my four boys organized a team that they called the "Stix"; made up of some of Patrick's younger friends, and some of Brian and Phil's older friends, and started playing organized hockey in an amateur men's ice hockey league at Racquet and Rink. Even their cousins, Greg and Jim Egan, joined the team and came down from Tarrytown to skate with them. Beside their regular Friday night "rent outs," they were also playing in "Men's League" games at least one or two nights a week.

Nick, Philip, Brian and Patrick - THE STIX - 1980.

The Men's League games were played against other teams, and, over time, heated rivalries developed between the Stix and some of the other teams, and even personal vendettas between players. These rivalries made for a lot of rough, tough and exciting hockey games. Needless to say, the entire family, including wives, kids and girlfriends, spent a lot of time at the rink in those days.

~~~

One night I went up to the rink to watch them all play, and I was standing by the dasher boards with Nick's wife, Phyllis, and Brian's wife, Debbie, when the referee who was going to call the game came

Jimmy Gillen, Laura and Michael.
Racket & Rink circa 1978.

over to the three of us and asked if we knew anybody who knew how to keep score. Phyllis and Debbie both pointed at me and said, "She does." So I agreed to keep the score sheet for him, and he helped me shuffle across the ice to a seat in the penalty box, where he gave me a pad of "scoring summary" sheets, to keep a record of all the goals, assists and penalties during the game. That was the first time, but not the last time, that I sat in the penalty box during my sons' hockey games. Some of the refs got to know me, and whenever they were in need of someone to keep the score sheet, or run the clock for the game, they would ask me. I was pleased to do it but I don't think any of my boys were. They were embarrassed to have their mother sitting in the penalty box, between the team benches, keeping the scoring stats. All of the boys on the Stix had to watch what they said whenever they were penalized and had to come sit in the penalty box with me. Instead of uttering some curse word in the heat of the game, they had to restrain themselves by saying things like,"Oh, gee" or "Darn it," when complaining about the refs or the opposing players. Even the players on the other teams were chastised and confronted by my sons and their teammates for using foul language in front of me. I finally had to stop keeping score during games when the boys all pleaded with me not to do it anymore. I'm not sure if it was more because they were so embarrassed by it, or because they were tired of getting five minute fighting penalties and getting ejected from games for going after opposing players who failed to display the proper measure of decorum in my presence.

Brian - STIX circa 1978.

One night I got to the rink late, and the game had already started. When I looked out on the ice, I could see Brian and Philip out skating in the game, and Nick was sitting on the bench, but I didn't see Patrick. When I turned, I saw Patrick standing in the bleachers behind me, dressed in his street clothes.

"What happened?", I asked, "Did you get in a fight?", thinking maybe he had been thrown out of the game or something.

He looked at me in his stoic way and said, "No." Then he bent down closer to me and quietly whispered, "Now Mom, I don't want to make a big deal out of this, so don't make a scene, but I broke my tooth."

Of course I overreacted and shrieked, "WHAT? YOU BROKE A TOOTH?"

Well, so much for not making a scene. It was one of <u>his</u> front teeth that had gotten broken during the game, but that was only one of the many such hockey injuries that <u>I</u> had to endure over the ensuing years.

Hockey Mom - Circa 1981.

Phil and Kim's annual skating party - February, 1999.

Hockey became a major part of the McFadden family lifestyle for many years, and Racquet and Rink was our home away from home. The boys were all New York Ranger fans and I was the lone New York Islander fan, so there was always a lot of needling each other.

I remember one night that I was over at Philip's house watching a game between the Islanders and the Rangers. The Rangers had been leading for most of the game, but the Islanders tied it, and then won the game on a late goal. After I got done claiming bragging rights from Philip, I just couldn't resist the urge to harass Nick, so I picked up the phone and called his house. Later, he told me that when he heard the phone ring, he looked at Phyllis and said, "I'm not gonna answer that, it's probably my mother." But finally he picked up the phone and said, "Hello," and I just gave him the "raspberries." I made the "Bronx cheer" sound as loud as I could, and then just hung up without saying a word.

But and Nick has gotten his revenge many times over the years by doing the same thing to me on nights when the Rangers beat the Islanders.

Karma, I guess.

The night that Brian's oldest son, Danny, was born, April 5th, 1979, the boys had all been playing in a hockey game up at Racquet and Rink, and I had gone up to watch them. Brian didn't play in the game because he had gone to up to Central General Hospital in Plainview with Debbie when she had gone into labor that afternoon.

After the hockey game ended, I went with Nick, Philip and Pat, over to the hospital so we could all give moral support to Brian, who was sitting anxiously in the waiting room. As we were all gathered in the waiting room, someone came out of the maternity ward and made a comment that, "…a big baby had just been born." Then, a little while later, a nurse came out and said that Debbie had delivered the baby, so we all got up and went to the nursery to welcome Daniel Patrick McFadden into the world. He weighed 10lbs., 2ozs., when he was born, and was "...the big one" that was the talk of all the nurses in the maternity ward that evening.

I remember standing in front of the windows of the nursery, delighting in my fine new grandson, Danny, then glancing over at Nick, Phil and Patrick; who were all standing with their arms around Brian's shoulders, and I could see that they all had tears in their eyes as they proudly looked in at the newest member of the McFadden clan. Another young Crooked Disciple.

Nick, Patrick, Brian, Philip and Jack - 1966.

~~~

Chapter Eleven

HEART'S DELIGHT

Jack was born on February 25th, 1947. He weighed nine pounds, two and a half ounces. I didn't get to see him until the next morning because I had been knocked out during his delivery, but when I finally saw him for the first time, I thought, "Oh, what cute little dimples." In those days, you were kept in the hospital for two weeks after giving birth, much different from today. These days they give you the heave-ho within a day or two, as long as you or your baby aren't bleeding to death.

I just thought that Jack was the greatest thing that ever happened. Whenever I would take him out for a walk in his carriage, and run into someone I knew, I would gush, "Isn't he cute? Isn't he just the cutest little boy?"

Jack at one year old - 1948.

Then one day John asked me, "What are you going to do if someone says, 'Nah, I don't think he's so hot'?"

But truthfully, I really couldn't imagine anyone ever thinking that Jack wasn't just as adorable as I thought he was.

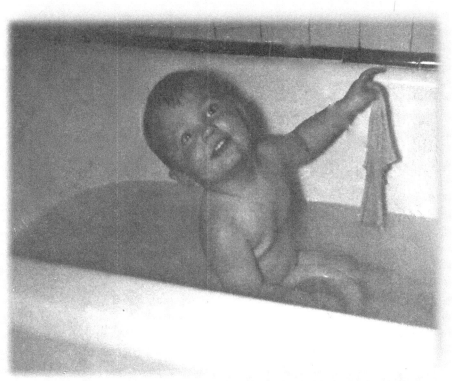

Jack at 18 months old - August, 1948.

~~~

We had a birthday party, in Pocantico, for Jack when he was one year old. All the little cousins were there; Larry and Mary Ellen Dick, and Eileen Budney. Nick was three weeks old and Greg Dick was about a month old. I can still see all the kids; lined up in their highchairs, eating birthday cake and ice cream, and Mary Ellen crying in her playpen in the living room. She was always crying as a baby.

For a couple of weeks when Jack was little, he had a terrible habit when he was around other little kids. He would lean in toward them like he was going to kiss them, and we'd all be standing around saying, "Oh look how cute Jack is, kissing so and so...," but then he would lean in and bite them on the cheek. I would have to grab him away from the other baby, mortified that my perfect little boy would do such a thing.

Jack, Eileen, Larry Jr., Mary Ellen, Alan Bruhn Jr., Aunt Mary with Greg, Tapa Egan with MaryAnn, Alan Bruhn Sr. with Jimmy and Fifi holding Nick - 1949.

~~~

My mother and father loved Jack. I would leave him with them to babysit sometimes, and they loved having him. My mother would dote over him, and just as she did with Helen and Mary's little ones; Larry, Mary Ellen and Eileen, she called him her "Heart's Delight."

I remember one day when we were still living in Pocantico, and Jack was about three years old. I had some beautiful crystal candlestick holders, that John and I had gotten for a wedding present, out on the kitchen counter to wash. Jack came into the kitchen and got a hold of one of the candlestick holders and dropped it into the sink, thinking he was helping me. But it chipped when it hit the bottom of the sink, and I got very upset and scolded him, and told him to go stand in the corner. He toddled over into the corner, his head bowed and shoulders hunched over, and started quietly sobbing. Then I heard his little voice imploring, "Heart's delight. Heart's delight," in between his sobs and sniffles. Of course that immediately made me melt. His little heart was broken because I had scolded him, and mine was broken for having done so.

Jack - 1949.

"Heart's delight" became a term of affection and endearment that I used to call Jack all through his childhood and youth. In his later years, he would always send birthday cards or Christmas cards to me and sign them "Heart's delight".

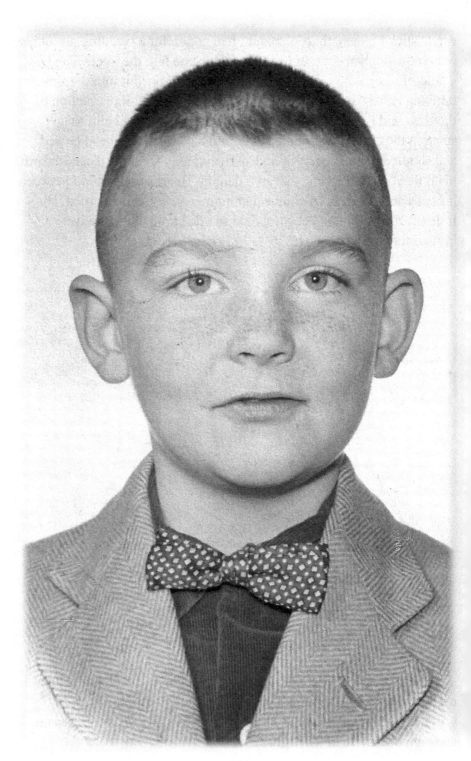

It was obvious from the time that he was just a little boy that Jack had a natural talent and aptitude for music. We had a baby grand piano in the playroom of our house in Ossining, and he took maybe two lessons from a piano teacher when he was very young. When he was only about eight or nine years old he started to develop an uncanny ability to play music by ear. He would hear commercial jingles on the television or radio, then run over to the piano, sit down, and after only a few minutes of working at it to figure out the melody, start to play the measures that he had just heard.

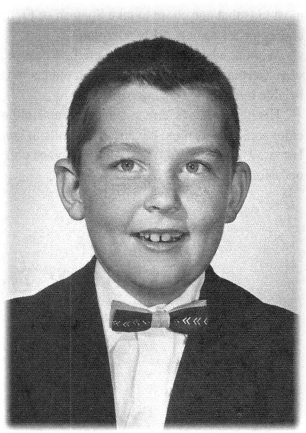

Jack, taken in April, 1955 - 8 years old, in 3rd grade.

When we first moved to Long Island Jack was still in the seventh grade, and I remember taking him up to Seaford High School to get him enrolled in school, and talking to the guidance counselor. Jack spoke to him about how he wanted to do something in the field of music after he got out of school.

It was required in those days that kids take a language in junior high, so when the guidance counselor asked him what language he wanted to take, Jack replied, "German."

The counselor and I both looked at each other in surprise, because most kids that age chose to take Spanish or French. Then the guidance counselor asked him, "Why German?"

Without hesitation Jack answered, "Because all the great Masters were German, and wrote all the great operas in German, and I want to be able to read their manuscripts."

His high school German teacher, Frau Kalthofer, would sometimes enter some of her more advanced students in language competitions at Hofstra University, and Jack won first place on more than one occasion.

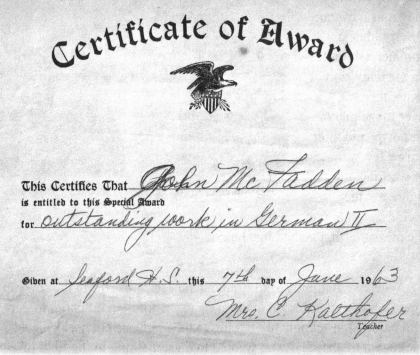

High school CERTIFICATE OF AWARD for German II - June, 1963.

Jack continued to study German all through high school and college. He became fluent in German through his classes, but it was by his listening and studying of the great German operas that he learned and understood the many subtleties and nuances of the German language. He attained such a mastery of the language that he could speak it, and understand it as if he had been born and raised in Germany.

~~~

One day, in the spring of 1964, Jack came home from school and informed me that the high school chorus was going to be having their spring concert the following Friday evening. Then he modestly announced, barely containing his pride, that he would be performing a solo and asked if John and I could come. So I told him that I would tell his father to come home early that night so we could go to the concert.

That Friday evening, John, Nick and I were going to go up to the school. John got home from work early and went up to take a shower. After he got dressed, he was coming down the stairs and enquired, "So, what's this bit I hear about Jack going to be singing a solo tonight? Have you heard him practicing?"

"Well," I said, "I've heard him singing in the shower, but I can't say that I've actually heard him really practicing. Why?"

He looked at me and fretted aloud, "I just wonder if we're going to be embarrassed tonight."

John's insensitive remark got my goat to the point that I was almost speechless, and all I could muster was a caustic, "Well, I'm sure Mr. Mech wouldn't have Jack singing a solo if he thought it would be embarrassing to you," but I just wanted to kick him.

In any event, we went up to the school and sat through the elementary school band and chorus, the junior high school band and chorus, and the high school band and orchestra. Finally it got to the high school chorus. They performed a couple of songs as a group, then Mr. Mech, the chorus director, walked to the front of the stage and announced, "Tonight we are pleased to present a wonderful performance by Mr. John McFadden. He will be singing Schubert's 'Sereanade.'"

Jack walked down the risers, from the rest of the chorus, and took his place on stage next to the pianist. He was completely calm and confident. He performed the song the way it was originally written, in German, and when he finished singing he got a loud standing ovation from the entire audience. Except for three people. John, Nick and I were blown away, and my heart was pounding so hard, and was so full of pride for Jack, that I could hardly breathe.

Jack - High school senior yearbook photo.

After he graduated from high school in 1964, Jack went on to study at the State University of New York at Fredonia, near Buffalo, which was a college that was primarily for musically inclined students. He won many accolades for his performances in concerts and in operas such as "Falstaff," which he was perfectly suited for because of his heavy build. He also started to conduct some of the opera and choral groups that he taught and worked with. His professors at Fredonia recognized his talent, and ardently encouraged him to pursue his studies of music and opera.

Jack as FALSTAFF - Fredonia - 1967-68.

~~~

Jack loved to laugh, and had the most wonderful sense of humor. I remember one night in the late sixties, when Jack was home from college and Nick's girlfriend, Phyllis Smith, was over at the house. We were all getting pretty hungry, and decided to order some Chinese food. Nick asked Phyllis to call the order into the Chinese restaurant, so we could go pick it up. Then, while she was busy asking everyone what they wanted and writing down the order, Jack slipped away, downstairs to the playroom without anybody noticing, and picked up the phone extension. Phyllis picked up the phone in the kitchen and dialed the Chinese restaurant, but Jack was already waiting for her and answered the other end using a silly Chinese accent. Unsuspectingly, Phyllis said that she wanted to place an order, and Jack, posing as an English-challenged waiter at the restaurant, asked, "What name?", in this silly, fake Chinese accent.

She said, "McFadden."

Jack replied, "Missaden?"

"No," she corrected, "McFadden!"

"Mifallen?", Jack responded.

"No, no," she insisted, her voice rising, "McFadden."

This went on for another minute or so with Jack coming up with all kinds of silly mispronunciations of our name, in his dopey sing-song accent. And the more he did it, the more frustrated Phyllis got.

Then she started spelling it for him, "M-C-F-A-D-D-E-N."

And he would misspell it back to her, "N-E-S-A-P-P-E-M."

We could all hear Phyllis getting louder, and more and more agitated. Finally, Jack couldn't contain himself anymore and started laughing out loud, and we could all hear him upstairs. The rest of us had caught on well before Phyllis did, and we all had a good laugh. Then even Phyllis had to laugh, once she caught on to Jack's silly prank.

~~~

Then there was one time when I had bought a big basket of fresh peaches, and I would serve them to the kids in all kinds of ways. I cut them up in their cereal for breakfast. I served them with ice cream for dessert. I even tried my hand at making a peach pie. I was giving them to the boys all the time, trying to use them up. Then one night, after dinner, I put a bowl of sliced peaches on the table for dessert. I went into the kitchen, and when I came back to the dining room table a minute later, I happened to look over at Jack. He hadn't said anything, and was just sitting quietly at the table, but he had a slice of peach hanging out of each of his ears. He still didn't say anything, but the insinuated message was that he had been eating so many peaches that they had started coming out of his ears. We all got hysterical,

Jack fooling around at the piano.
Year unknown.

laughing at him, but he continued to sit there as if he had no idea what everyone thought was so funny.

~~~

The first summer that Jack was home from school, following John's heart attacks, he got a job working nights so that he could be home with his father during the day, while I was at work. I depended on Jack's salary to supplement our income, as John was not working.

The first job that he got was working as the night desk clerk at the Hempstead Hotel, in the city of Hempstead, New York. It was in a pretty seedy area of the city, and about half of the hotel was set aside for welfare residents.

Jack would usually leave to go to work at around seven o'clock in the evening, but one night, as I was expecting him to leave, he came to me and said, "Mom, I'm not going to work tonight. I don't work at the hotel anymore."

"Why?" I asked, "What happened?"

"I quit my job" he confessed, and then I noticed that his hands were shaking.

I immediately knew that something had to be wrong. It just wasn't like Jack to be so unnerved. So I took his hands in mine and repeated softly, "What happened, Honey?"

He proceeded to tell me how at work, he would always lock the front entrance to the hotel lobby at around 9:00 p.m.. From where he stood behind the front desk he could see the front door, and anyone who wanted to come in would have to ring the bell. If he didn't like the look of them for any reason, he would wave them away and say that there were no vacancies, especially late at night.

But two nights before, a man had come to the door during the night, and rang the bell. He was a well dressed black man, and after giving the guy the once over, Jack buzzed him into the lobby. The man walked over to the cigarette machine and reached into his pockets for change. Jack thought to himself, "Oh hell, he doesn't want a room, he just came in to buy cigarettes." Then, after fumbling around with some loose change, the guy walked over to the counter and asked Jack if he could change a dollar bill for him, and Jack said, "Sure."

There was a cash drawer under the counter, and Jack had the key to it attached to a ring on his belt. He bent down to unlock the cash drawer, and when he stood back up the guy reached over the counter and grabbed him by the front of his shirt with his left hand, then pulled him up against the counter and put a knife under his chin with his right hand. Then the guy jumped over the counter and slammed Jack up against the wall and threatened, "Don't push any buttons or try to sound any alarms," the whole time holding the knife under Jack's chin.

Off to one side of the counter was the manager's office and the guy told Jack, "Get in there," so they went into the office and he sat Jack down at the desk. "Who else is working in the building?", he demanded.

Nobody else was working that night, but Jack told him, "The janitor. He's working up on the top floor."

Then the guy asked where the safe was. It was behind a cabinet, but Jack told him that he didn't know the combination. He said, "The only one that knows the combination is the bookkeeper, and she won't be in till the morning."

Then he ordered Jack to, "Give me your wallet," so Jack threw his wallet on the desk. There was only twenty dollars in it, which the guy took, then he demanded, "What are those boxes out under the counter," and pointed through the door to the counter were he had first grabbed Jack.

"They're safe deposit boxes," Jack told him, and so the guy went back out by the counter and started to try to open some of the safe deposit boxes, leaving Jack sitting at the desk in the office.

Jack told me, "Mom, when the guy went out, it was like my arm wasn't even attached to my body. I reached over and slammed the office door shut. It locked automatically, so the guy couldn't get back in."

He could hear the guy dropping change on the floor as he rifled through the cash box. Then he reached over and pushed the alarm button, under the desk, that would summon the police. He could hear the footsteps of the thief, running across the lobby, but he didn't hear him leave, and didn't know where he went. After a few minutes of silence he opened the office door, and stood half in and half out; where he could keep an eye on the lobby door to let the police in when they arrived, but jump back inside the office if the thief was still there. A few minutes later the police arrived, and Jack let them in. They searched the building, but couldn't find the guy.

The police called the owner of the hotel, and when he arrived and was told about what had happened, Jack told him the he was resigning. "Ah come on," said the owner, "don't make such a big deal about it, it happens all the time."

Jack looked at him in disbelief and barked, "Well, not with me it doesn't"

The owner asked Jack if he could give him another day or two to find someone to replace him, and said he would have someone stay with Jack overnight if it would make him feel better.

So, the next night, Jack went back, and the janitor stayed and slept on the couch in the lobby. At around midnight, Jack heard the elevator start coming down from one of the upper floors. It stopped at the lobby, but no one got off, and from his position behind the counter Jack couldn't see into it to see if anyone was still inside. Then the elevator doors shut again and it continued down to the basement. Then he heard the basement door, which went out to the parking lot, open and close.

The police hadn't found the guy when they searched the building the night before, and Jack started to think that maybe he had hidden all night and day somewhere in the hotel and was just coming down now to make his getaway. So Jack went over and woke up the janitor, and told him that someone had come down in the elevator and gone out through the basement door. The janitor got up, and the two of them went down to the basement to check things out. They looked out the basement door to the parking lot, where they saw an old woman, one of the welfare residents, walking over to a bar across the street. They relocked the door from the inside, and when she came back a few hours later, she had to come to the front door, for Jack to buzz her in.

The next day, the police wanted Jack to come to the station to look at some photos of suspects, but he never went, and he never went back to work at the hotel.

~~~

Following his graduation from SUNY Fredonia, where he received a Bachelors Degree in music, Jack went to Southern Illinois University to study for his Masters Degree. One of his earlier female professors at Fredonia, Elaine Wallace, had been instrumental in securing a grant for him to go there. She was now teaching at Southern Illinois, and had kept abreast of his progress at Fredonia.

At that point, Jack's interest was starting to gravitate more towards conducting than singing.

394

One night, at Southern Illinois, Jack attended a program to listen to some of the other graduate students who were performing recitals for Ms. Marjorie Lawrence. For those who aren't familiar with her, Marjorie Lawrence was an Australian born woman who had become one of the worlds most celebrated opera stars, singing at all of the major opera houses in Europe and the Metropolitan Opera in New York City, prior to and during World War II. She was especially known for her energetic portrayals of the great German heroines of the master composer Wagner, due to her youthful beauty and physical presence on stage. But as a young adult, at the height of her career, she was stricken with polio and crippled, and could no longer perform on stage. After years of rehab and therapy, her husband, an American doctor by the name of Tom King, suggested that she visit some of the veterans' hospitals and sing for the many soldiers who had been sent back from the battlefield wounded and crippled, to try to raise their spirits. At first she said, "No," that her "...singing career was finished," but he persisted. Finally she agreed, and when she sang for the wounded soldiers, they loved her. She started to perform a little more at various Veterans Administration hospitals, then the Red Cross heard about her and asked her to go sing at other hospitals. Eventually the Red Cross sent her to Europe, to sing for the troops there. Little by little she regained her confidence on stage, even though she was confined to a wheel chair. Soon, the opera world welcomed her back. Stage settings were devised to make it look like she was sitting on a rock or mounted on a horse or something, but staged so that she wouldn't have to walk or stand during her performances. She ended up having a very successful second career in the opera, despite her disability. She wrote her autobiography, entitled "Interrupted Melody," which was made into an academy award winning movie starring Glen Ford and Eleanor Parker in 1955.

Following her retirement from the opera, she and her husband bought a ranch in Hot Springs, Arkansas, so that she could be close to the natural hot springs which helped her with her therapy and rehab. She named the ranch, "Harmony Hills," and had since become the "Artist in Residence" at Southern Illinois University.

In any event, Jack attended the recital that evening to hear some of his fellow graduate students perform for Marjorie Lawrence. One of them was a young man named Roger Keyes, who had been studying with Jack. At the end of the program, Ms. Lawrence summoned Roger over to speak to her, and to compliment him on his performance. "Your German is perfect," she extolled, "how long did you study in Germany?"

He confessed that he, "…had never been to Germany."

"So then," she prodded, "where did you learn to speak it so fluently?"

"I've been studying with Mr. McFadden," he proudly revealed.

Jack had already left the auditorium and was getting into his car when a student ran up to him in the parking lot and gushed, "Miss Lawrence would like to speak with you," so, filled with curiosity as to what she might want to speak to him about, he went back inside and met her for the first time.

Jack with Marjorie Lawrence and Dr. King - Date unknown.

After graciously greeting him, she said to Jack, "I've been enjoying the performance of your friend Roger tonight, and he tells me that you are the one responsible for his perfect German."

Jack thanked her for the compliment.

Then she continued, "He also tells me that you have a beautiful voice in your own right."

Again Jack thanked her for the compliment.

Then she asked, "Would you sing something for me?"

So Jack sang for her. I don't remember what he sang, but, when he finished, Ms. Lawrence sat quietly; reflecting pensively for a moment. Then, peering up at him, probing his eyes, smiled warmly and impassioned, "Oh. My dear boy, you owe it to the world to sing."

Jack with Marjorie Lawrence - August, 1973.

Marjorie Lawrence and Doctor King became fast friends of Jack's, and they spent a lot of time together. Jack would often drive to Hot Springs to visit with them at their ranch. At some point she asked Jack to be the Assistant Director of her "Summer Opera Theater" that she ran in Hot Springs, and Jack continued to work there during the summers when he wasn't working at Baylor University.

Jack with Marjorie Lawrence and Dr. King.
Hot Springs, Arkansas - 1974.

In the spring of 1973, Philip and his fiancée Claudia were planning their wedding, and they asked Jack if he would sing during the ceremony at the church. He said that he would be proud to, and would select the music for their ceremony.

A week before the wedding, Phil's friends threw a bachelor party for him, and Jack, Nick and Brian all went. The party was held at a bar in Suffolk County that featured topless dancers. Apparently, these girls not only danced provocatively for the boys, but flirted with them in an effort to get tips.

Jack was the oldest one there, and was sitting quietly, sipping a beer, when one of the dancers tried to get him more engaged. She removed Jack's eyeglasses, then seductively slipped them down the front of her G-string, and danced with them there, in front of him for a few minutes. All of the boys got a big kick out of this, and hooted and howled at Jack's good fortune of the attention that he was getting from the dancer. I think Jack just found it a bit embarrassing, but took it all in good sport. He related the whole story to me when he got home, late that night.

The next day, Jack was sitting in the living room reading the newspaper, when my neighbor, Mary Gillen, came over to see me. I was telling her the story about the dancer taking Jack's glasses from him and putting them down the front of her G-string. Mary wasn't quite sure how to react to this sordid revelation. She laughed nervously, then looked over at Jack and commented, "Oh my God, you've got to be kidding me."

Without missing a beat, Jack looked up at her from the newspaper, took off his glasses and, pointing to the bridge of his nose, quipped, "No, I'm not kidding, and I've even got the rash to prove it."

Well, Mary and I laughed so hard we almost wet our pants.

In the days leading up to Philip and Claudia's wedding, I told everyone to come early to the service because Jack and his friend Ingrid, a girl that he knew from his days at Fredonia, were going to be singing.

That day, as people were filing into the church, Jack and Ingrid were singing a beautiful rendition of "And this is My Beloved". Nick was Philip's "Best Man", so the two of them were up on the altar, awaiting Claudia's entrance to the church, when Jack first started to sing. They had never really heard Jack perform like that before, and when he first started to sing they both looked at each other in disbelief, both thinking the same thing to themselves; "Oh my God, that's Jack."

It was magnificent, and their voices filled the church, but that was just the beginning.

During the Mass he sang "Ave Maria", and people were turning their heads to see where this beautiful, powerful voice was coming from. Then he closed the ceremony by singing an operatic version of "The Lord's Prayer". The range and tone of his voice was glorious, and his expression of the song was filled with power and passion. It brought chills down my spine. And it still does, even to this day.

After the Mass, when we were all at the reception, our neighbor and good friend, Jack Gillen, came over to me and said, "You know Fifi, I've heard you talk about what a good singer Jack was, but I just wasn't ready for this. He had the rafters shaking at the end of 'The Our Father.' He was just fabulous."

A year or so later, my niece, MaryAnn Budny, was getting married in Kingston, New York, and my sister Helen flew Jack up from Waco to sing at her wedding. They too were all blown away by Jack's magnificent voice.

~~~

There was a year or so in the early seventies that Jack took time off from his studies in Southern Illinois University to stay home and help me with the bills and the running of the house. During this time he started doing some substitute teaching in the Bethpage School District, and then became a full time teacher at the Charles Campagne Elementary School, just off the Seaford-Oyster Bay Expressway. The woman who was the principal of the Charles Campagne School got to know Jack very well, and admired him. Her name was Mary Quinn, and she was very pleased that Jack was a member of her faculty, but she confided to him, "You're too talented to be wasting your time here. You should be working at a higher level."

He worked there for a full school year before returning to Southern Illinois University, in the summer of 1972, to complete working on his Master's Degree.

Jack's Bethpage Elementary School choir - Circa 1970.

~~~

Jack had sent out some demo tapes to several colleges and universities, and one day, in the summer of 1973, I was home and got a telephone call. The female voice on the other end asked for, "Mr. John McFadden," to which I asked, "Which one?"

I could hear her ask someone next to her, and they replied, "The one that sings."

"Well, he's not here right now," I explained, barely containing my exuberance, "but I'll have him call you as soon as he comes in."

I was bursting with excitement, so I called Jack right away and gave him the number that they had left. Then he called them and, to his delight, they said they were interested in talking to him about a teaching position in the "Voice Department," and asked if he would come down to Baylor University, in Waco, Texas, to interview with them.

So, a few days later, Jack flew down to Waco. They picked him up at the airport and booked him into a hotel near the campus. Over the next couple of days he interviewed with the head of the Music School, and had to sing for some of the faculty and spend some time teaching a class so that they could see him interact with some of the students.

Then one evening, all the heads of the various music departments met at one of the director's houses for a dinner party where they all got a chance to speak to Jack. This was an opportunity for them to talk to him about his background and training, and to get a feel for how he would fit in with the music school faculty and administrators. By the end of the evening, the head of the music school made him an offer to become part of their faculty, but Jack was asking for more money than they were offering and he was sticking to his guns. So they said they would have to think about it, and took him back to his hotel.

The next morning, when they picked him up to bring him back to the airport, whoever it was that was driving told Jack, "You must have really impressed them. You got everything that you asked for."

Well, Jack was thrilled to finally have a chance to make his living in the field that he loved most, music.

Jack's publicity photo at Baylor University. 1974.

BAYLOR UNIVERSITY
Abner V. McCall · President
Waco, Texas 76703

July 18, 1973

Mr. John McFadden
Villa Inn Motel
4401 Central Avenue
Hot Springs, Arkansas 78901

Rank (1973-74)__Instructor of Voice____
School of Music
Salary (1973-74)_____$9,000.00*____
Annuity Payment____$____

Dear Mr. McFadden:

Your academic rank, salary, and the amount appropriated by the University
for annuity have been approved for 1973-74 as indicated above. Your salary,
less withholding for income tax and social security and for other items which
you may authorize, will be paid in ten equal monthly installments beginning
September 1.

Appointments to the rank of Instructor are on an annual basis. Otherwise,
it should be understood that rank and salary will continue as indicated until
further official notice.

Summer session salaries are based on the salaries for the preceding regular
academic year, conforming to the plan adopted by the faculty in 1956.

Policies describing the mutual responsibilities of Baylor University and the
faculty are set forth in the Personnel Handbook.

Please sign and return one copy of this contract to the Office of the Dean of
Instruction by May 4. August 3.

Sincerely yours,

Abner V. McCall

Abner V. McCall
President

I accept this contract. _____

*The University will pay two-thirds of your household moving expenses up
to but not exceeding the amount of one salary check. Please contact Mr. Earl
Newland, Director of Purchasing, concerning your moving arrangements.

Baylor University - Contract offer - July, 1973.

403

I can remember him telling me about the first time that he walked into the Baylor University School of Music, and saw his name listed in the building's directory as, "John McFadden - Assistant Professor", and got chills up and down his spine. It was everything he wanted and had worked so hard for. He had his own private teaching studio and piano where not only would he work with his students, he could exchange ideas and share music with his fellow faculty members, and spend time honing his own skills for the many concerts and recitals that he gave.

It was a very happy time for him, and he made a lot of good friends in the music school. He told me about one day when he was driving through Waco and saw a large illuminated community signboard in front of a bank that heralded;

Tonight

Mr. John McFadden

In performance at the Baylor Arts Center

It was all very exciting.

A few days after Thanksgiving, following John's death, Jack was still home and he received a phone call from a mutual friend of his and Marjorie Lawrence. The friend told him that there was going to be a presentation ceremony for Ms. Lawrence, at the Metropolitan Opera, during which she would be presented with a portrait of herself, in Wagnerian costume and mounted on a horse. The portrait would be hung in the opera house and the whole thing was going to be a surprise, so Ms. Lawrence knew nothing of it, only that she was going to be attending the opera that night in New York City. Jack asked me if I would like to go so that I could meet Marjorie Lawrence and her husband, Doctor King, and of course I jumped at the chance and gave him a resounding, "Yes."

When Ms. Lawrence saw Jack at the ceremony, she was delighted that he was able to attend, especially in light of our recent family events. It was a memorable evening for me, meeting her and Doctor King, because they were both so gracious and had so many wonderful things to say about Jack. She was very pleased with the portrait that had been commissioned for her, and it turned out to be a very exciting evening.

Letter from Dalton Baldwin inviting Jack to Master Classes in Geneva. January 30, 1978.

GENEVA
MASTER CLASSES
PIANO - VIOLIN - CELLO - VOICE
14 AUGUST — 2 SEPTEMBER 1978
AT THE GENEVA CONSERVATORY OF MUSIC

Pierre FOURNIER
14 - 29 August

Nikita MAGALOFF
14 - 31 August

Henryk SZERYNG
15 August - 1 September

Gérard SOUZAY
and Dalton BALDWIN
16 August - 2 September

Program for Master Classes in Geneva.
August / September, 1978.

406

CONSERVATOIRE DE MUSIQUE DE GENÈVE

Samedi 2 septembre 1978, à 20 h. 30

CONCERT

donné par les participants au cours d'interprétation de

Maître Gérard SOUZAY et Maître Dalton BALDWIN

PROGRAMME

1. Le promenoir des deux amants . . . . Cl. Debussy
   a) Auprès de cette grotte sombre   b) Crois mon conseil, chère Clymène
   c) Je tremble en voyant ton visage
   Kurt OLLMANN (U.S.A.)

2. a) La Dame d'André . . . . Fr. Poulenc
   b) Dans l'herbe . . . . Fr. Poulenc
   c) Air vif . . . . Fr. Poulenc
   Shigeko KAMADA (Japon)

3. Air de Leila des « Pêcheurs de Perles » . . . . G. Bizet
   Ilona VERNAY (France)

4. a) Lachen und weinen . . . . F. Schubert
   b) Der Musensohn . . . . F. Schubert
   Linda SKORSKY (U.S.A.)

5. Extraits des cinq Mélodies populaires grecques . . . . . M. Ravel
   a) Le réveil de la Mariée - b) Là-bas vers l'Eglise - c) Quel Galant ! - d) Tout gai !
   Takamasa HIROOKA (Japon)

6. Chanson perpétuelle . . . . E. Chausson
   Pleurez ! pleurez mes yeux ! . . . . J. Massenet
   Extrait de l'opéra « Le Cid »
   Michèle BOUCHER (Canada)

ENTRACTE

7. a) Réponse d'une épouse sage . . . . A. Roussel
   b) La statue de bronze . . . . E. Satie
   c) Le chapelier . . . . E. Satie
   Brian BENNETT (U.S.A.)

8. a) Mein Liebster singt am Haus . . . . H. Wolf
   b) Du denkst mit einem Fädchen . . . . H. Wolf
   c) Phidylé . . . . H. Duparc
   Janet WHITMOORE (U.S.A.)

9. a) Morgen - b) Die Nacht - c) Zueignung . . . . . . R. Strauss
   John MC FADDEN (U.S.A.)

10. a) Le colibri . . . . E. Chausson
    b) Air de La lettre de l'opéra « Werther » . . . . . . J. Massenet
    Takako TAGUCHI (Japon)

11. a) Pantomine - b) Clair de lune - c) Apparition . . . . Cl. Debussy
    Extraits de Quatre Chansons de Jeunesse
    July HOLLAND (U.S.A.)

12. De l'Oratoire « Jephta » . . . . G.-F. Haendel
    a) Récitatif : Deeper and deeper still - b) Waft her, angels, thro' the skies
    Ingemisco du Requiem de . . . . G. Verdi
    Wayne WILLIAMS (U.S.A.)

Au piano : Mary DIBBERN - Gérard LUTZ - Rut PERGAMENT
Tina de ROOS - Ursula RUTTIMANN - Dalton BALDWIN

Entrée libre

Program from concert at Geneva Conservatory of Music.
September 2, 1978.

407

During the late seventies and early eighties, Jack had been receiving a lot of meaningful accolades and recognition from many people in the academic and professional fields of classical music and opera. Some of the people that he had studied with in Europe, and who he had met through Marjorie Lawrence had told Jack that they thought that if it wasn't for his being so overweight, that he could be a leading man at the Metropolitan Opera. They felt that he certainly had the talent, but his physical build was holding him back. So in the spring of 1982 Jack decided that it was time that he lost some weight, and took a shot at seeing where his voice could carry him.

Jack - June, 1982.

SOUTHERN ILLINOIS UNIVERSITY
SCHOOL OF MUSIC
MEMORANDUM

TO: Jack McFadden

FROM: Mary Elaine Wallace

DATE: May 4, 1972

REFERENCE: Graduate Recital

_ _

The voice faculty was pleased with your recital
preview and OK'd you to give your recital on
May 26, as scheduled.

The next fifteen minutes of the meeting were
spent in discussing your talent and your future.
I have been authorized to say that we agree to
the person that you have very little chance of
becoming a renowed singer...something we all agree
you might really be.... unless you begin to lose
weight now and continue until you have the physical
appearance and stamina to be something besides a
Falstaff. You can probably do oratorio like Ingrid
and Judy any time that you want, or you can probably
gain back the weight if you ever become famous and
nobody will care, but as a "young singer" you cannot
be fat and expect to really go places.

Personally, I think if you would discipline yourself
to lose weight, Marjorie Lawrence would work hard to
find someone to back you but she doesn't think you
stand a chance as long as each breath you take means
moving that hulk of yours.

Like your mother always said....this is for your
own good.

Affectionately,
MEW

Southern Illinois University - Letter from Elaine Wallace about losing wieght.
May 4, 1972.

409

He consulted his doctor, who recommended him to a weight loss clinic in Waco where he would undergo a drastic weight loss program for people who were at high risk to their health because of their weight. He was put on a liquid diet where the only thing he ate was protein shakes, and given a strict regimen of physical exercise. It was a highly monitored program that required that he go to the doctor's office twice a week at which time they would take blood samples, monitor his heart and other organs, and record his weight. And he committed himself to it. He joined a gym and started exercising. He even bought a bicycle and started biking. And soon he started to see results. He was losing so much weight that he even told his brothers that he would get on the ice and play hockey with them, the next time that he got home for the holidays.

Counting calories.

OBESITY & RISK FACTOR PROGRAM

3420 PINE AVENUE
WACO, TEXAS 76708
(817) 753-0928

RICHARD L. GIBNEY, M.D.
DIPLOMATE - AMERICAN
BOARD OF INTERNAL MEDICINE
AND NEPHROLOGY

JOHN J. BARDGETTE, M.D.
DIPLOMATE - AMERICAN
BOARD OF INTERNAL MEDICINE
AND NEPHROLOGY

TO WHOM IT MAY CONCERN:

This patient is being treated in a physician operated and directed, multidisciplinary treatment course aimed at the reversal of the condition of morbid obesity and recovery from longstanding related complications such as hypertension, diabetes mellitus and hyperlipidemia. It is prescribed only on physician referral and is offered only to patients who are 20% or more above their ideal weights; in most cases this represents a minimum of 50 pounds.

This is the only facility in this area implementing a unique and rigorous approach to these problems, consisting of weekly physician visits, a supplemented fast, therapy in the form of behavioral modification directed by a behavior modification specialist, nutritional education and counseling, physical activity sessions and laboratory testing to carefully monitor physical status as often as needed, but with a minimum of every two weeks. A total of 5 hours is spent each week among these various disciplines.

Patients adhering to this program experience a minimum weight loss of 3-3½ pounds per week for women and 4-4½ pounds per week for men. Our experience has shown a greater weight loss in a significant number of patients.

Such a rigorous and carefully monitored treatment course assures swift, but safe reduction in weight which is mandatory for the welfare of the patient. This medically proven regimen has been carefully researched and has been implemented in more than 25,000 patients, the largest single groups have been at the Mount Sinai Hospital in Cleveland, Ohio, and the University of California at Los Angeles. Hypertensive patients become normotensive within 3-5 weeks of beginning this treatment and antihypertensive medications are discontinued or markedly decreased in amount in almost all. Patients with adult onset diabetes mellitus become normoglycemic without further need for oral hypoglycemic therapy in 3-5 weeks as well. Elevated triglycerides normalize in essentially all patients, cholesterols in two-thirds.

Patients undergoing this individually monitored course are able to tolerate prolonged fasting on an ambulatory basis. The protein-sparing supplement counteracts the metabolic effects and prevents the complications of prolonged food withdrawal. Muscle breakdown, metabolic acidosis, hypoglycemia, and electrolyte imbalance are prevented. Fasting causes increased urinary potassium losses which are appropriately replaced.

Obesity & Risk Factor Program - 1 of 6.

411

Because of the rigorous nature and potential hazards of this treatment course, we are uncompromising in our demands of patient participation; patients are discharged for inattendance or non-compliance. The risks of non-supervised fasting are too great to allow anything less. A physician is on call 24 hours a day.

As salt and food are reintroduced later in the course of the patient's treatment, continued weekly visits are critical to detect possible return of hypertension or hyperglycemia. All other treatment modalities continue as weight reduction continues during the readministration of food. During this entire period of treatment, monthly progress reports are sent to the patient's referring physician.

Please find attached an Information Packet which describes in detail answers to common questions regarding this program. If you have questions that are answered in this packet, do not hesitate to ask. Please read this packet carefully as well as letting your family become familiar with the program and keep this packet handy for referring to.

Sincerely,

Richard L. Gibney, M.D.   John J. Bardette, M.D.

RLG/JJB:srh

OBESITY & RISK FACTOR PROGRAM
Information Packet

The following information is being supplied to you as an orientation to our clinic. This packet includes many items that will help you learn how the program operates. Included are:

1. PROGRAM BUSINESS CARE -- For any business related problems, contact the office (9:00 a.m. - 5:00 p.m.) at 817-753-0928. There is a 24 hour medical emergency and information service, 817-752-5503. This is for a medical emergency only and a nurse or M.D. will be contacted. For any questions relating to the program that are not of an emergency basis, please call during office hours.

2. EMERGENCY DIET -- This diet is only for emergency circumstances. It should be used only after speaking with a physician or nurse!!

3. MEDICATION SHEET -- This is a list of all medications that are allowed while on the diet. Any OTHER MEDICATIONS SHOULD BE APPROVED by the physician in the clinic.

* If for any reason you are going to discontinue the program, you must call the nurse or M.D. on call and she will give you instructions on how to start re-eating. Our services include talking with the staff in planning to start re-eating should you decide to discontinue. Unsupervised "re-eating" may precipitate a variety of medical illnesses.

* It is advisable for you to make copies of this information packet and place them where you may need them, i.e., work, school, etc.

* Inform us of any change in personal information, i.e., address, employment, phone number, etc.

* Please be advised that if you miss two consecutive appointments with our clinic, YOU WILL BE DROPPED from our program. This is for your own well being. We feel strongly that it is not fair to you or to the program to go medically unsupervised while on this diet.

I. Supplement - 35 packs per week:

1. Take 5 packs per day, at 3-4 hour intervals. It is extremely important that you take all 5 packs daily to have sufficient protein to avoid breakdown of muscle tissue.
2. The supplement is made from egg albumin - it will congeal if mixed with hot liquids and must be kept refrigerated (or in a thermos) if mixed in advance.
3. The supplement may be mixed in a blender, with wire wisk, or a fork - if foaming occurs, drink the foam as well (it contains protein).

II. Potassium:

You have been given a prescription for potassium chloride. You must begin taking potassium as soon as you begin your fast and we recommend taking it with your supplement. The potassium you need is available by prescription only and the potassium found in health food stores is not the same thing. Potassium is critical for muscle and heart tone. Failure to take potassium as prescribed can be very dangerous.

III. Fluids:

Fluid intake must be a minimum of 2 quarts (8 - 10 glasses) a day. Beverages which you may drink include:

1. Water
2. Tea (black)
3. Coffee (Black decaffeinated recommended to avoid gastric irritation.) May mix with supplement when cooled.
4. Soft drinks having less than 2 calories per serving. (May mix with supplement.) Citrus flavored soft drinks often contain significant amounts of sodium and are not encouraged.
5. Lemonade may be made from frozen, bottled, or fresh lemon (juice only - no pulp!)
6. Artificial sweeteners may be used, however, it is recommended to limit the intake of them due to possible fluid retention.

The above listed are the only ones allowed on the fasting program. They have been researched and proven to have of little or no effect on your weight loss process. Anything else will interfere with the rate of weight loss and is not advised.

-REMINDERS-

Diet Gum -- Sugarless
Saccharine

Do not make any rapid change in position.

The following must be avoided in order to avoid low blood pressure, fainting, and loss of consciousness: Hot steamy baths, whirlpool baths, sauna baths, scuba diving, swimming alone, diving off diving boards, piloting a plan, horseback riding and motorcycle riding.

DO NOT cross your legs at the knee. This may result in nerve injury.

DO NOT go on vacation during the first two months of the program. The fast cannot be safely without close supervision during this period. If deciding to go on vacation, you need to discuss this with the physician prior to that time.

Obesity & Risk Factor Program - 4 of 6.

413

OBESITY & RISK FACTOR PROGRAM
Supplemented Fast - Reminders and Side Effects

1. If you have any fast-related medical problems, you can call the office and ask for the person on call. There is a nurse or physician on call at all times.

2. The emergency food list is for emergency circumstances only, to be implemented only on advice of clinic personnel.

3. Remember to go from lying or sitting to standing positions SLOWLY.

4. Most of you will urinate a great deal over the first two weeks as your body releases excess water due to the low salt content of the supplement.

5. It is important not to miss a clinic visit while on the fasting portion of the program.

6. Inform us of any change of phone number or other personal information.

7. The following side effects have been experienced by some people on this regimen:

Skin rash -- will disappear with the first week and you may use calamine lotion or bathe in baking soda.

Dry skin -- use generous amounts of skin lotion.

Brittle nails -- do not take gelatin capsules (Knox).

Hair loss -- Use conditioners and Do Not tease, dye or permanent.

Cold intolerance -- dress accordingly.

Muscle cramps -- flex foot, walk, keep fee warm, do not massage, and do not cross legs at the knee.

Orthostatic hypotension (light-headed) -- change positions slowly and get out of bed slowly, avoid hot baths, steam baths, whirlpool, sauna, diving, horseback riding, motorcycling, swimming alone, weight lifting, and piloting an airplane.

Halitosis (bad breath) -- may chew sticks of sugar free gum per day if necessary, and should use good oral hygiene.

Constipation -- if very uncomfortable, or goes beyond one week, notify clinic. No enemas.

Obesity & Risk Factor Program - 5 of 6.

MEDICATION SHEET

If the following medications are needed, they may be taken for minor complaints. If the symptoms continue, your family physician should be notified.

Headache or mild pain elsewhere:
Tylenol - up to two (2) tablets (600 mg.) four times per day

Colds:
Nose drops or sprays - use as label directs
Cough syrups - any brand which does not contain sugar (ask your pharmacist)
Antihistamines - any over the counter or prescription cold remedy which does not contain aspirin

Constipation which is causing discomfort:
Inform your physician at your next office visit
Milk of Magnesia (no chocolate or mint flavored) two (2) tablespoons at bedtime. Repeat next morning if no bowel movement
Dulcolax suppository
Glycerine suppository
Fleets' enema (green box)

Diarrhea:
Kaopectate or Pepto-Bismol
Persistant diarrhea or vomiting - call clinic

Indigestion or Heartburn:
Any antacid - liquid or tablet for occasional use
Low-sodium Riopan for regular use

You may take any antibiotics or sulfa drug prescribed.

YOU MAY NOT HAVE ANY OF THE FOLLOWING:

Aspirin
Amphetamines
Tranquilizers — unless previously discussed with our physican
General anesthetics (Sodium Pentothal). NOTE — Local (novocaine-type) anesthetics are okay, gas (dental) is also okay.

Obesity & Risk Factor Program - 6 of 6.

OBESITY & RISK FACTOR PROGRAM

Exercises

Tension-Release Exercises:

1. HEAD ROLL - Sitting relaxed, close your eyes and roll your head slowly clockwise.
2. SHOULDER SHRUGS - Sitting or standing, palms flat, raise and lower shoulders.
3. SHOULDER CIRCLES - Sitting or standing, palms flat, arms at side, roll shoulders forward then backward.

Body-Tone Exercises:

1. ARM CIRCLES - Arms extended, palms down, three size circles counterclockwise, 15 repetitions of each size. Palms up, three size circles clockwise, 15 repetitions of each size.
2. TRICEPS EXERCISE - Use 3# weight for females, 4# weight for males. Arm raised straight in air, elbow next to ear. Palm facing to the rear, bend at elbow, touching weight to back.
3. SIDE BENDS - Bend at waist from side to side, hips stationary facing forward.
4. LOWER BACK EXERCISE - Lying on carpeted floor, bring one bent leg to chest and hold, then repeat with other leg and hold. Then both and hold.
5. ABDOMEN EXERCISE - Lying on carpeted floor, slightly bend one leg. Raise the other leg straight up as high as possible, keeping the knee straight. Lower the raised leg slowly till it is 3" from the floor and hold it for 10 seconds. Release. Repeat with other leg.
6. ABDOMEN EXERCISE - Bend forward, palms on thighs. Exhale forcefully all air in your lungs. Hold for 10 seconds. Release. Inhale forcefully to the full extent. Hold breath for 10 seconds. Release. NOTE: Please do this exercise one or two times at the beginning of the session, midway and at the end.
7. NECK-TIGHTENING EXERCISE - Lock fingers in front of you. Place palms on forehead and press head against palms tightly. Hold for 10 seconds. Bring still-locked palms to the back of head. Press tightly for 10 seconds.

Things to Remember

You must do the Body-toning exercises a minimum of three times per week in order for them to do any good.

Tension-release exercises can be done as often and as much as you need.

None of these exercises require a great deal of calories to perform, but they will aid you in toning your body as much as is possible for your own body type.

Always start out slowly when attempting new exercise activity. Be careful not to overdo—you can always increase your exercise capacity a little bit at a time until you reach a good exercise level that is vigorous, but not strenuous.

Obesity & Risk Factor Program - Exercises.

416

OBESITY & RISK FACTOR PROGRAM
3420 PINE AVENUE
WACO, TEXAS 76708
(817) 753-0928

·RICHARD L. GIBNEY, M.D.
DIPLOMATE - AMERICAN
BOARD OF INTERNAL MEDICINE
AND NEPHROLOGY

JOHN J. BARDGETTE, M.D.
DIPLOMATE - AMERICAN
BOARD OF INTERNAL MEDICINE
AND NEPHROLOGY

Guidelines for a Smooth Reintroduction to Food

Beginning to eat normally after fasting for a long time is a
simple process but it does need to be done by degrees. Your body
has adapted itself to a low calorie, low fat, and low salt diet.
Eating large quantities of food, particularly high fat foods, can
be medically dangerous if you haven't built up to it gradually.
Because of this, refeeding is done over a period of 3 weeks:

WEEK 1:   3 packets of supplement & 400 calories of food

WEEK 2:   No supplement & 500 - 800 calories of food

WEEK 3:   Full maintenance calories

The food choices are up to you, but we advise you to avoid high
fat content foods and include some protein source each day. Keep
in mind that good nutrition is a matter of eating a variety of
foods, increasing the amount of complex carbohydrates you take in,
and decreasing the amount of fat.

Obesity & Risk Factor Program.

417

Around the end of that August, after I was done teaching summer school that year, I took a trip down to Waco to visit him. During that time, Jack and I drove to San Antonio, where we stayed at a hotel on the River Walk and did some sightseeing. There were lots of cafes and entertainment there. We also the Alamo.

Jack and Jane Abbott, a wonderfully talented pianist who often accompanied him in concert, were scheduled to give a recital at Jane's mother's home, in the hill country outside San Antonio in several weeks. Jane was still back in Waco, but Jack and I visited her mother and stayed overnight at her house.

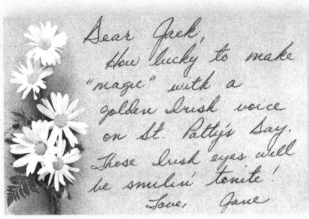

Florist's note from Jane Abbott to Jack on St. Patrick's Day.

Jack with Jane Abbott and Allan Smith - Concert at Bandera, Texas.
September 12, 1982.

The next day, on our way back to Waco, we stopped at a mall and Jack bought some new clothes for himself, which he needed because he had lost so much weight and none of his clothes fit him anymore. He was thrilled because it was the first time in his life that he was able to buy clothes off the regular sizes rack and didn't have to go to the "Big and Tall" shop. But as proud and happy as he was with his new physique, he wouldn't let me take any pictures of him while I was there as he wanted to surprise all of his brothers, when he came home for Christmas, with how much weight he had lost.

By early that fall he had lost just about one hundred and twenty pounds in the five months that he had been on the program.

Jack - Concert at Bandera, Texas - September 12, 1982.

~~~

Then, around the second week of October, 1982, Jack called me from Baylor one evening, and, as we were talking, he off-handedly mentioned that he hadn't been feeling very well that day. So the next night I called him back to see if he was feeling any better. He said he felt lousy, and that a lot of the students and faculty on campus had been coming down with some kind of flu-like symptoms. He told me that if he didn't start feeling better by the next day, he might consider going to see his doctor. The following afternoon he called me again. This time, to tell me that he was feeling even worse, and had checked himself into the hospital. That's when I really started to worry.

The next day I was home. Brian and Debbie and their two little boys, Danny and Ben, had come back from Florida and were living with me at the time. The phone rang, and when I answered it, it was one of the doctors from the hospital in Waco, and as worried as I had been the night before, I wasn't prepared for what he had to say.

The doctor soberly advised me that Jack was, "…very sick, and we had to put him on a respirator."

"Okay," I allowed, somewhat staggered by the weight of what he had just said, "I'll get a flight to Waco this afternoon and be down there as soon as possible."

But he wasn't done yet, and his next statement hit me like a bludgeon when he uttered,"I don't know if he'll still be here by the time you arrive."

I immediately became extremely upset and panic-stricken. I felt terrible guilt that I hadn't gone down there sooner, but it seemed impossible that he could be that sick. Whatever was going on, it happened so quickly that I felt like I just got punched in the stomach.

When I got off the phone with the doctor, I was beside myself with fear and worry. Debbie took the phone and tried to contact Nick, Phil, Brian and Patrick, who were all at work for the day. Then I called some of Jack's friends in Waco, to see if they could pick me up at the airport in Dallas. They were all shocked to hear that Jack's condition had turned so. They said things like, "That can't be, we just saw him yesterday."

I continued to call the airlines to try to get a flight, and over the next hour or two all the boys and their wives arrived at the house. It was all very chaotic as Nick and I were trying to finalize arrangements to fly to Dallas that evening, to get to Jack's side. It felt like a nightmare that couldn't possibly be happening for real. As bad as the news had been, we were all praying, and holding out hope that everything would be okay. There was just no way that we were going to lose Jack.

Then the phone rang again, and it was the doctor again. Philip had answered it and the doctor gave him the bad news. Jack was gone.

Philip had to deliver that terrible message to the rest of us. There would be no waking from this nightmare, and we all cried inconsolably, long into that dark, grief-stricken night.

~~~

By the next morning, I started to get calls from some of Jack's friends and colleagues in Waco. They too had by now gotten the bad news, and were calling to convey their grief and their condolences. Some of them that had been very close to Jack asked me if it would be all right if they kept him there in Waco for an extra day, so that they could have a day of mourning amongst themselves at a local funeral home, and I agreed. I told them to have Jack dressed in his new clothes, the ones that he had been so proud to buy on our way back from San Antonio a few months earlier.

At the service that was held for Jack in Waco, there was a Priest, a Minister and a Rabbi that attended. They all spoke very highly of Jack as he had either sang at their churches and synagogues or conducted their choirs at the services of all the various faiths in and around Waco over the years. There was also string quartet that played during the service.

~~~

Baylor University was generous enough to pay for three of Jack's colleagues from the School of Music, who were also his closest friends, to accompany his casket to New York. They stayed for the wake and the funeral.

Jack's wake was held at the William E. Law Funeral Home, on Jerusalem Avenue, in North Seaford. The funeral Mass was held at Saint Barnabas Church, in Bellmore, the same church were he had sung so gloriously for Philip and Claudia's wedding years earlier. Then the hearse took him to be laid to rest at Washington Memorial Park, in Mount Sinai, near where Nick and Philip lived. The plot that I bought at Washington Memorial Park has room for seven more of us next to Jack, when the time comes.

~~~

A few days after Jack's funeral, Nick, Phyllis and I flew down

Gannett Westchester Newspapers
Friday, October 29, 1982

Obituaries

John J. McFadden II

John J. McFadden II, 35, of Waco, Texas, a Tarrytown native and former Ossining resident who became a star opera singer in the southwest, died Tuesday at Providence Hospital in Waco after a brief illness.

Mr. McFadden was born in Tarrytown, Feb. 25, 1947, to John J. Jr. and Kathryn Egan McFadden. He attended grammar school there before moving to the Torbank section of Ossining.

He graduated from Seaford High School in Long Island and the State University of New York at Fredonia. He earned a master's degree from the University of Southern Illinois at Carbondale.

Mr. McFadden joined the faculty of Baylor University in Waco 10 years ago as a professor of voice. For the past four years he was Baylor's musical director and opera theater conductor.

He had sung professionally in Europe and was a concert soloist in the southwest.

Mr. McFadden was a grandchild of the late Nicholas and Ellen Egan of Tarrytown and John and Laura McFadden of Pocanitco Hills.

Mr. McFadden is survived by his mother, of Seaford; and four brothers, Nicholas and Philip of Mount Sinai, N.Y., and Patrick and Brian of Seaford.

to Waco to get Jack's things in order. We had to close up his apartment and bring his car back to New York. While we were there we stayed in his apartment, packing up all his belongings; his clothes and his huge music collection, which consisted of hundreds of classical albums; many of which were priceless collectors items, and boxes and boxes of valuable sheet music and opera scores. But most precious to me were the many recordings of his own highly acclaimed performances; timeless oratorios and immortal operas.

422

In Memoriam: JOHN McFADDEN, 1947-1982

"We have lost a good friend and colleague; the world of music has lost an artist. We are all fortunate to have known John McFadden as a part of the university family and the community."

- Elwyn A. Wienandt

John McFadden, assistant professor of voice and music director of the Baylor Opera Theater, died Oct. 26 in a Waco hospital following a brief illness. Funeral services were held Oct. 28. McFadden, 35, had been a member of the Baylor music faculty since 1973. In addition to his university position, he was choir director at Central Presbyterian Church in Waco at the time of his death.

Born in Tarrytown, N.Y., McFadden graduated from high school in Seaford, N.Y., and earned a bachelor's degree in music education from the State University of New York, Fredonia. He was granted a master's degree in voice from Southern Illinois University in 1972.

McFadden appeared frequently as a soloist in recitals, oratorios, concerts and operas. He had planned to present a recital at Baylor on Nov. 13 with renowned accompanist Dalton Baldwin. In addition to his work with Baylor opera, he spent several summers as associate director and conductor of the Marjorie Lawrence Opera Workshop in Hot Springs, Ark. He was a member of Alpha Psi Omega, Phi Mu Alpha Sinfonia, Pi Kappa Lambda, and the National Association of Teachers of Singing.

McFadden is survived by his mother, Mrs. John J. McFadden, of Seaford, Long Island, N.Y., and four brothers. Burial was held in New York.

Donations may be made to the John McFadden Memorial Scholarship Fund, Office of University Development, Att: Judy Maggard, Baylor University, Waco, TX, 76798.

Baylor University News.

While we were there, we got a message that the President of Baylor University wanted to see us before we left. I thought it would be just a perfunctory meeting, but I was wrong. Instead, Doctor Reynolds spent over two hours telling us about all that Jack had done to raise the profile and enhance the reputation of Baylor University, through his performances, his reputation as a teacher and musician, and how he had become so beloved and respected by his colleagues and students.

A day or so later, Nick and Phyllis packed all of Jack's personal belongings into his car and drove it up to New York, and I flew home. Over the following days and weeks, I received many beautiful letters from all over the country. They were from many of Jack's friends, colleagues and present and former students, sharing their grief and many memories of Jack with me. All those notes and letters were a great source of strength for me during those dark days, and fueled my pride in Jack, to know that he had touched so many people with his personality, his humor and his music.

THE MAGIC FLUTE

Opera in Two Acts

Music by Wolfgang Amadeus Mozart

Text by Emanuel Schikaneder

English Version by Ruth and Thomas Martin

by arrangement with G. Schirmer, Inc.

Conductor	Douglas Newell
Producer and Director	Daniel Scott
Costume Designer	James W. Swain
Set Designer	William T. Sherry
Lighting Designer	Timothy M. Logan
Production Assistant	Elem Eley

-IN MEMORIAM-

John McFadden, Music Director of Baylor Opera Theater from 1978 until his death October 26, 1982, was a primary force in planning and casting this production. THE MAGIC FLUTE was one of his particular favorites, and we can only hope that it is a fitting memorial. This production is dedicated to his memory.

Program from THE MAGIC FLUTE. Dedicated posthumously to Jack on his birthday. February 25, 1983.

424

Karen Peeler
1624 South Tenth Street
Waco, Texas 76706

October 28, 1982

Dear Mrs. McFadden, Nick, Brian, Phillip, and Patrick — and all who loved Jack —

I want to add my voice to the dozen from here who would love to be with you and will surely write you. Many of you I'm sure know only vaguely of Jack's life here; I do guess you know how happy he was.

...fine students. He was eager to see you Christmas and "show off" his new self.

You should know that he was adored by his students here — and all of his colleagues are devastated. He is irreplaceable for countless reasons — we will feel the void of his leaving as long as you. He gave us all a great deal. He was fabulously good at what he did — respected by everyone. He has taught so much to so many —

nieces & nephews — often. He was every inch Irish, Catholic, from "New York" — and wonderful.

Jack and I shared much — similar tastes, love of opera, good sense of humor — we fought, argued, joked, partied — I'll never forget him and carry some of him with me always. We are all in a way a family here — Jack's older students have seldom left each other, and remained with Alan and I

I want to tell you that he was in the middle of a very full, complete, productive, and important life. In the last few months especially he had pulled aspects of his life into focus and order in a marvelous way. He looked wonderful, was singing beautifully, and was teaching well. His new church choir adored him and he was excited about the opera and symphony concerts ahead. He loved his new house and was thrilled

no one knew Jack without liking him and feeling the strength of his music, his fine mind, his great personality. Calls are going literally all over the world now to students and friends — we can not imagine life without him here. I wish you could see the grief and love that surrounds him now.

He was so proud of his family — and spoke of you often. He displayed family pictures — especially

at the funeral home all evening — they are truly his "children" and will always live his music and his memory.

Forgive my incoherence it is very late, but you are all in my heart — my love to you in your loss. Please call upon me or anyone here if we can do anything for you.

Karen Peeler

Karen Peeler's consolation letter - October 28, 1982.

425

The suddenness of Jack's passing left us with many questions but few answers. Because Jack was so young, only thirty-five at the time, the Waco coroner's office was legally bound to perform an autopsy to determine the cause of his untimely death.

Philip, once again, happened to answer the phone when the doctor called with the results of the autopsy. He told Phil that they had found, "... a growth on Jack's aorta." He said it was, "... a viral cluster that had coagulated to about the size of his thumbnail, and looked like a small piece of cauliflower." It had somehow developed on his aortic artery, and flared-up to the point where it weakened the arterial wall, causing it to rupture.

He blamed it on the virus that had been recently going around the campus, and said that under normal circumstances Jack would have fought off the contagion. But he was in a physically weakened state because of the his severe weight loss over the previous five months, and unable to stave off the infection.

That revelation made Jack's brothers and me very bitter and resentful toward the doctors and staff that ran the weight loss clinic that Jack had been going to. We even had a discussion about suing them for "wrongful death", and negligence. How could Jack have gotten that weak if he was under their scrutiny and being monitored so closely?

But in the end I made the decision not to pursue it. What would be the purpose? Jack was gone and there would be no bringing him back. To pursue a lawsuit against the doctors who ran the clinic would only have served to prolong the agony of his loss, and I didn't think that I was up for it. At that time in my life all I could do was lick my wounds, and try to come to terms with what had happened.

~~~

For a long time I fell into deep despair over the loss of Jack, and for a while, I could barely contain the anguish that howled in my head and clawed at my heart. It got so bad that one night, probably about six months after Jack had died, I was driving out to Nick's house for a family gathering, up Route 83, near Bald Hill, and I couldn't stop crying. How could we be having a "family gathering"? My family had been shattered, and I couldn't make any sense of it. I found myself literally screaming at the top of my lungs, raging at the windshield and the thin air. Anyone driving next to me would have thought I was crazy, and they probably would have been right.

When I pulled up in front of Nick's house I stayed out in the car for a while, trying to compose myself and fix my make-up. But I couldn't. Every time I thought that I had regained a little self control, I lost it and started sobbing again.

After a little while, Philip came outside to see what was taking me, and he saw me crying. He knelt down next to the car door, and got me to open the window. "What's wrong Mom?", he asked, although I'm sure he already knew.

But I couldn't look at him. I could only sit there, slumped down in the front seat of my car, and sob. It felt like the last bit of strength had been drained out of me. "Come on Mom, come inside.", Philip gently coaxed, "Everything will be all right."

"No, no it won't," I railed, still looking down at the floor of the car, "It's not all right. Jack is gone! How can anything be all right?"

We stayed there like that for what seemed like a long time, neither one of us speaking. Then, shaking my head in despair, I wailed, "I don't think I can handle it. I just don't think I can keep going on like this anymore."

Philip was quiet for a little longer, but when he spoke his tone had changed. "I don't get it Mom," he said, "do the rest of us mean so little to you?"

Suddenly, I felt ashamed. Of course the rest of my boys and their families were important to me. They were more than important, they were my life. And maybe more importantly at that time, they were my reason for living. But I had lost sight of that. My grief for Jack had blinded me to taking in the whole picture. But Philip's words had brought me up short.

After a few more minutes I collected myself and we went inside. It was a struggle, but I managed to refocus after that, with the understanding that life is hard sometimes, and often unfair, but you have to take the good with the bad, and hopefully, be able to embrace the good and leave the bad behind.

~~~

I had bought a fairly expensive electric organ earlier in 1982, with the idea that Jack would be able to play Christmas music on it when he came home for the holidays that year, but he never got the chance. To this day, whenever I think of Jack, I always imagine that he is still with us, just away. Still living and teaching in Waco, at Baylor University.

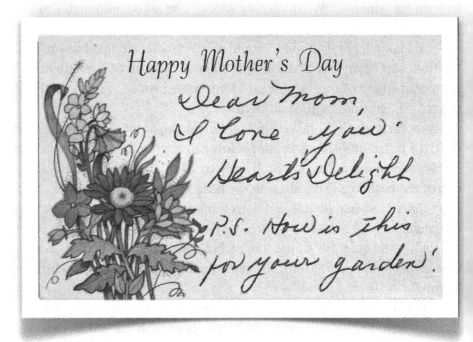

Chapter Twelve

WORLD WITHOUT END

My greatest joy in life these days comes from seeing how my family grows and prospers. Starting with my own generation, my two sisters and I, along with my husband's two sisters, brought twenty-three children into the world between us. That generation parented another wonderful group of young men and women, all born between 1970 and the 1990s, which has in turn started marrying and cultivating their own families.

Patrick,Michael, Nick, Phyllis, Nama Nell, Uncle Larry and Aunt Mary.
September, 1970.

The family tree that has its roots planted firmly in Ireland now has many new limbs and branches that have spread across America. There are McFadden, Egan, Dick, Bassett, Mulligan, Suddarth, and Paul families that have branched off into Kurz, Giordano, McDowell, Murray, Murphy, Moro, Mendelsohn, White and Stephenson families. Which if brought all together in one place would resemble a small army, ranging in age from their late eighties, (moi), down to newborn infants. And that doesn't even take into account all of the Nelson, Hamill, Foley, and Aurdick cousins.

Mcfadden Cousins Family Reunion - Hershey - August, 1992.

431

Dick Family photo - circa 1982.

Helen and Walter's 50th Wedding Anniversary - January 19, 1996.

432

Bassett family photo - Hershey - August, 1992.

Mulligan family photo - Hershey - August, 1992.

433

Naturally, I am filled with love and affection for all of the members of our extended family, but I have to admit that the overwhelming abundance of pleasure in my old age has come from the experience of having grandchildren and great-grandchildren, and the pride and joy that I get from having them around me, and watching them grow.

I was first made a grandmother at the tender age of forty-eight, by my son Nick and his wife Phyllis, when my first grandson, Michael, was born in 1970, and after that it seemed like the babies started coming fast. Laura came along in 1973, Aubrey in 1977, Erin and Danny in 1979, John and Ben in 1981, Katie in 1987, and Matt and James in 1988. Lots of diapers, lots of crying, lots of birthday and Christmas presents. Lots of laughs and lots of love. And lots of stories.

Aubrey and Erin - August, 1979.

Nama and Danny - Florida - August, 1979.

Nama and Ben - Florida - April, 1981.

Aubrey, Erin and John - 1981.

Kate and James - Christmas, 1989.

Each one of the grandchildren added their own chapters as they grew, and those episodes ran the gamut of emotions. Some were goofy and laughable, others evoked anger or heartbreak; and still do if I linger on them. But most are just the stuff of life, and make me smile. They are about growth; physical, emotional and spiritual, and about learning; through one's own experience, and through the lessons and experiences passed on from others. And they are about finding one's own place in the world.

Matthew - August 14, 1993.

As parents and grandparents, it is our responsibility to nurture and teach each new child as they come into the world and make their way through life. But it's funny how much we can learn about life when we open our minds and hearts to the lessons that our children can teach us.

Fifi's 69th birthday - dancing with Kate and James - August 2, 1991.

436

~~~

One of my favorite stories, perhaps because he was my first grandchild, is about my grandson Michael. When Michael was about four years old, his father was trying to learn how to play the guitar, and one of the songs that Nick used to practice was called "*BAMBOO*", by Peter, Paul and Mary, and the first verse went like this;

> *You take a stick of bamboo*
> *You take a stick of bamboo*
> *You take a stick of bamboo*
> *And throw it on the water*

Anyway, Nick used to practice, and Michael learned to sing the song with him.

Well, one day I had Michael in the car, and he was sitting on the armrest next to me as we were coming home from grocery shopping. He looked over at me and said, "Let's sing a song, Nama."

"Sure," I smiled, "what song do you want to sing?"

"Bamboo!", he enthused.

"Okay," I played along, "but I don't know the words. You'll have to teach me."

"Okay Nama," he chirped, and he began singing, "You take a stick of bamboo...."

I started to sing along with him, but apparently not to his liking. He abruptly held up both of his hands and ordered, "Stop! Stop!"

"What's wrong, Honey?", I asked.

Michael - 3rd grade - 1979.

He got a very serious look on his face and instructed, "It's 'Bamboo!", emphasizing the "boo."

So I repeated after him, "Bamboo."

But it still wasn't right. He repeated, "Bamboo," again over accentuating the "boo."

And again I tried, "Bamboo," in the way that I thought he was looking for, but to no avail.

Exasperated, he sighed heavily. It was becoming painfully evident to him that there was little hope for me. "No Nama, no," he admonished, this time leaning forward, very close to me, and taking my face in his hands to squeeze my cheeks and mouth into the desired shape. "Look at me," he insisted, "its bamboooooo," pursing his lips together at the end.

Well, I started laughing so hard that I hit the brakes and poor Michael almost slid off the seat, onto the floor. He was so cute, I'll never forget it.

~~~

Then there was the time that Laura wanted to have her ears pierced. I had mentioned one time to Phyllis, that I was thinking of getting my ears pierced because I was always losing one of my earrings. Laura was about ten years old and had wanted to have her ears pierced for some time, but Nick didn't want her to, and wouldn't allow it. Finally, after a while, Nick relented, so Phyllis called me one day and said that Nick had finally agreed, and that she was taking Laura to get her ears pierced, and asked me if I wanted to go with them to have mine pierced too. I said, "Okay,"

Phyllis and Laura - 1979.

and off we went to a jewelry store where we could have it done.

When we got to the store and went inside, the woman there said that she would do Laura's ears first. She said that she preferred that Phyllis and I didn't come in with her, and took Laura into a separate

438

room, by herself, and sat her down. There was a glass panel between the rooms, so Phyllis and I could watch what was going on.

We watched as the woman spoke to Laura and explained the procedure, but we couldn't hear her. Then the woman picked up an aerosol can, to spray some kind of numbing agent on Laura's earlobe, but, before she even touched her, Laura started to wail. We still couldn't hear her, but we knew she was crying because her mouth was wide open and her face was turning red. The woman tried to calm her down, but Laura wasn't having it. Finally, the woman brought Laura back out of the room and explained, "I'm sorry, but she's too upset. I can't pierce her ears today."

Then she motioned for me to come into the room with her, but by now I had started to get scared too. I really didn't want to go into the room because Laura's weeping and gnashing of teeth had gotten me so upset that I started to have second thoughts about allowing this stranger to pierce my poor delicate flesh with that cold steel spike, and I almost walked out of the store. But then I decided that I couldn't let Laura see me be so fearful. I gave myself a little pep-talk and was able to conquer my own apprehension, got over it, and in I went. And my

Nama and Laura - First Communion - May, 1981.

fears proved to be unfounded, as it turned out to be really no big deal. It didn't hurt at all.

I don't remember how much time passed after that day, but, eventually, Laura overcame her own fears and finally had her ears pierced too.

There are undoubtedly countless other stories about my ten grandchildren. Their births and their birthdays, first days of school and graduations, dance recitals and athletic events, illnesses and injuries. The things that made me laugh and the things that made me cry. The things that gave me pride in their accomplishments, and the nights that I lost sleep either due to excitement for them, or worry about them, just as I did with their fathers as they were growing up.

There was plenty of inter-family competition. I can remember Philip's son, John, and Brian's son, Benjamin, shirtless and flexing

their muscles in a "pose-off", in Patrick's backyard when they were little boys of eight or nine. And there always seemed to be a boisterous game of street hockey or touch football going on outside. Inside, there was always a heated table hockey play-off game going into overtime, or Rock Em' Sock Em' robots raucously battling it out on the dining room table.

Brian, Michael and Patrick playing Rock Em' Sock Em' robots - 1973.

There were the dance recitals that Laura, Aubrey, Erin and Kate performed in when they were little girls, always it seemed in an overstuffed school auditorium with no air conditioning, on the hottest day of the year.

There were dozens of basketball games that I proudly went to see Danny and Ben play in when they were in junior high and high school. And just like so many years earlier, watching their father playing in games, I was compelled to zealously comment and critique the

Aubrey as Josie and the Pussycats
June 17, 1990.

performance of the coaches and referees during the course of their games. Much to the chagrin of the boys and their father.

I sat huddled against the weather on more cold, wet March and November days than I care to count, to watch all my grandsons compete

Dan and Ben - Little league.
June 24, 1991.

James and Nama - West Babylon lacrosse.
May 3, 2001.

in baseball, football and lacrosse games from the time they were only about nine years old, right through high school and college

John Philip and Phil - Pace University - September 30, 2000.

There were all the horse shows that I sat through, in the penetrating cold rain or chocking, dusty heat of some remote farm field, to cheer the kids and their parents on as they competed in western events of barrel racing or cow penning. Watching them, galloping at breakneck speeds around the arena on horseback, I couldn't help but think about my husband, John. He would have been extremely pleased, in his understated way, to see how his passion for horses had been carried on so enthusiastically through our sons and their children.

John on "Mercedes" - WIS horse show. Summer, 1994.

Brian, Nick, John, Phil and Danny - WIS horse show - August 14, 1994.

I watched Laura and Aubrey do their cheerleading routines that brought me back to my days when I was a cheerleader at Washington Irving High School in Tarrytown. And I was so proud to have Katie represent us at my old alma mater when she chose to attend college at Mount Saint Vincent in Riverdale.

Laura's dance moves - Christmas at Brian and Debbie's. December 25, 1990.

Matt and James - Batman costumes, August 1, 1992.

And I remember all the holiday gatherings that the kids put their signature on. There was the Christmas day at Brian's house, in 1990, when Aubrey, Erin and Laura were all showing their dance moves to the rest of the family, gyrating around the living room to MC Hammer's, "U Can't Touch This", that had us all in stitches. Or the Halloween that James and Matthew both dressed up in their Batman costumes and posed, so seriously, as the Caped Crusaders.

443

There were all the aspiring boyfriends and girlfriends that I gave notice to, had to get my seal of approval before I would allow them to date one of my grandchildren. The kids always laughing that off because they thought that I was just kidding, and for the most part I was, but not completely.

Aubrey and a potential boyfriend - January 9, 1993.

Nama, Kate and James - Patrick's Birthday - December 9, 1992.

I baked countless angel food cakes drizzled with chocolate icing, and the kids could never get enough. And I cooked more turkey breasts for family gatherings than you could shake a stick at, because all the kids loved it. There was always potato chips and a bowl of onion dip on the coffee table because it was a family staple. And always lots of laughs and hugs and smiles and kisses whenever my beautiful grandchildren were gathered together around me.

Christmas at Nama's - 1989.

But as I sit here today, it is with the realization that I am the last surviving member of the Egan clan. The only male child of any of the Egan families to survive childbirth was my older brother Bart, who was born in 1915, but died when he was only a couple of months old. There were eight Egan females; between myself, my two sisters and five cousins, but no males to carry on the Egan name.

My husband, John, was the only male member of his family that could carry on the McFadden pedigree, and we were blessed to have five wonderful sons. Although Jack never married, and died very young, Nick, Philip, Brian and Patrick, all had children, sons and daughters, totaling ten grandchildren. Six grandsons and four granddaughters.

These grandchildren, in turn, have been prolific in bringing another generation into the world. Nick's son, Michael, has three children. Their names are Kayla, Jillian and Michael Nicholas. His daughter, Laura, has a daughter, Katelyn Ann, and two beautiful stepchildren; Matthew and Olivia.

Fifi and Kayla- 80th Birthday Party - August 2002.

Philip's oldest daughter, Aubrey, has a son; Ethan Philip, and a daughter; Evan Faye and is now expecting another son this coming November, 2011. His daughter Erin has four beautiful children; Talia Rose, Callista Ashley, Lukas Colin and little Hailey Madison, born this past

Ethan and Evan - Fall 2010.

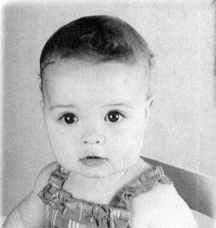

Sarah Eileen - Spring 2011.

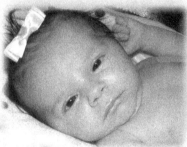

Hailey Madison - Spring, 2011

Talia, Lukas and Calista - Christmas, 2009.

May. His son, John, and his wife Kelly were blessed with their first child, a daughter named Sarah Eileen, last October, 2010. So as of today I have thirteen great-grandchildren, with one "in the oven", and still counting.

Nick's son; Matthew, Brian's two boys; Danny and Ben, and Patrick's two children; Kate and James, aren't married and have not yet had children. But I am sure that, in time, they too will add to the growing number of McFadden / Egan progeny.

The Grandchildren and Great Grandchildren.
Aubrey and Jasons Wedding - August 16, 2008.

And so the family grows. Through good times and bad. Just as it has since the old days back in Abbeyfeale, Ireland, and in Tarrytown, New York.

And life goes on.

Amen.

~~~

Chapter Thirteen

LESSONS LEARNED ALONG THE WAY

The world has changed so much from the time that I was a little girl. We have become too materialistic. We have lost the idea that the family is the core of society. People seem to have lost the value of life and treat it far too casually. Every day we hear about violence in families, and things like drive-by shootings; and I wonder how some people could attach so little value to life.

I was raised as a devout Catholic, and have tried to be true to the teachings of the Catholic Church, where one of those teachings is tolerance. I adhere to my Catholic beliefs but accept the fact that others embrace different religious tenets. They are all good as long as one is true to the concept of right and wrong.

My faith in God has been very important to me for all my life, and has carried me through many of the hardships that I have seen. What I have found is that the fundamental knowledge of right and wrong is important as you go through life, and my belief in God has always helped me to discern the difference, and make the right choices along the way.

In my latter years, I seem to spend a lot of time reflecting on the miracle of life. When you look at how our bodies and minds develop from birth and how we are given fingers to touch and feel; our senses for sight, smell and sound; how our minds work to recognize and form thoughts; and how we are able to communicate, you start to see that a human life is truly an amazing thing. Perfect in conception and design, and something that could only have been engineered by the hand of God.

I regret that my husband John didn't have a chance to see how his sons have matured, and to know all of their children and grandchildren. As I have said before, I think he was a sad man, but I think that had he lived, his grandchildren and great grandchildren

449

would have been able to replace much of that sadness with joy. He would have loved having them all around him, to have known the love and happiness that I have come to know from each and every one of them. He would have been so proud to watch the next generations of our family grow and succeed, and they all would have benefited from having their "Tapa" in their lives.

Anytime we all get together for holidays or special family occasions, I am so proud to be able to look around the room and know that I am responsible for over half the people there. It is especially pleasing to know that none of my sons or their children have done anything that would sully the Egan or McFadden names. They have all been solid, upstanding and hardworking, and a credit to John and me.

Fifi's 80th Birthday Party - August, 2002.

What I have learned is that when times get rough, you'll always have your family to back you up. That isn't to say that we haven't had our issues, all families do, but when the chips were down, anytime a crisis came, our family has always stood together and supported each other.

Every individual member of our family and each new addition, contributes to the whole in more ways than you can imagine. Each one brings their own joys, their own love, and their own stories.

I remember that when I was pregnant with Nick, I thought there was something emotionally wrong with me. I just loved Jack so much that one day I said to my mother, "Mom, I love Jack so much, I don't know if I can love another baby as much as I love him."

She said, "Don't worry honey, each child is different. Every baby brings its own love." And it's true, you love each one unconditionally for all the special things that make them each unique in their own way.

I have come to strongly believe that every person that comes into your life is meant to be in your life at that time. That everything happens for a reason, and that there are no accidents or coincidences in life. Very often, the reason for something happening doesn't reveal itself to you for months or even years, but every event and every person that comes into your life is meant to be there at that moment in time.

Sometimes I sit alone in the quiet of my room and ponder the question of why I have been granted such a long life, when others have been snatched away in their youth, when they still had so much to offer. But I believe that God has a plan, and that they were called away for another purpose. And then something tells me that the reason that I have lived this long is that I was given a mission to perform, and I'm still not done yet.

~~~

451

EPILOGUE

Throughout the pursuit of this personal calling to bring my mother's proclamations that she "...*should write a book*" to fulfillment, I have had an opportunity to learn much more about my family and myself than what I had previously been aware of. I've been given new insight into my parents as people, and the dynamics of the time and place that they lived in, that have shaped our family into what it is today. And I have had the time to reflect on many things that I had previously been ignorant of, had simply faded from memory, or had, in a few cases, conveniently evaded the narrow scope of my own self-absorbed field of view.

There is nothing profound about any of my mother's stories when taken individually. They are just tales of some of the various occasions in her life. For that matter, I would guess that you could easily change a few names and places, and many of her stories could apply to a lot of other families from her era, first or second generation Americans who were taught the value of living by the Golden Rule, if not by the Ten Commandments. Like so many others from small towns across America that married their high school sweethearts and then watched them go off to war, never knowing if they would return. They raised their families through good, bad and indifferent times, with grace and dignity.

But when these stories are strung together and viewed in a broader context, they create a record of something bigger. What is revealed is not only a vivid picture of an exceptional woman, but also of her extraordinary peers and the momentous period in American and World history that they simultaneously influenced and were influenced by.

One of the driving forces that compelled me towards taking on this assignment is an invaluably significant concept known as "filial piety". This is a term that was first introduced to me around 1994, but something that I would like to think that I have practiced, even if unknowingly, all of my life.

Essentially, "filial piety" is a deep respect and reverence for our ancestors and elders, especially our parents and grandparents, for no

I

other reason than that they <u>are</u> the older generation. This way of thinking is deeply ingrained into almost all Asian cultures and is one of the strongest pillars of Eastern societies. Sadly, it is a commodity that has all but vanished in today's Western culture. We Americans, to our detriment, seem to have lost touch with that ideology to the point where it appears to be on the brink of vanishing altogether.

An elder's accomplishments in life have little or nothing to do with this philosophy. Their level of worldly success or failure has no bearing whatsoever on the level of respect, honor and support that senior members of society are accorded in Asian cultures.

This doctrine of unconditional respect for the elders trickles down and has a profoundly positive impact on everyday life in Eastern societies. Teachers, shopkeepers, police officers, etc., are shown a high level of respect from younger generations. Asia's elderly are venerated and important. Their age related infirmities are accepted and dealt with as part and parcel of their inherent value to the community. But not so in modern American society.

This is incomprehensible to me, and America's loss of respect, honor and support for our elders is especially disconcerting when we consider my mother's generation, for they have earned our reverence and adulation perhaps more so than any other generation before or since.

The parents of the Baby Boomers have become known as the Greatest Generation, but that description of them seems to fall short as one of the greatest understatements that I can think of. To my mind, they are a generation of men and women the likes of whom we will never see again.

They were innocents, born into a world that was changing at an unprecedented pace; politically, industrially, and economically. Born in the 1910s and 1920s of a collective optimism, fearlessness and faith that they would bring to bear to overcome the Great Depression of the 1930s.

They would come together, against overwhelming odds, to face and defeat the evils of tyranny on opposite sides of the globe during World War II. A feat that required unimaginable sacrifice, hard work and a steely national resolve. And they saved the world for all of us that would follow.

I quote an excerpt from the noted war historian, Victor Davis Hanson, who observed in a June 30, 2010 essay; *"History is not equal, and whether we like it or not, strange things happen during wars that don't transpire as often in peace time. We have to nurse the next generation on some knowledge of the collective sacrifice of prior generations, otherwise the society won't understand what it gave up in the past to enjoy in the present."*

During the ensuing decades they faced the threat of Communism and confronted injustice around the world and at home. They made great leaps of progress in civil rights, and had the audacity to think they could put a man on the moon, and then did it. They built our cities, our highway system and our infrastructure. They made vast contributions in the fields of science, communications, education and the arts. And they did it all with the courage and conviction that comes as second nature to inquisitive, resourceful minds; tenacious, resilient spirits; and passionate, principled hearts.

There wasn't anything they couldn't do. There wasn't an enemy that they couldn't defeat. They were bigger than life. Giants, steadfastly watching over us, lighting the way and keeping us safe. They weren't perfect. Certainly they all lived imperfect lives. But they strove to overcome their collective flaws, and made the world a better place. They did it with an unmatched work ethic, boundless enthusiasm and a resolute character that was founded in their faith and supported by their core values. We would all do well to learn from their example, and we should understand that when we fail to respect, honor and support our elder generations, we ultimately lay the groundwork for our own "winter of discontent", and our society will deteriorate by degrees, insidiously, generation to generation, until only a hollow shell of our culture is left.

But now that Greatest Generation has all but run its course. It turns out that our parents are mere mortals after all. The ones that we always looked up to for guidance and affirmation are finally succumbing to the attrition of age, and, soon, all we will have left of them will be old photographs and documents to prove that they even existed on this earth at all. But their legacy must be greater than that. We must pass on their steely determination, their belief in their fellow man and their faith in God, their humor, their energy, their hope and humility. And we must live up to, and pass on the example that they set for us.

Now, as they fade into memory, we should embrace their spirits, and cherish and savor all that they gave to us Baby Boomers, and we should make a real effort to assure that their stories are told, to ensure that their character and accomplishments are never lost to future generations. That the generations still to come gain the knowledge of what their predecessors did for them, and know that they have big shoes to fill. A very daunting task indeed, but they have the ability to succeed. It was bequeathed to them by their grandparents and great grandparents; a legacy passed down to them in their genes, just like the color of their eyes and the dimples in their cheeks. It's there, inside. All they need to do is embrace it, honor it, and the rest will take care of itself.

Our parental heroes are no longer putting our dinner on the table each night or showing us how to bait a hook on Saturday mornings. They have handed those and countless other responsibilities off to us, and we must prepare our children to accept them when their time comes.

The ones that cleared the way for us, in historical fashion, are now passing on to be part of history, and fading into posterity. But the spirit of that generation, myth-like in quality, will continue to live on in us and those who follow, generation to generation, if we honor their venerable accomplishments, their sacrifices and their memories. And if we practice "filial piety" through word and deed.

There is a great tendency on my part to look at our past history through the lens of my mother's stories. They give me a strong perspective on how it is that I and the rest of my family have arrived at where we are today. Consequently, I believe that the youth of today need reference points to understand their own place in the world as individuals and as a group. But how can they appreciate where they are if they don't know where they've come from. Perhaps Fifi's stories will provide them with a rear view mirror of sorts, to help them put their own world into better perspective.

Fifi McFadden is the quintessential example of our Greatest Generation, and has earned a place of reverence in our extended families' lore. The pages of this book are not just fables, they are written, first hand accounts of life from an era gone by, and there is much to be learned from them. She is one of the very last of one of our greatest resources, our heritage.

Thankfully, as I write this, my mother is still here with us, and that is due in no small part to her great passion for life. By her own admission she is a "tough old Irish broad," still full of piss and vinegar. But having spent so much time with her over the past fifteen months, I have seen first hand how she struggles physically just to move around to get in and out of her chair, or to get up to use the bathroom, or go out to the dining room to eat her meals. She is in tremendous pain and every step is a struggle for her, but she keeps on fighting the good fight, putting one foot in front of the other, and embracing the life that she has been given. She has done many inspiring things over the course of her life for my brothers and me, but to watch her now, in this stage of her life, is to be inspired anew, and it just adds another dimension to her, that even in her old age, she refuses to throw in the towel. There's just no "quit" in her.

But the number of her wonderful contemporaries shrinks every year, and has dwindled to a precious few. She is one of the last members of a very prestigious group, and I can only hope to honor her and her memories as much as the life that she has led does honor to her own generation and all of us who have followed. She has shown us our heritage through her example and her stories, and they, along with her sons, her grandchildren and her great grandchildren, will be her legacy.

This book is intended as a tribute to my mother, and a celebration of her life. If it comes across as a eulogy then I have failed in my purpose, for she is still very much "alive and kickin", and there will be time for eulogies on some other, sadder day. But when, inevitably, the time comes for Mom to leave us and go to join my father, my brother Jack, her parents and her sisters, she can go in peace with the confidence and knowledge that she did her part in all aspects of life. With her head held high that she lived her life faithfully, with honor and integrity, humor and humility. With the knowledge that she is loved and revered by many who extend far beyond our familial ties. And she can take her rightful standing among all the others that have gone on before her to the place where myths dwell.

In our hearts.

Our willing hearts.

~~~

The Last Unicorn

When the last eagle flies
Over the last crumbling mountain.
And the last lion roars
at the last dusty fountain.
In the shadow of the forest,
though she may be old and worn,
they will stare, unbelieving,
at the last Unicorn.

When the first breath of winter
through the flowers is icing,
and you look to the North
and a pale moon is rising,
and it seems like all is dying
and would leave the world to mourn,
In the distance, hear her laughter,
It's the last Unicorn

When the last moon is cast
over the last star of morning,
and the future is past
without even a last desperate warning,
then look into the sky, where through
the clouds a path is torn.
Look and see her,
how she shimmers,
it's the last Unicorn.
I'm alive! I'm alive! I'm alive!

Jimmy Webb

ABOUT THE AUTHOR

Philip McFadden was born in Tarrytown, NY in 1951 and was the third of five sons. His family moved to the south shore of Long Island in 1959 where he grew up in the village of Seaford, NY. He lived most of his adult life in Mount Sinai, NY, where he raised his three children. In the wake of a divorce in the late 1990s, he returned to the site of his family roots in Westchester County, NY, where he remarried in 2000. His love of family and his desire to express himself moved him to try his hand at writing. "The Last Unicorn" is his first offering.

Philip McFadden, cousin Michael Sheehan (grand nephew of Ellen "Nellie Horgan Egan), Patrick McFadden, and John Philp McFadden holding daughter, Sarah Eileen. In front of the Horgan homestead. Abbeyfeale, Ireland. - June 13, 2011.